HOW TO SAVE THE UNDERCL[

How to Save the Underclass

Robin Marris
Professor Emeritus of Economics
Birkbeck College
London University

First published 1996 by
MACMILLAN PRESS LTD
Houndmills, Basingstoke, Hampshire RG21 6XS
and London
Companies and representatives
throughout the world

ISBN 0–333–66949–5 hardcover
ISBN 0–333–66950–9 paperback

A catalogue record for this book is available
from the British Library.

10   9   8   7   6   5   4   3   2   1
05   04   03   02   01   00   99   98   97   96

Printed in Great Britain by
the Ipswich Book Company, Suffolk

Published in the United States of America 1996 by
ST. MARTIN'S PRESS, INC.,
Scholarly and Reference Division
175 Fifth Avenue, New York, N.Y. 10010

ISBN 0–312–16208–1

Contents

List of Figures

To Rachel, who succours me,
to E, who introduced me to the underclass
and to Robert Reich, who set me thinking

Preface and Acknowledgements

The problem discussed in this book is profoundly political, profoundly moral and profoundly current. It has already provoked a major literature. Inevitably most of the leading writers are propagandists as well as researchers: they would not be human if they were not. That applies on both sides of the political spectrum. I therefore think I should give a brief indication of where, politically and as a professional economist, I come from.

A British subject whose line can be traced to an actual Norman who fought with the invaders at the Battle of Hastings, I have been of voting age for 14 General Elections and cast my ballot for the Labour Party in all but five. In three out of those five I voted Conservative. For a short time in the past I was the resident economic writer for the left-wing weekly, *The New Statesman*, then under the editorship of Paul Johnson, who later changed his spots and became a passionate supporter of Lady Thatcher. I too, after the mid-70s, became estranged from Labour, hostile to socialism and highly critical of the power of unions. But I never swung *spiritually* to the political right, as did a significant handful of leading British intellectuals. I must also add that at no time have the ideas of the so-called radical Right, on either side of the Atlantic, attracted me one little bit. In the past five years I have swung back to my old support of Labour (which makes me a liberal in the American sense). I am satisfied that there is indeed a serious problem of an underclass in the modern affluent society, but I am still enough of a political centrist to be wary of exaggeration and to dislike one-sided selections of statistics.

I do hold the view that the primary purpose of paid employment is to serve the consumer, not the employee. But in saying that I recognise a certain personal hypocrisy, in that I am a person who has been lucky enough (maybe also determined enough) to have obtained a career where the work has been exceptionally interesting and rewarding. I have four children aged 21 to 35, the youngest of whom has a rather bleak view of the London labour market, but quite enjoys earning five dollars an hour in a brasserie in the American West. Each of the others has interesting work they currently enjoy and whenever in the past one or another has found this was not the case, they have succeeded in changing jobs, direction or career appropriately. Finally I believe that the very great shake-up of the British job market that resulted from the Thatcher era, while indeed creating much painful insecurity, also brought much prosperity to a large section of the population. In so many sectors where it was not previously the case, the consumer (or client, or patient) is now treated as such, rather than as a nuisance. The other side of the coin is the underclass.

As an economist, I was trained in Cambridge by people who were closely associated with Keynes and I have remained proudly Keynesian (not 'post-', not 'neo-', not 'new-') ever since. The fundamental Keynesian theory is to me a simple model of the macro stabilities and instabilities of any practical market economy, which is no more capable of being 'wrong' than the laws of gravity. In the past decade, however, I began to see that one particular aspect of the way Keynes presented his theory – namely in such a way that it would hold true in an imaginary 'perfectly competitive' economy – was a major error. In the first quarter century after the theory was published this did not matter much because economists simply ignored it: Keynes-based statistical models correctly assumed that practical competition in the real world was necessarily imperfect. Then came the Monetarist and General-Chicago counter-attack on Keynes, whereupon (in my opinion) the latent error in the Keynesian theory became an Achilles Heel. I have published one book and some papers on this theme whose significance will reappear in Chapter 3.

In the middle period of my career I worked on the economic theory of the modern large capitalist corporation, and at that time became symbiotically associated with the parallel 'institutionalist' work of John Kenneth Galbraith. (I do claim to have been the first economist to predict the importance of take-overs, where he at the time was sceptical.) In today's context it is worth remembering that as early as the 1960s Galbraith was arguing that poverty was a permanent problem for the affluent society and that the only permanent effective way to combat poverty would be by maintaining a permanently fast rate of economic growth. It would never be politically feasible,

Galbraith argued at that time, to solve the poverty problem by redistributive taxation alone.[1] The central theme in the chapters below endows Galbraith's then-implied prediction with much credit; for when, after the mid-70s, economic growth did slow down, the problem of poverty, which had been declining, began to increase again.

Finally, in the past few years I have become intensely interested in current research on the biological mechanism of the human brain and especially in what is known as neural computing. This, as I hope to show in Chapter 5, has given me, I believe, a new approach to the controversial question of the relation between human economic performance and innate intelligence. That, in turn, I claim throws new light on the problem, or more precisely the paradox, of meritocracy.

From the foregoing it will be seen that there is not too much in my professional history to justify a book in a field where I have not previously worked and where many others have. I was in fact drawn to the subject by watching a BBC TV programme on unemployment and low wages, written and compered by Peter Jay, which showed interviews with, among others Robert Reich, currently US Secretary of Labor and author of a seminal book called *The Work of Nations*.[2] He captured me by remarking that if it were true, as some had argued, that the US had less unemployment than Europe on account of lower wages, US citizens were not necessarily better off than Europeans: they were merely trading one form of poverty for another. I began wondering about the 'macro' implications of the comparison. As compared with Europe, what commodities were the lower-paid US employees producing and who was buying them? The answer had to be services for affluent 'alrights' (people earning good money and fully employed), who, in the US, gained both from cheap labour and from paying less in welfare taxes. I offered this thought to Anatole

---

1   In a recent (January 1996) television programme he seemed to have forgotten his earlier view and extolled the merits of progressive taxation! I think Galbraith's most distinctive talent is for ideas that are ahead, but only slightly ahead of their time – ideas whose time, helped on by his own remarkable prose, is just about to come; or, in this case, come again.

2   Reich, 1991, see References.

Kaletsky, economics editor of *The Times*, who kindly commissioned two articles, which duly appeared and in turn provoked a flattering invitation from Tim Farmiloe, Macmillan's head of academic publishing, to write a quick short book, as now follows. My justification for having accepted that challenge is that I shall try to introduce a wider range of elements into the discussion than has been possible for some deeper researchers and that I shall thus be giving the story some, I think, new emphases.

I think that my emphasis on the causal role of the economic-growth slow-down is new in *current* discussion; and I believe I have made major progress in answering the question, which has so far defeated the economics profession, of *why,* after the mid-70s, economic growth in the rich countries did slow down.[1] I would also claim some other distinctive elements, such as on the role of intelligence in the income distribution and in the discussion of the economics of welfare. I also do face certain questions, such as whether the rise in labour-force participation by women may have contributed to the weak market for men, which are not much discussed in the economic literature, possibly because they are considered politically incorrect.

Finally, in the last chapter, I have stuck my neck out to make definite proposals to a greater extent than is usually thought judicious. These imply radical reorientation of public policy, nationally, internationally and globally and have major implications for bodies such as the EU.

Writing in London, I bow with humility to the depth and breadth of the research of my professional colleagues on both sides of the Atlantic and especially on the Western side. I think it is a considerable moral and practical credit to our trade that so much careful and detailed research is being devoted to this major social problem of our

---

1   'Why did the magic economy go away? Hundreds of books have been written on that topic. .... But let me cut to the chase: the real answer is *we don't know.*' Paul Krugman, 'Peddling Prosperity', p 5. [In speaking of 'hundreds of books', I think the gentleman doth exaggerate a little; I would challenge him to find that many: also, as will be seen in my Chapter 3, there is a major question, which he doesn't face, as to whether in the US there ever was, in the technical sense, a productivity slow down – RM.]

time.

In the matter of political correctness I completely agree that the use of 'he' when one means 'one' is a form of male chauvinism, but I do not agree that the fault is corrected by saying 'she'. Wherever possible I will use 'one', and where not, 'he or she' or 'her or his' according to alphabetical order.

A major question arises as to whether the actual title of this book is not itself politically suspect. It can well be argued that the term 'underclass' is patronizing,[1] that to speak of 'saving' 'them' is infelicitous and that the implied objective is boastful. But the term is now widely used[2], most especially among liberals, and the publisher believed a less ambitious title would be bad for business. The reader shall judge at the end.

Acknowledgements
The roles of Anatole Kaletsky and Tim Farmiloe has already been mentioned: without their support and initiative respectively this book

---

1 Mr. Chris Smith, MP, British Labour Party spokesman on social security, suggested this to me. There is also an interesting-sounding book, not available in England yet, by Herbert Gans, *The War against the Poor*, which I understand argues that the term 'underclass' morally disenfranchises the poor.

2 I personally first heard the term in the late seventies, from Frank Levy, distinguished US urbanist, now full Professor at MIT, and subsequently one of the most important opinion-formers in the field (see especially *Dollars and Dreams*, 1987, and his chapter in *The State of the Union* (Russell Sage), 1955). Around 1977 he read a paper to the Economics Dept at the University of Maryland, College Park, where I was then chair, entitled, 'Is there an American underclass?' His affirmative answer was based on the observation that among US blacks, in the past, owing to discrimination, there had been less variation of income than among whites; now, as emancipatory policies took effect, the income distribution among blacks was becoming more skewed. In short, Frank Levy was anticipating the advent of the meritocractic paradox discussed first in Chapter 1 and again in Chapter 5 below: one reason for the existence of an underclass is equality of opportunity for entry into the overclass. I was impressed by Frank Levy's data, but unhappy with the findings; for at that time, because I was in my conservative political phase, I did not want to believe them. Had someone told me then that what Frank Levy was observing among American blacks was to begin happening among all races and classes throughout the First World, I would have expressed disbelief and surprise. As we now know, I would have been wrong.

would not have happened. I also single out for special mention the help I have received from my brother Stephen Marris, from Adrian Wood and from Robert Solow. The first has given me the benefit of his wide knowledge of international public policy in a series of long discussions which have provided the intellectual backbone of the whole thesis on macroeconomic policy and growth. The second who, as readers will know, is a leading authority on the trade aspects of the problem, gave me constant encouragement, advice and support, and provided a large quantity of data and documents. The third in Cambridge, Mass., has responded rapidly in a running correspondence with factual and theoretical comment of a kind which, so typically of his mind, each time hits the target and goes beyond.

I also single out the Director and staff of the University of Lausanne Pareto-Walras centre for material help and moral support in the documentation of Pareto, in Chapter 5.

In addition, the following professionals, listed in alphabetical order, have helped with advice, data or other information, often substantial. My thanks go out to all.

Ed Balls, Gary Burtless, Juergen Elmeskov, Richard Freeman, Christopher Frith, Peter Gaskell, Amanda Gosling, Will Hutton, Peter Jay, William Keegan, Robert Lawrence, Frank Levy, Steve Machin, John Martin, Patrick Minford, Steve Nickell, Angela Nugent, Paul Ormerod, Mary O'Mahony, Robert Plomin, Chris Smith, Mahlon Strasheim, John Taylor.

Although the usual acknowledgements to typists and assistants are missing (my pc and spreadsheets were my assistants, and, supported by WP-6, I was the typist and typesetter[1]), I should surely mention Sunder Katwala, my editor at Macmillan, for great efficiency.

---

1 Has technology destroyed these jobs? Yes it has. But I think they were basically rather horrible jobs. With adequate economic growth, new and more rewarding jobs will be created. Without it, there's the problem.

1. The Problem and its Causes

Many people today believe there is a serious problem of an underclass. What is this problem? It is partly that between ten and 20 per cent of society are in serious risk of poverty and 'non-employment'. It is also the problem that another 20 or 30 per cent feel insecure, and that the whole income distribution seems to have moved from too much equality to excessive inequality.

*The problem is an aspect of the paradox of **meritocracy** – we create an equal-opportunity society and then find we have created a new elite of brains. But the extreme version is not inevitable. There are severe and moderate forms of meritocracy. In both, the distribution of personal ability is bell-shaped. In both, the resulting distribution of economic rewards is skewed. But in the one version the skewness is much less severe than in the other.*

The kind of meritocracy we get depends on the macroeconomic environment – most especially on the long run buoyancy of the general labour market. The meritocracy has become worse in the past quarter-century because long-run economic growth has been sluggish.

During this same period, however, there have also been four additional forces – each inevitable and in itself desirable – with major adverse side-effects reinforcing the effects of the growth slow-down.

*These are **technology, trade, services, women**.*

*'**Technology**' means the effect of the new technology on the comparative earnings of people with high and low education and/or intelligence. '**Trade**' means the effect on the relative earnings of skilled and unskilled workers of the opening up, through increased trade, of a global labour market. '**Services**' means the effect of the shift (that comes with affluence) of consumer demand from manufacturing to services sectors, where the wages of less-educated workers are normally low: it is also associated with 'de-industrialization' and 'de-unionization'. '**Women**' means the effect of the addition to the **supply** of labour of the large number of additional women who, in all the rich countries bar Japan, have desired to enter the labour force. Did they inevitably push men out of work and/or push down wages?*

*On top of all this, **public policy**, by 'tightening up' the welfare state, has aggravated the situation.*

The background
In 1994 and 1995 the British Gallup Poll asked a series of questions about social problems,[1] one of which was,

> There is talk at the moment of the growth in Britain of an 'underclass' – people, many of them living in inner-city areas, who have no jobs and no skills and seem destined to spend the rest of their lives largely cut off from the rest of society. Do you think an underclass is appearing in this country or not?

To this, *eighty five per cent* of respondents answered 'yes'. Nearly fifty per cent said they were 'very worried' about the problem. Seventy per cent said they thought poverty was a very important problem in Britain today, compared with 66 per cent when the same question was asked a decade earlier. Only 13 per cent, compared to 33 per cent a decade earlier, thought lack of effort was mainly to blame if a person was poor.

The same polls showed more than half the population regarding themselves, family or friends to be in danger of unemployment, and large segments expressing fear about crime and social breakdown directly resulting from current economic conditions and the existence of an underclass.

In the United States, the problem is in many ways even more politically acute, and has been the subject of major and continuing academic research for at least the past decade.

What, then, is the nature of this problem?

The problem
On January 12 1996, Margaret Thatcher gave a speech in London praising public policy during the time when she had been Prime Minister:

> Public spending as a share of the GDP fell, which allowed tax rates to be cut and government borrowing was reduced. We repaid debt. Three hundred and sixty-four economists who claimed it was madness to think you could get economic growth by cutting government borrowing were proved wrong.[2]

Needless to say, she made no mention of poverty. But you can't eat disinflation or clothe yourself with a budget surplus. Economic growth in the 1980s did not recover its earlier pace and this affected

---

1   See Gallup, 1995, in References.
2   *The Times*, London, Jan 12, 1996.

Welfare and welfare

In economics jargon the *'welfare'* of an *individual* is the person's economic well-being.

> (The 'law of diminishing marginal utility of money' is the proposition that $100 a month increases the welfare of a person whose monthly income is $1000 more than it does the welfare of a person whose monthly income is $5000.*)

Total welfare is an aggregate of the personal welfare levels of all the people who are considered to belong to a society. The problems of defining this are discussed in Chapter 5, page 157 after.

The Welfare State is a society where, in order to maintain total welfare, a publicly-financed safety net is placed under personal welfare.

---

* Ragner Frisch – of Norway, the first economist to receive a Nobel Prize – found a way of measuring the rate at which the marginal utility of income declines, and James Mirrlees, distinguished contemporary Cambridge economics professor, has made classic use of the law of diminishing marginal utility in his work on optimal taxation (Frisch, 1959 and Mirrlees 1971).

---

not only the level, but also the distribution of income. A society does not increase its total welfare merely by increasing its average real income. Because people with low incomes benefit more from given gains than people with high incomes, it is perfectly possible for an increase in the average, if accompanied by an increase in spread, to mean actual decline in total welfare. Nor on the other hand does a society increase total welfare merely by reducing inequality.

Lady Thatcher is reputed to have said, 'There is no such thing as society. There are only people.' Unfortunately, in the context of public policy, the statement has no logic. All acts of public policy, such as cutting down government expenditure or using only monetary weapons to combat inflation, will affect different people differently. If you are not prepared to think about society as a whole you have no criterion for choosing between one policy or another.

The problem we actually face today is a triple one, all three aspects coming out of a general tendency to greater inequality in the 'Anglo-Saxon' countries (Britain and the US) since the middle seventies. On the west European continent the same causes have produced similar problems, but more spread out among the general population.

A Secession of the Successful?

Extracts from US Labor Secretary Robert Reich's Commencement Address at the University of Maryland, December 1996*

Between 1950 and 1978, the wealthiest fifth of America's families saw their incomes double. And so did the poorest fifth. We grew together. That was how it worked in America. .... From Beijing to Berlin, courageous women and men took on tyrants in the name of the American ideals of personal liberty and shared prosperity.

That global triumph of the American model makes all the more troubling the current condition of the American Dream. Instead of an America that is growing together, the Class of 95 has been handed an America that is growing apart. From 1979 to 1993 – the years you were growing up – our economy continued to expand. But almost all the growth in income went to the wealthiest fifth of American households. The poorest fifth saw their incomes *fall*....

The American economy is again percolating with possibilities. But not for everyone.... Gone for ever are the assembly lines that used to provide lifetime jobs with rising wages and benefits to people straight out of high school. The winners in this new economy are those who can identify and solve problems, manipulate and analyze symbols, create and manage information. The degrees you are earning today signify your competence at doing these tasks. You are thus likely – not guaranteed, but likely – to end up on the happier side of the great divide.

Indeed, you may even come to see yourselves more as inhabitants of the global economy ... than as citizens of a particular community ... And this ability to *succeed* in the information-rich global economy may lead you to withdraw, to *secede* from that part of America which remains trapped in the old economy, on the other side of the great educational divide. ...

We are witnessing a retreat from common ground ... from the very idea of shared aspiration and common responsibility. And as the successful secede, they ask with ever louder voice...why should we care?

With the degrees you will soon receive, many of you have been handed a ticket to secede, if you wish to. But let me urge you to resist. Not because commencement speakers are obliged to offer lofty sentiments. But because you will not want to live in a society sharply divided between winners and losers.

Consider for a moment those who are being left behind. As I travel across America I hear their fears and see their disillusionment....For all these people, the vaunted American dream seems a cynical lie. Some turn to crime. Others to demagogues seeking easy targets to blame....

The underlying question is this. Are we simply an economy, in which the only thing binding us together is the business we transact with one another? Or are we still a society, whose members have responsibilities toward one another, who continue to join together to create opportunity for all?

---

*   by kind permission of the University.

The *first* aspect is the underclass itself, ie the between ten and twenty per cent of the population who are long-term likely to experience poverty or need public help to avoid it.

The *second* aspect is that the next ten or fifteen per cent of the population now feel at risk of falling into the underclass - a probability of a probability, but none the less real for that.

The *third* aspect is that *within* economic groups income has become more spread out.

A quarter of a century ago many reasonable people thought that society had become too egalitarian. Incentives for able workers were inadequate and there was too much, rather than too little security. Today, equally reasonable people are concerned that the pendulum has now swung excessively the other way. In Britain, from the end of World War II until the mid sixties, the inequality of the distribution of personal income remained more or less constant. Then it fell steadily and quite strongly until the mid seventies, when the trend was so sharply reversed that by the mid eighties UK inequality had almost surpassed any previous post-war level.[1] After that the government suppressed the figures, but one may reasonably assume the new trend continued.

In America, there were similar, if not stronger, tendencies as the reader can see dramatically described in a speech summarized in the box on the opposite page given by Robert Reich, US Secretary for Labor, at the University of Maryland only three weeks before Lady Thatcher spoke in London.

The underclass

The concept
The term 'underclass'[2] has replaced such terms as 'working class' only recently. It is an economic concept. The working class was a cultural as well as an economic entity. One was born into that class;

---

1   See Table 1.1 in Tony Atkinson, *Incomes and the Welfare State*, 1995, in References, a typically authoritative collection of essays and research papers from this author (Warden of Nuffield College, Oxford and ex-Professor of Political Economy at Cambridge) which is required reading for anyone wanting more hard information on income distribution and the Welfare State not only in Britain but also in the rest of Europe and the US.

2   See the Preface for more discussion and reference to Frank Levy.

Labour Force Terms

Employed
In paid employment or actively and profitably self-employed.
Unemployed
Not currently employed but fit to work and considered to be actively
seeking work.
Labour force
All those of working age* who are either employed or unemployed.
Non-employed
A person in the working-age population who is not employed, ie is
unemployed or 'non-participating' (not in the labour force).
Disguised unemployment
The 'involuntary' subsegment of the non-participating segment of the
total non-employed, ie excluding eg male-supported working-age
women who are content to stay at home or men who have retired early
by choice.**
Non-employment rate
The non-employed as a percentage of the working-age population.
Unemployment rate
The unemployed as a percentage of the labour force.
Participation rate
The labour force as a percentage of the working-age population.

---

*   Definitions of the relevant age range vary. In this book I use 25 to 64. Obviously
     there are many active workers aged 16-24, but I cut off at this age to allow for the
     large and increasing proportion of that age range who are students.

** 'Disguised' unemployed people are also described as 'discouraged workers'. For
     an excellent further discussion see John Eatwell, *Disguised Unemployment*, 1995,
     in References.

one could prosper in it and be proud of it. In the underclass, one may
be content, but unlikely to be proud, and never, by definition,
economically comfortable. Being raised in a poor home increases the
chance of joining the underclass after leaving home, but the concept
is not hereditary as such. Although it is obviously wrong to define a
person as 'in' the underclass if he or she happens to be unemployed
or earning low wages for only few months, it is clearly possible for a
person or household to move into or out of the underclass at different
times in their lives.

   The definition
So we say that a person or household is in the underclass if they have
a long term *probability* of needing state support to avoid poverty

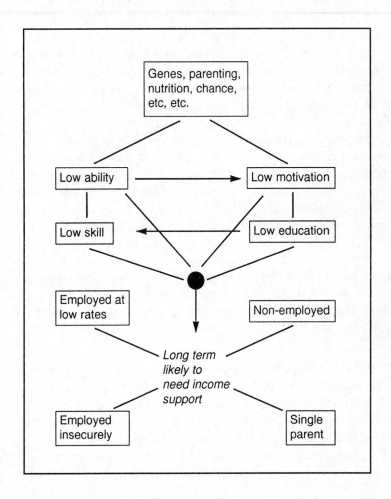

Figure 1.1   The underclass syndrome.

and/or starvation.[1] Unless one believes it would be feasible to have a society in which every household had the same income, one must accept that there will always be people who have less than the average. The current widespread belief that an underclass has become a problem is due to believing that in recent years the income and total economic well-being of the bottom group has fallen *too far* below the average. In the US it has in fact fallen absolutely as well as relatively.

That is a problem for the whole community. It is a problem not only on account of crime and social breakdown – grave though these may be – but also because a society with an excessively disadvantaged underclass is a society with low economic welfare.

The problem is in many ways self-reinforcing. For at least the past thousand years, human societies have put safety nets underneath the economically disadvantaged.[2] Today, in 'first world' societies there is usually a minimum level of support. Given that, an increase in the size of the underclass automatically increases public expenditure. That in turn means higher taxes or increased government deficits. If higher taxes are indirect, they are also paid by the underclass. If direct taxes are increased, work and business incentives are reduced. If fiscal deficits are increased, the public finances are generally de-stabilized and long term real interest rates may be pushed up. If real interest rates are high, macroeconomic growth is slowed down, reinforcing the general problem.[3]

The syndrome

Figure 1.1 describes the situation. If, through accidents of genes, chance or whatever, one is born with or raised into low ability, one is likely to be a slow learner and so feel discouraged. Alternatively one may receive negative motives directly from one's peer group. On both sides of the Atlantic there is currently much concern about negative peer-group pressure on schoolboys from underclass or working-class

---

1 From here and through the next sub-section I acknowledge some influence from the ideas of Will Hutton, author of *The State We're In* (1995, in References) – a radical polemic, not all of which I agree with, that has had record sales.

2 See eg Brian Pullen, *Rich and Poor in Renaissance Venice*, in References.

3 See Chapter 3, p 104, and also later in the present chapter for the reasons why slow overall macroeconomic growth since the mid-1970s has been the prime cause of the current underclass problem.

families. With low ability and/or low motivation one will perform badly in educational selection tests.[1] So one is twice likely to get a bad education - for example to drop out of high school in the US or in Britain leave the system around age 16 with no GCEs or other qualifications. Therefore, maybe around age 20, one will be a person of low skill and not much to offer the job market. One may then drop out of the market altogether, subsisting on welfare-based income support, if available, or in the grey labour market or worse (drug dealing, crime) if it is not. Or one may become a single parent. Statistically one has become 'non-employed' (see the box). Neither the fact of insecure or low-paid employment nor the fact of non-employment automatically puts one in the underclass (the non-employed include some affluent and contented bodies). But either increases the likelihood.

The basic problem is inadequate demand for your services. Whether the result is low-paid work or non-employment will depend on circumstances, including the ease or difficulty, as the case may be, of getting welfare support. Whether the cause is to be seen as your own inadequate employability – the 'supply side'– or inadequate demand, or both, is the topic of this book. What is sure, however, is that if an economy does suffer from deficient general demand for labour, then the more liberal the welfare system, the greater will be the tendency for the demand deficiency to show up in non-employment. Conversely, if income-support is difficult to obtain, the general demand deficiency is more likely to show up in employment at low wages.

The concept of meritocracy
Both the above patterns are aspects of an excessive meritocracy.

The concept
Thirty-eight years ago, Michael Young (now a Lord, in his eighties and flourishing) published a profoundly original book, part-satirical, part academic, entitled *The Rise of the Meritocracy, 1870-2033: an essay on education and equality,*[2] in which he described the paradox

---

1 In the middle classes, parents, concerned for a child's future may spend more, rather than less money or effort on the education of a less able child.
2 See Young, 1958, in References.

that when we create equality of opportunity we also open the way for a new elitism of merit and ability. He forecast our contemporary end-of-century dilemmas with remarkable accuracy. Although they do not list him in their references, Young's analysis, albeit in a contemporary right-wing American colouring, lies behind the arguments of Richard Hernstein and Charles Murray in their highly controversial 1994 book, *The Bell Curve*.[1] Meritocracy is also the shadow lying over the contemporary world as seen by Robert Reich,

> ....Regardless of how your job is officially classified .... your real competitive position in the world economy is coming to depend on the function you perform in it. Herein lies the basic reason why incomes are diverging. The fortunes of routine producers are declining..... But symbolic analysts – who solve, identify, and broker new problems – are, by and large, succeeding in the world economy.[2]

Alternative Meritocracies

It is my passionately held opinion, whose propagation will take up much of this book, that the perverse meritocractic scenario is not inevitable. I believe there are two versions of meritocracy, severe and moderate, or '*SM*' and '*MM*'. For reasons discussed further in Chapter 5, the social system transforms the natural curve of human ability, which is bell-shaped, into a curve of earnings which is highly skewed. Some skewness is inevitable, but

> **Tony Blair on Meritocracy**
>
> ".... We need entrepreneurs and people who are going to go out and be wealth creators and who are going to become wealthy by their own efforts. I support that, I want that, a succeful economy needs that.... *I am an unremitting meritocrat in that sense.*"
>
> – from an interview with the leader of the British Labour Party reported in the London *Evening Standard*, 23 May 1996.

its amount can vary. A severe meritocracy has high skewness of employment incomes; a moderate meritocracy, moderate skewness. What decides whether we experience one kind of meritocracy or the other? The answer is the macroeconomic environment. If the demand for all kinds of labour is healthy, people who initially lack the best labour-market skills will nevertheless be drawn in, and, in the

---

1 See Hernstein and Murray, 1994, in References
2 Reich, 1991, first page Ch 17, in References.

The Bell Curve and the J-Curve

A *'Bell Curve'* is a type of graph in which data are arranged in groups, eg one group could be the number of people earning between £8000 and £10,000 a year and the next group those between £8000 and £6000. The centre of each group range is plotted on the x-axis and the number of people reported as being in that range on the y-axis. If the resulting curve is flattish topped and symmetrical, it is called 'bell-shaped'. The point on the x-axis corresponding to the peak of the curve is called the 'mode': it is the mid-point of the range of the group containing the largest number of people – the modal income is the 'typical' income. Because the curve is symmetrical, the modal income is also the average income: there is an equal number of people on either side of the mode and an equal number of people with above-average and below-average income.

This kind of curve is predicted by mathematics for any kind of data where the differences between people are the result of the sum of a number of small effects. It is also the curve that occurs naturally in data on the sizes and weights of animals and humans and *also human performance in exams and intelligence tests.*

A *'J-Curve'* is a bell curve which has been 'skewed' to the right: there is a long right tail where small numbers of people have very large earnings. The average is also pulled out to the right and most people are below the average. Income, property and the sizes of firms follow this type of curve. More precisely, the curve is a *J* turned round, and – because the largest group does not have the lowest income – the curve also has a short bent-over tail to the left.

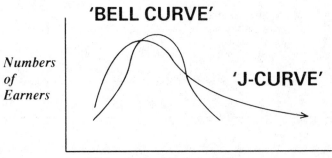

'BELL CURVE'

Numbers of Earners

'J-CURVE'

Mid-points of Earnings Ranges

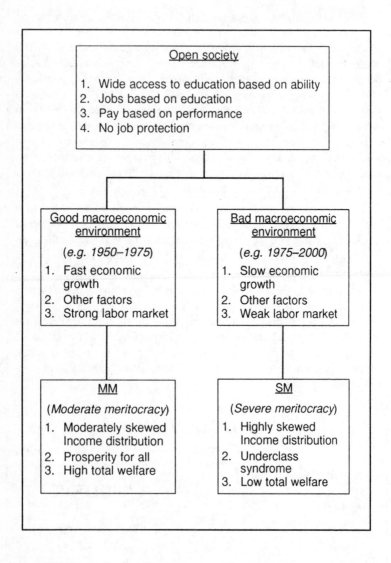

Figure 1.2 Alternative meritocracies.

process, will learn on the job and so be upgraded. In addition, employed people whose abilities are currently under-utilized will be promoted, leaving vacancies for others. Why? Because, in the presence of a sellers' market for labour, buyers, ie employers, will have the incentive to do whatever is necessary to make the available labour employable. On the other side, with vacancies available, it is easier for workers to match their particular abilities to the best paying jobs.[1] In the third quarter of the 20th century, economic growth was brisk and the demand for labour chronically buoyant. During those years we did not hear much about the social problems of meritocracy (mostly we heard about the problems of living with a labour shortage) and although Michael Young remained a strong influence on British public life, his book was forgotten. In sharp contrast, after 1973 – the year of the first great oil-price shock – the dominant concern of macroeconomic policy became the containment of inflation; economic growth slowed down (the one thing being surely partly, if not wholly, the result of the other), various other awkward things began to occur, the underclass syndrome began to emerge and other signs of *SM* also began to appear. The logical structure of the story is depicted on the tree in Figure 1.2. Before 1973 we were on the left hand branch, after, on the right hand.

The macroeconomic environment

In Figure 1.2, I show economic growth as the main factor distinguishing between the alternative configurations in the macroeconomic environment. I have also mentioned other factors. In fact, during the actual period 1973-1995 (stylized as '1975-2000' in Figure 1.2) 'other factors' (some of which had set in already) were very important indeed. Briefly, in short-hand, they were *technology, trade, services, women and public policy*. The first refers to the effects of the IT (information-technology) revolution, the second to the so-called globalization of international trade, the third to the shift of demand and employment from industry to services and the fourth to the large

---

1   A counter-argument is that with well-paid unskilled work easy to obtain, and skill differentials in wage-rates reduced, there is less incentive on the workers' side to acquire skills. I believe this is a valid point, whose dangers in the future should not be ignored.

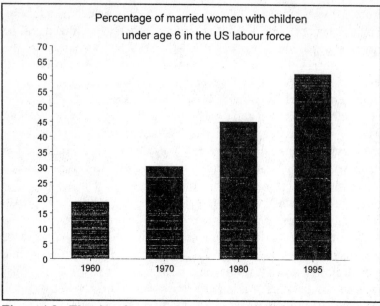

Figure 1.3   The rise of maternal employment in the US 1960-1995.
Source: Statistical Abstract of the United States, 1993, p 391 (1995 extrapolated from 1993).

and continuous increase that has been taking place in the proportion of the female population of working age who desire paid employment. The 'services' item also embraces the ideas of '*de-industrialization*' and '*de-unionization*'. Finally, by 'public policy' I refer to the effects of the tightening-up of the qualifying requirements for unemployment and income support which occurred on both sides of the Atlantic: for example, in the United States, for persons of either sex without children, after six months, there is no support at all. Significant though it may be, this last is not a topic which will be further pursued in this book. One reason is that I am not technically qualified to pursue it in detail, another that, being the result of a series of political decisions, it is also politically reversible.[1]

---

1   Tony Atkinson, who, in contrast, is highly qualified on the topic, considers this factor has indeed been important, both quantitatively and, as it were, qualitatively, in the on-going situation. See especially Chapters 1 and 9 of his 1995 book

Several of the items above are closely connected with or dependent on growth. Taken together with growth, and riding the escalator of meritocracy, the group represents a unique nexus of features of the economic history of the final quarter of our century. There is nothing intrinsically bad about any of the members of the nexus: they were things that were inevitable, desirable or both. But, taken with the macro environment, they have nevertheless led us down the bad right branch of Figure 1.2.

Although growth and trade will have separate chapters I now discuss them in an introductory way, and also the other items.

Economic growth

The definition

'Economic growth' means the long term trend of the annual percentage increase in GDP per capita, ie GDP[1] per head of total population. It is in turn the sum of three corresponding component growth rates; the growth rate of employment per capita, the growth rate of annual hours per employee and the growth rate of GDP per employee-hour, ie productivity. The distinction between the whole and the parts is not always made clear. When economists speak of 'growth'[2] sometimes they mean GDP per capita, sometimes productivity and sometimes both. They are obviously not the same, because for all kinds of reasons the figure for total annual employee-hours does not necessarily grow at the same rate as the population. However, the distinction between per capita GDP growth and productivity growth is crucial to

---

(already referred to, in References.)

1   GDP is a statistical measure of the real value of all the goods and services produced by the national economy, including public goods such as education and defence. The value is taken at constant 'market' prices, ie final selling prices.

2   Among financial and economic journalists the word 'growth' has unfortunately also come to be widely used in a short term sense, eg 'in 1995 the Japanese economy grew by 5 per cent'. If a major part of the 5 per cent represented recovery from a recession, the economy has not grown in long term GDP-producing capacity, it has merely shifted to a higher utilization of its capacity. The proper words are, 'in 1995 the Japan's GDP increased by 5 per cent'. I believe the misleading usage reflects a short term emphasis which, since 1975, has flowered among economic writers in conscious or unconscious deference to the 'short-termism' of their main readers - the operators of financial markets.

our problem. Why? Because the relationship between the two determines the long term state of the labour market.

Growth and the labour market

Whether, in the long run, there is to be a weak or strong labour market depends, obviously, on the balance of long term trends in the macro supply of and the macro demand for employment.

The *supply* of labour is the number of persons desiring paid employment multiplied by their average desired annual working hours. It is often identified with the 'labour force' (total employed plus total unemployed – see box on labour market terms). But during the past quarter century, this identification, for rather obvious reasons, has become obsolete. First, there has been a general increase in non-employment among men, a large part of which may have resulted from inadequate demand, rather than from a socially induced decline in supply. Second, as Figure 1.3 dramatically illustrates, the supply of women workers has increased much faster than the female population of working age. The causes of this are certainly very much social, and may also be partly economic, but whatever they are they are surely mainly a form of supply-, rather than demand-effect.

The effective labour supply

We therefore need a better measure of the labour supply. I will call this the *effective labour supply*. It is the sum of the *actual* number of participating women aged 25-64, times their annual working hours, *plus* the corresponding numbers and hours of participating men calculated *not* at the actual participation rate but *as if* the male participation rate had remained constant.[1] Clearly, the new measure is only a rough guide: it does not tell us how many women actually wanted paid work, only how many found it. Nor does it allow for men who left the labour force for reasons other than discouragement.

Obviously the new concept need not grow at the same rate as the general population. Therefore we also need a concept of *per capita* growth rate of the effective labour supply: the growth rate of the effective labour supply less the growth rate of the population.

Figures 1.4 and 1.5 show the growth of per capita effective labour supply, since 1970, for the UK and the US.

---

1   At the 1970 level, pre-dating the general rise in male non-employment.

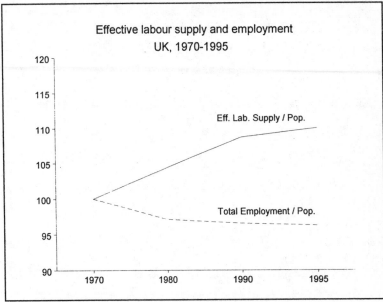

Figure 1.4   The employment gap in the UK, 1970-1995.

Sources: See Statistical Appendix to Chapter 2.

Definition: Effective labour supply = actual number of participating
females + males calculated as if their non-employment rate
was constant at the level of 1970.

The same graphs also show actual employment, relative to
population. In a society whose age pattern was fairly constant, the
population of working age would grow at roughly the same rate as the
total population. If the proportion of people who wanted to work was
constant, effective labour supply would grow at the same rate as
population. If all those who wanted work found it, employment would
grow at the same rate as population. If all these things happened, all
the lines in these two figures would be horizontal. But none of them
happened, and they are not.

In both countries the per capita effective labour supply bursts
upward on account of the increased participation of women. In both
countries employment could not keep up. The resulting gap between
employment and supply was, however, much higher in the UK than
in the US. In fact, as has been widely pointed out, the US employ-

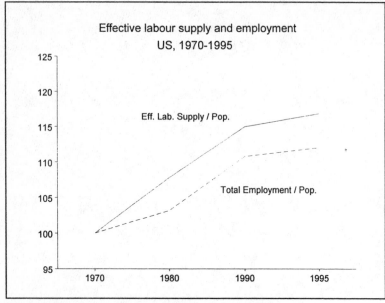

Figure 1.5   The employment gap in the US, 1970-1995.
Sources: See Statistical Appendix to Chapter 2.
Definition: – as UK (see Figure 1.4).

ment performance appears impressive. In the UK, in sharp contrast, there was an actual fall in the proportion of the population who were employed.

Table 1.1 shows the employment gap in percentage terms in 1995 for seven additional countries, as well as for the UK and the US.

The role of wages
The reason for the difference between the UK and the US, and also for a similar difference between the US and France and Germany lies, of course, in the opposite story of wages. As we shall see in Chapter 2, over the same period, the ratio of US real wages to European real wages sharply declined. Among the lowest paid workers, real hourly earnings in the US today range from three-quarters to a half typical West European levels. Only if the US had shown superior performance on both the employment and the wage front would one have been able to say that as compared to Europe, the US had maintained a superior growth of demand for labour relative to effective supply.

Table 1.1   **The Employment Gap in Nine Countries in 1995**
(The excess of the effective labour supply over actual employment, as a percentage of effective labour supply.)

Japan	2.5	*US*	7.4	*Italy*	11.7
Norway	6.0	*UK*	11.8	*Germany*	14.3
Sweden	6.3	*Australia*	11.9	*France*	14.7

Definitions: see text.
Source: calculated from *OECD Labour Force Statistics*, 1995, in References.

A substantial amount of research has shown that major factors in the performance of low-end wages in the Anglo-Saxon countries were the economic weakening of labour unions and the repeal or weakening of minimum-wage legislation.[1] Had this not occurred, the employment performance would presumably have been correspondingly weaker.

The demand for labour
The macroeconomic *demand* for labour, measured in total person-hours is the amount of employment required to produce the current GDP. In other words, GDP divided by productivity (GDP per worker-hour). The per capita *growth-rate* of the demand for labour is therefore the growth-rate of GDP per capita *less* the growth rate of productivity.

Supply and demand
The long-run balance of supply and demand for labour is uniquely set by the relation between the growth rate of effective labour supply and the growth rate of demand. So we get the fundamental equations shown in the box on page 27. If the equation is not satisfied, a long term gap between labour supply and demand will emerge, and, so long as the two growth rates continue to differ, will be ever-increasing. The mathematics leads to a crucial conclusion: to avoid imbalance, *the growth rate of per capita GDP must equal per capita effective labour supply **less** the growth rate of productivity.* Suppose the effective labour supply per capita were constant, but productivity were growing at two and a half per cent. Then if labour-market balance is to be

---

1   See Freeman, 1991, Borjas, 1995, Gosling and Machin, 1995, in References.

sustained, in the sense that workers displaced by productivity growth are readily re-employed, per capita GDP must also grow at two and a half per cent. If the per capita effective labour supply is also growing, GDP growth must be correspondingly faster.

How weak growth causes SM

But per capita GDP growth is precisely what I mean (see above) by 'economic growth'. If it falls below the required rate, the labour market must be progressively weakening – which is precisely how slow growth after 1973 contributed to the bad macroeconomic environment shown on the right-hand arm of Figure 1.2. After 1973, the long-run growth rate of GDP per capita in the OECD slowed down by about one and a half percentage points. What happened to the *required* growth rate is a more complex question waiting to be discussed in Chapter 3. For the sake of argument suppose that the required growth rate did also slow down by, say, half a point. That would imply after 1973 a long term gap of one percentage point between labour demand growth and labour supply growth. Compound interest at one per cent for 22 years increases the principle by nearly a quarter, implying an excess supply of all kinds of labour by 1995 of the same amount. Of course, we have not seen open unemployment rates of 25 per cent. Part of the gap has been closed in other ways.

As a matter of fact, in the whole OECD, in 1995, the average non-employment rate among working-age so-called 'Low-Ed'[1] males is, currently, at least 25 per cent. The burden has almost certainly fallen disproportionately on the lower end of the labour market, thus contributing, as I have said, to the gradual replacement, since 1973, of *MM* by *SM*.

The simple theory lying behind the foregoing calculations is by no means new, but it has suffered a period of neglect. The basic equations were first worked out in the late nineteen thirties, in the wake of Keynes's theory, by Oxford economist Roy Harrod[2] and Cambridge-Massachusetts economist Evsey Domar[3]. Harrod called the required

---

1 People with no more than lower-secondary education, eg in Britain someone who left school with no GCEs or other qualifications or, in the US, 'dropped out' of high school, ie left without a graduation diploma.

2 Harrod, 1939, in References.

3 Domar, 1946, in References.

Labour-market algebra

(1) $Gr(demand) = Gr(supply)$

(2) $Gr(GDPC) - Gr(productivity) = Gr(ELSPC)$

(3) $Gr(required) = Gr(ELPC) + Gr(productivity)$

Definitions:

$Gr(x)$	=	growth-rate of x
$GDPC$	=	GDP per capita (ie per head of population)
$ELSPC$	=	effective labour supply per head of population
$Gr(required)$	=	$Gr(GDPC)$ required for labour-market balance.

Note: in earlier versions (eg in Harrod's 1939 version, listed in References and further discussed below) equation (3) was written

(3a) $Gr(GDP) = Gr(Pop) + Gr(productivity)$

– the two versions being the same only if ELS grows at the same rate as population, which, in our time, it has not.

---

rate of growth the 'natural' rate of growth. The implications were later tellingly pursued by the Cambridge-England economist, Joan Robinson, in her book entitled *The Accumulation of Capital*, published in 1956.[1]

In 1961, Robert Solow (MIT – Cambridge, Mass.) published a brilliant mathematical model in which a condition of excess supply in the labour market might drive down real wages and therefore reduce incentives to economize labour. Labour productivity would therefore fall off its trend line. So the economy might resume balanced growth at the cost of a one-time reduction of wages. The model became the professional economist's standard and in due course Bob Solow received a Nobel Prize for it.

The simple message, therefore, is that if the actual growth rate falls below the required (or 'natural') rate, there must be increasing non-employment, lower wages, lower productivity, or all three. Like the original Keynesian theory, as mentioned in the Preface, this is an economic proposition akin to the law of gravity. If one ignores gravity, one will be confused. From 1973 to 1990, although faced with an evident actual/natural growth-rate gap (whose more detailed anatomy will be discussed in Chapter 3), both policy makers and economists were seemingly trying to forget the Keynes-Harrod-

---

1 Joan Robinson, 1956, in References.

Domar-Solow laws, causing not only intellectual confusion, but worse, ie *SM*, social distress and the underclass syndrome.[1]

Technology

I believe that slow economic growth, in the manner described above, has been the dominant element in the whole story. Other people, with strong arguments, believe the dominant factor has been the effects of the new technology. Their argument is not that technical progress, as measured by hourly productivity, has accelerated (it hasn't) but rather that the new technology is biased against the employment of people with lesser education or intelligence, most especially the latter. The very nature of computers makes the argument convincing.

The phenomenon is elusive because it is hard to observe. Many of the jobs lost to computers are in white-collar occupations. When the jobs go, other jobs open up for the new people working on direct line from screens and keyboards. Are the new people a different socio-economic class, better educated, more intelligent? The answers are by no means always necessarily, 'yes'.

Because of this elusiveness, the topic of technology will get less space in this book than it deserves. There are however some valuable American economic studies on the subject[2] and a further major American contribution which I now discuss.

In 1992, John Bound and George Johnson published in the *American Economic Review*[3] a very important and profoundly professional paper in which they studied the employment, output and earnings in ten distinct worker categories (education level, age, sex, etc) in twenty industries over fifteen years. By careful theoretical and

---

1 On Jan 9, 1995, *The Times* economics editor, Anatole Kaletsky, wrote, 'it is a simple arithmetical fact that unemployment can only be reduced if the economy grows by more than the growth of productivity plus the growth in the number of people who want to work'. Such a remark, in such august columns, was an important sign of 'new times'. I doubt if a search of the paper over the previous ten or even twenty years would yield anything similar. Only a year earlier the OECD Jobs Study (OECD, 1994, in References) contained few signs that the authors understood the simple arithmetical fact.

2 See, in References, the works of Ann Bartel and Frank Lichtenberg, and of Jerome Mark, in 1987; and of Alan Kreuger in 1991.

3 'Changes in the structure of wages in the 1980's: an evaluation of alternative explanations', in References.

statistical modelling they were able to estimate how much the relative wages of each category *should* have changed according to various explanatory factors such as demand and supply. For example, if Low-Ed men were disproportionately employed in industries or services where demand, as indicated by changes in final output, had comparatively declined, this would show up as a quantified negative factor for the group.[1] The corresponding 'supply' factor would be the changes in relative numbers of available Low-Eds.

Having calculated the changes in demand and supply for each category, Bound and Johnson then estimated how much effect the combined changes should have had on the categories' relative wages. By similar procedures they also estimated the effects of changes in productivity levels within industries and the effects of varying degrees of unionization within industries.[2]

Have done all this, Bound and Johnson then, in effect, compared their equations' predicted results with actual results and naturally found major discrepancies (prediction errors, or 'residuals'). These they largely attributed either to technology or to changes in the quality of the labour force itself. The latter they attributed to the classic problem of meritocracy, namely that as a result of the expansion of education, the pool of blue-collar labour had been emptied of its most intelligent members.

In Figure 1.6, I present a summary of Bound and Johnson's main results, the black bars showing the actual, the grey bars the predicted

---

1 An average of all the industry-sector relative output changes weighted by the initial share of total Low-Ed employment accounted for by the relevant industries.

2 The model therefore has the valuable feature of being able to pick up the results of the following widely-suggested scenario: (i) declining relative demand for manufactures (ii) disproportionate employment of Low-Eds in manufactures (iii) higher unionization in manufactures, all leading to (iv) lower economy-wide wages for Low-Eds as they move out of the unionized manufacturing sector into less unionized services sectors.

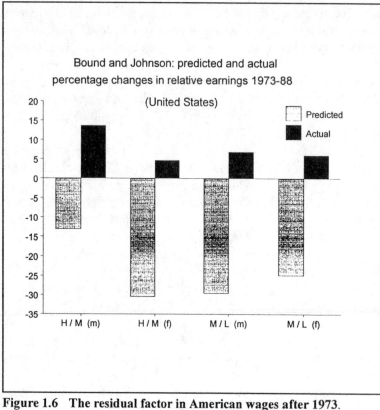

Figure 1.6   The residual factor in American wages after 1973.

    Source: Calculated from John Bound and George Johnson, 1992, in References.

    Definitions: H-Ed = 'High-Ed'   = some college education

                M-Ed = 'Mid-Ed'   = high school graduate, no more

                L-Ed = 'Low-Ed'   = less than Mid-Ed.

                Changes in relative earnings are the difference, from beginning to end of period, in the percentage change in one indicated group as compared to the other (eg H-M = percentage increase in H-Ed minus percentage increase in M-Ed).

    'Predicted'   Changes predicted by (i) changes in supply [eg increased numbers of college graduates] (ii) changes in demand derived from changes in the final demand for products (iii) industry wage-effects [eg effects of greater unionization in industries especially employing the indicated type of worker] (iv) industry productivity effects [eg changes in the productivity of a particular type of worker in particular industries].

results. For example, the first pair of bars, labelled 'H - M (m)' indicate that the model predicted that the percentage earnings gain for higher-educated males should have fallen *below* that of 'middle-educated' (high school but no college) males by 13 percentage points.[1] But the actual result was a 14 point change in the opposite direction, making a positive 'residual' of no less than 27 points! Much the same story is obtained for females and, it will be seen, for other categories right across Figure 1.6. There are very substantial positive residuals for every comparison of higher with lower education levels. Bound and Johnson attribute the upper-end effects mainly to technology and the lower-end effects, by implication, to meritocracy, ie they suggest that the pool of remaining Low-Eds has become less intelligent. The implications of suggestions of this type are discussed in Chapter 5.

Some economists have criticised these conclusions on the ground that residuals are no more than residuals: if a residual is unexplained, it is unexplained and that is that. Nevertheless, one must surely accept that, given the intuitive expectation that something has happened, the results do give food for thought.

A major problem, however, is that the Bound and Johnson 'experiment' is necessarily based on actual history. It is based on the macroeconomic environment that actually occurred. It cannot tell us what would happen in a different environment. If overall economic growth during the period had been different, the Bound and Johnson industry effects would have been different and their residuals would have been different. For example, with a brisker demand for labour, employers would have found ways of effectively using 'less intelligent' Low-Eds and of affording to pay them higher wages.

The general conclusion is that it is likely that technology effects have played a significant role in our story, *interacting* with the macroeconomic environment, in building up our post-1973 '*SM*' story.

1　The main reason for the prediction, as with most of the others in the figure, was the large increase in relative supply. As college-education numbers have increased dramatically, the middle group has remained roughly constant, losing numbers upwards while gaining from below as the number of Low-Eds has equally dramatically declined.

Trade[1]

This topic is more fully discussed in Chapter 4. The basic argument is that since around 1980 the export capacity of the 'South' (meaning loosely the Third World – all non-OECD countries except Eastern Europe and ex-Soviet Union) has sharply increased, causing an increase in actual or potential competition from the South within the economies of the 'North' (ie within the OECD). Inside the South there is a much smaller supply of skilled labour relative to unskilled labour than in the North. Therefore, in the South, as compared to the North, the price of unskilled labour, relative to the price of skilled labour, is much lower. The opening up of trade has a similar effect to the opening up of labour migration: it brings the relative prices together. Inevitably this means a fall in the relative wage of unskilled labour in the North.

A major variation on the theme is that increased exports from the South to the North have mainly affected the most unionized sectors of the economies of the North, where previously less educated male blue-collar workers had been able to earn good wages, with similar effects.

Few economists disagree with the theory but there is a good deal of debate, backed up on both sides by statistical research, as to how important a factor it has been in practice, at least up to the present. Because I devote the whole of Chapter 4 to the topic I say very little more here. I simply report that Adrian Wood's calculation[2] suggests that the cumulative effect in the North up to 1990 was of the order of 20 per cent. That is to say, if the skilled-wage/unskilled-wage ratio had been constant, the quantity of unskilled labour demanded, relative to the quantity of skilled labour demanded would have declined by 20 per cent.

Trade and growth

Before the seventies, when the OECD countries were 'industrially autarkic' (ie not importing industrial goods from the rest of the world), they were also, as it happened, growing briskly. With not

---

1   The outstanding current exposition of this topic is in Adrian Wood's already classic, *North-South Trade, Employment and Inequality* (Wood, 1994, in References) especially pp 27-9 and 32-42.

2   Wood, 1994, p 149, and 1995, Table 1, in References.

much more than a tenth of the world's population, they had more than half the world's real GDP and much more than half of her economically productive assets. The real gap between their average per capita GDP and the rest of the world was about equivalent to a factor of ten, and was neither closing nor widening.

Subsequently growth slowed down and trade increased. I do not suggest that one thing caused the other. Far from it. The latter thing was inevitable and desirable, the former was neither. But, as in the case of technology, the historical coincidence of the two events is striking.

Services, de-industrialization and de-unionization
When average income in a modern society becomes high, the growth of consumer demand for industrial goods falls behind the growth of demand for services. Unless one or both of two other things also happens, the share of employment in industry must fall. This is called *de-industrialization*. De-industrialization leads in turn to de-unionization, because on balance unions tend to be stronger in industrial as compared to other sectors of the economy.

Unless the growth of *productivity* in industry also slows down, or the growth of industrial exports accelerates, these trends are inevitable. Thus de-industrialization is itself inevitable and has in fact been occurring to a varying extent in different OECD countries for some time past: the share of private-sector services in total OECD employment, for example, rose between 1970 and 1990 from 37.5 per cent to 50.5 per cent.[1]

De-industrialization has two closely connected effects on the macroeconomic environment, a *wage effect* and a *growth effect*.

The wage effect
Wages earned by less educated, less skilled workers in the services sector are generally lower than the wages these people would have earned in industry.[2] With an increasing share of the total demand for Low-Ed labour occurring in services, the Low-Ed economy-wide average wage is pulled down. Faced with the prospect of no work in

---

1   *OECD Jobs Study,* Part I, (1994, in References) Chart 4.5, p 159.
2   See eg, 'Are services sector jobs inferior?' (Dupuy and Schweitzer, 1994, in References).

industry or low-paid work in services, some people may prefer non-employment. So the wage effect of de-industrialization is a possible contributor to *SM*.

The growth effect

For the past half century, according to statistics the average 'productivity' of the services sectors has been growing less rapidly than that of the manufacturing sector and the former is now significantly lower than the latter. Since we cannot directly compare motor cars with hamburgers, we must ask what this actually means. The answer is that it means that the average service employee, in an hour of work, contributes statistically less to GDP than an average industrial employee. In short, service work creates lower value added (per worker hour) than industrial work.

If employment shifts from industry to services, although average productivity (in value added) in neither sector changes, productivity averaged over the whole GDP, by simple arithmetic, necessarily declines.[1] This effect, which is called 'the structural-shift effect' causes a slow-down in the economy-average growth rate of GDP per worker-hour and, therefore, a fall in the required rate of growth. Consequently, it should be a factor tending to favour long-run demand over supply in the labour market, ie tending in the direction of *preventing SM*: a weak economy-wide demand for labour may be partially 'sponged away' by the labour-intensive needs of the expanding services sector.

Thus as far as concerns our problem, the wage effect and the growth effect of the shift to services appear to go in opposite directions. But I believe that is only the beginning of the story. *Why* are Low-Ed wages low in services? The conventional answer is because productivity is low. But why is productivity low and why has it been slowing down? The conventional answer is that services are inherently labour-intensive; hamburger-cooking cannot profitably use as

---

1   In extremely valuable research work we shall be seeing again in Chapter 3, Angus Maddison, economics graduate of Cambridge, England, then on the staff of the OECD, then senior research worker at the OECD and currently Professor of Economics at the University of Groeningen, Netherlands, has quantified the effect for six countries from 1950 to 1988. See Maddison, *Explaining the Economic Performance of Nations*, 1995, Tables 20-22, pp 66-7, in References.

much equipment per worker as car assembling.

The effect on the labour-market gap measurement

I have another idea about this, however. Suppose there is an underlying weakness in the actual rate of economic growth. Although consumers are switching away from manufactures, their corresponding increase in demand for services is not very strong and rather price sensitive. To attract customers and profitably employ labour, services prices must be 'competitive'. Now, given that, as already mentioned, the output of services is measured by value added, what this means is that in the presence of weak economic growth we will see a low-wage, low 'productivity' shift to services. Had growth been faster, the shift could have taken a different form – higher prices, higher wages and higher 'productivity'. 'Productivity' is put in inverted commas because what is happening is not a genuine physical or technical effect; there has been no slowing down in the annual increase (if there is one) of hamburgers cooked per worker-hour.

If my idea is correct, it has quite wide-ranging significance. In Chapter 3 we shall see that in the United States there has in fact been a slow-down in the rate of growth of apparent productivity in services which has not so far been explained. Statistically this slow-down adds to the structural-shift effect and thus contributes to an apparent slowing down of US national GDP per worker-hour. This will also reduce the calculated value of the required growth rate.

In short, I am suggesting a circle of causes which begin with a major actual-growth slow-down, one of the effects of which is to *cause* an apparent slow-down in the required rate of growth, ie affect both sides of the basic equation in the box on page 27. The gap between actual growth and required growth opened by the initial slow-down, is therefore seemingly reduced. But the reduction is in effect a statistical illusion. The result is an *understatement* of the true labour-market gap.

Some leading American economists[1] have a parallel idea involving a different explanation of the productivity deficit which has, however, much the same implication for the labour-market gap. They have noted that in the US economy, the only sector whose apparent

---

1   See especially Grilliches, 1994, in References.

productivity has truly, in the long term, slowed down is the group of services sub-sectors whose output is most difficult to measure. The suggestion is that there has been an increasing downwards bias in their output as reported in the US GDP statistics. I discuss this further in Chapter 3. I and they hold common ground in suggesting that maybe in truth there never was a US productivity slow down.

Women

This extremely important subject – the economic effect of the social change in womens' aspirations – has already been mentioned several times. We now face a question that many economists seem to have thought unmentionable: have women pushed men out of the labour force and/or have they pushed down wages?[1] I personally suspect the question may be statistically unanswerable; certainly it cannot be answered definitively with any numbers presented in this book.

We can, however, say something definite about the logic of the question. We have already seen that the increased womens' labour supply means simply and clearly an increase in the effective *total* labour supply as compared with what it would otherwise have been, given the natural growth, if any, of the total population. Therefore women's 'liberation' inevitably implies an increase in the *required* rate of macroeconomic growth. If that does not happen, as certainly as night follows day, one or all of the following will happen: (1) some women will be frustrated in their desire to work, (2) more men will become non-employed than would otherwise have been the case, (3) men's and women's, wages, especially among Low-Eds, will be pushed down.

---

1 The *OECD Jobs Study*, Part I, p 33 (OECD, 1994, in References) does devote one
   paragraph to the question, as follows,
   > 'The boost to the labour force numbers has sometimes been seen as a factor behind
   > higher unemployment rates. However, a study by Elmeskov and Pichelmann*
   > suggests that there is in fact a negative relationship – both in levels and in changes
   > in the long-run – between unemployment and participation rates.... This is also the
   > case in the long-run for men and women taken separately.'
   > * – Elmeskov, 1994, in References.
   The paper cited is a valuable one, but surely not relevant here. The authors'
   correlations show, as one would expect, that in countries with a buoyant labour
   market there will be relatively low non-employment – either high participation,
   low unemployment or not; but that is a different point.

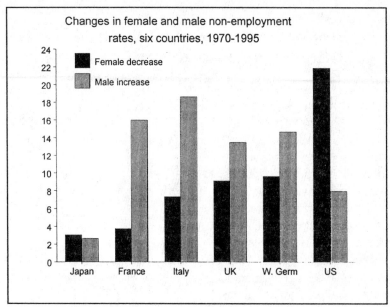

Figure 1.7 **Non-employment in six countries:** *decreases* **in female rates matched against** *increases* **in male rates, 1970-1995.**
Definition: Changes in percentage points.
Source: Calculated from OECD *Labour Force Statistics*, 1995.

If it were possible somehow to show that women had pushed men out of work and/or pushed down their wages, the 'culprit' would be whoever or whatever was responsible for the economic system having proved unable to match its actual rate of growth to accommodate people, of either sex, who desired to work.

Figure 1.7 gives the broad story for six countries. In every one, even including, by a tiny amount, Japan, the past quarter-century has seen a fall in female non-employment rates (meaning, of course a rise in labour-force participation: the women were not previously doing nothing, of course, but they were not in paid employment) and in all countries, even including Japan, there has been a rise in male non-employment rates. The figures for Japan reflect, on the one hand, a relatively small social-cultural change (over the period as a whole; in the nineties things are said to be changing) and, on the other, a vigorous market for all kinds of labour associated with Japan's spectacular long term growth.

At the other extreme, the American story, whatever the economic interpretation, certainly stands out. The US decrease in female *non-employment*, at 22 per cent, was more than double the figure for the UK which was around ten per cent. At the same time, the US increase in male non-employment, at under ten per cent, was *lower* than that of any other country bar Japan.

These remarkable American figures again underline the significance of the fact that, as we shall see again in Chapter 2, the US also stands out from the other countries in another way, namely the virtual stagnation, over the whole period, of *family* real income, as compared to brisk or at least moderate growth in all the other countries: after 1970 the annual growth rate of *median*[1] US family income slowed down from a previous long term figure around three per cent, to a figure up to 1995 of little better than one half of one per cent. It has been shown that the main cause of this adverse performance for US family units has been, in fact, the pattern of development of individual earnings. One might say that the great increase in

---

Women, Men, Work and Earnings

In an important paper,* Dr. Gary Burtless has shown that in the US, between 1969 and 1989,

(1) The *rise* in US male non-employment was mainly concentrated in the *bottom* 20 per cent (quintile) of the income distribution,

(2) There was *no* fall in non-employment among women in the *bottom quintile*.

(3) As well as a the rise in non-employment among bottom-quintile males, since 1969 their *working hours* have fallen 30 per cent.

(4) The working hours of all employed women *rose*, most especially in the higher quintiles, by from 10 to 20 per cent.

---
* See Burtless, 1993, in References.

---

1   Remember from the box on page 18 that in a skewed distribution the median (the income level above and below which there is an equal number of earners) is not the same as the average. If average income increases with constant skewness, the median will also increase. But if skewness is increasing it is possible for the average to increase with no increase in the median at all. This is what appears to have happened in the US. *Average* family income did increase, but the whole gain apparently fell to the group of families who were already in the top fifty per cent, leaving the median family income unchanged.

paid work by American women only partly offset by the modest shift to less work by American men, has not apparently increased the buying power of average American *couples*, but on the other hand it has surely changed the distribution of economic power within the family, in a rather obvious direction.[1] It has also raised the welfare of women whose motive was that staying home is boring.

---

1   Juergen Elmeskov of the OECD has suggested to me that the average size of US families has also fallen so that the total economic picture for couples is less gloomy than I have painted it. The problem however, is that given widespread contraception, procreation has become a voluntary choice. Maybe economic pressure *caused* the reduction of family size. My guess is that the reduction is directly associated with increased womens' employment. Women reduced their families and went out to work presumably expecting a net gain in welfare. In the event, there was little gain in family earnings, and the best that could be said of the situation is that, had family size not been reduced, things would have been worse.

2. Education, Employment and Earnings

In the past quarter-century there has been a huge rise in education – for both sexes and for all classes and ethnic groups. Previously, in Britain, the system was not meritocratic: with two-thirds of the population receiving no more than a basic education, numerous able children were eliminated by the '11+' exam. Now, in Britain, as in the US, at least two thirds of the population get better than a basic education. In Germany that always was so, and the old region of West Germany today, despite a current economic crisis caused by an overvalued exchange rate, has only a moderate meritocracy – with a level of total welfare which may well be as high as any in the world.

The other side of the coin is the rise in 'non-employment'. Many non-employed are people who have taken early retirement or become state-supported invalids and some of these increases may reflect natural tendencies to reduce working life as we become more affluent. But the trends are also partly 'endogenous' to the weak labour market. If fewer people had become invalids or retired early, would they have found jobs? They might well have just transferred from one kind of non-employment to another. By the same token, if there really are single women who have deliberately conceived children only to get income support, in a weak labour market, the decision could be quite rational.

Neverthless, the scale of the problem of potentially 'involuntary' non-employment among the bottom educational groups should not be exaggerated. Because these groups have become a low proportion of the population, although their non-employment rate is high, they represent quite small percentages of the general population.

The other aspect of the situation is the rise of earnings inequality. Since the middle seventies, while US top-end real hourly earnings rose, those at the bottom actually declined. In the UK, since the beginning of the 1980s, top-end earnings had a bonanza. Low-end earnings did better in the UK, however, than in the US: among the bottom ten per cent of British earners, average real earnings are now actually higher than in the US. In Germany, bottom-end real earnings are now double the US.

The education revolution

No single graph could better illustrate the late 20th century education revolution than Figure 2.1. In the mid nineteen-seventies the cultural profile of British women of working age still reflected a class-based structure of secondary education. Parents with money could send their children to fee-paying schools, either day or boarding, where they would be prepared for exams, taken from the age of 16 onwards, today called GCEs. The range of syllabuses was wide, but all shared common features, namely,

(1) The syllabuses tended to be academic in character (eg finer points of French grammar or, in maths, at 'A' level, finer points of calculus).

(2) The exams were essay-type-question / memory-based.

(3) The syllabuses were designed and the exams were set and marked, not by the teachers, but by external boards.

If parents did not have money for fees, their children could get free places at an academic school if they 'passed' an exam called the '11+', taken at that age, which was a mixture of an intelligence and knowledge test, intended, at least, not to be amenable to coaching. Otherwise, in Britain, before 1970, the rest of the children went to schools called 'secondary moderns' where although it was theoretically possible to study for the GCE exams, this was in practice uncommon. Most of these children therefore left school taking no exam and were subsequently statistically classified as 'Low-Ed', having 'no qualifications'. By contrast, children who went to fee-paying schools mostly took the exams, and mostly passed, in at least four, and sometimes as many as ten academic subjects.

In 1970, 60 per cent of the women of Britain, aged 25 to 64, were Low-Ed. The percentage for men was little different (Figure 2.2). These were the British working class. Nearly two-thirds of the population, they had only a basic education and worse still, under Britain's weak regime for industrial training, a high proportion were unlikely to gain anything better than on-the-job enhancement of their personal human capital during their working lives. The system was not meritocratic. For the majority of the population, 'no qualifications' was the social norm. Many able children 'failed' the '11+'. By the laws of mathematics if two-thirds of the population, having taken

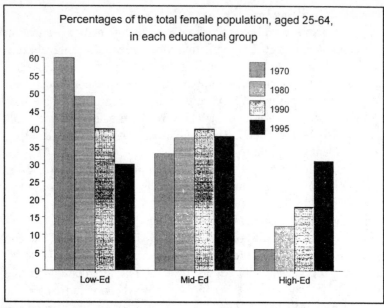

Figure 2.1 Female education patterns in the UK, 1970 to 1995.
Sources: – as next figure.
Definitions:
        H-Ed = 'High-Ed' = A-levels or above.
        M-Ed = 'Mid-Ed = O-levels or equivalent.
        L-Ed = 'Low-Ed' = no qualifications.

a test at age 11, are classified as unsuitable for further education after age 16, the median IQ of the other third must be well above the national average. That this was still the situation 17 years after Michael Young published his great book,[1] does not belie his prophecy, which was truly long term. In the United States there was also a working or 'blue-collar' class. But in proportionate terms it was substantially smaller. In contrast with the situation in the UK, fee-paying secondary education was rare. The great majority of the

---

1   Michael Young, *The Rise of the Meritocracy*, 1958, in References, already discussed in Chapter 1. In 1975, more than half the British working-age population had received their education before 1958, and more than a third before World War II. The legislation (partly drafted by my father) which created the 11+ system was enacted towards the end of the war.

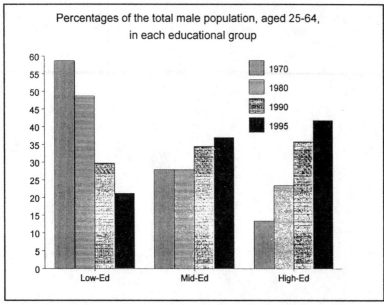

Figure 2.2   Male education patterns in the UK, 1970 to 1995.

Sources: Estimated   from Nickell and Bell, 1995 (in References),
Table 2b (their primary source is the UK General Household
Survey) and *Education Statistics for the United Kingdom*,
1995, in References.

Definitions: – as in Figure 2.1.

population attended, and still attend today, the local high school,
which is substantially financed from the proceeds of local taxation.
Educational stratification – and there is of course much of it – occurs
by means of strong class-based variation, between *localities*, in the
amount of money going in, and the quality of the education coming
out of the system.

At high school in the US one should take courses, pass internal
tests and acquire grades until one has sufficient credit to graduate. But
the law but does not compel one to graduate. If, for one reason or
another, one fails to graduate, in place of the British appellation, 'no
qualifications', one is loosely and even more pejoratively described
as a 'high-school drop-out' – the US statistical definition of 'Low-
Ed'. The difference of tone reflects a difference of outlook.

In 1975 only a third (see Figures 2.3 and 2.4) of all American

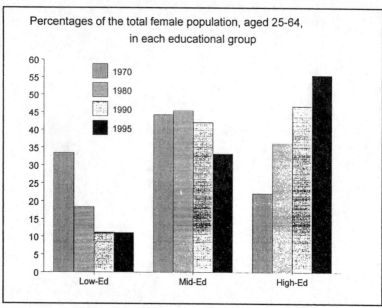

Percentages of the total female population, aged 25-64, in each educational group

1970
1980
1990
1995

Low-Ed   Mid-Ed   High-Ed

Figure 2.3   Female education patterns in the US, 1970 to 1995.
Sources: See Statistical Appendix.
Definitions:

  H-Ed = 'High-Ed' = 3 years college or more.
  M-Ed = 'Mid-Ed   = between Low and High.
  L-Ed = 'Low-Ed' = 'high-school drop-out'.

working-age (25-64) women and only a slightly higher proportion of men, were statistically classed as Low-Ed, ie had in fact 'dropped out' of high school. Among black people, however, the figure (not shown in the charts) was over 50 per cent, a difference which, bearing in mind that the Supreme Court had banned segregation in public education not many years earlier, is lower than might have been expected.

Thomas Sowell, the distinguished black US scholar of the history of economic thought, believes that de-segregation actually had the unintended consequence of reducing the quality of American black secondary education: before de-segregation, Sowell argues, the black communities, against much adversity, had created independent schools which gave good service to a significant minority of the

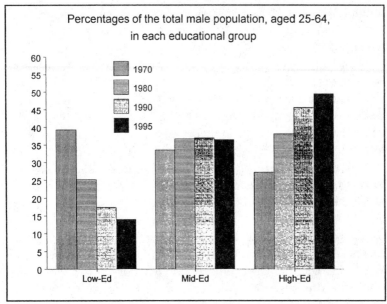

Figure 2.4 Male education patterns in the US, 1970 to 1995.
Sources: See Statistical Appendix.
Definitions: – as previous figure.

community: unfortunately de-segregation, by bringing black education under the aegis of self-serving bureaucracy, disrupted the old system without putting something better in its place.[1]

The revolution

So, then what happened? The answers for the total British and American working-age populations are there in the charts (Figures 2.1 - 2.4) which for simplicity do not show separate figures for American minorities. In fact, the broad trends for American blacks were little worse than the average: by the end of this century the proportion of Low-Eds among working-age US black males will have fallen to less than a fifth. Over the whole American social and ethnic spectrum, high-school drop-outs are now less than a seventh of the total working-age population and, as of 1995, the proportion was still

---

1   See Sowell, 1984, in References.

falling. Nearly a half of the whole US working-age population, females now even more so than males, has been to college and graduated.

In Britain, the proportion of female working-age Low-Eds came down from *60 per cent to 30 per cent*. For males the decline was even sharper. Male High-Eds rose from *13 to 40 per cent*. Women too made a spectacular gain, from seven per cent to 33 per cent – thus while the male percentage in higher education had increased three-fold, the female percentage had increased nearly five-fold.

In France and Germany, and indeed throughout the OECD, the story is similar. In France, over the twenty-five years, the proportion of Low-Eds (using OECD classifications) in the male working-age population fell from about two-thirds to about one-third. In West Germany, for reasons to be discussed in the final section of this chapter, in 1970, the situation was already completely different from that in the UK, the US or France: already *only a fifth* of German working-age men were classified as Low-Ed. Since then the figure has again halved and is now down to only a little over a tenth, a record today, as Figure 2.3 shows, that is matched only by American women.[1]

The question of standards
On both sides of the Atlantic, these developments provoked sugges-tions that standards had fallen. In the US there was talk of 'grade inflation' and also of the suspicion of downward drift in the scholastic content of the average high-school diploma. In the UK, the 11+ exam was abolished (in my opinion, rightly so) and the entire state system, in principle, homogenized. The GCE syllabuses were broadened and the grade range widened. If one took six but failed to achieve a 'pass' grade in all but five, the statistical system classified one as a person with some qualifications, ie, 'Mid-Ed'. If after two years' study one took six exams and received a 'D' – the highest 'fail' grade – in each, one was classed as 'Low-Ed'. I know of a number of people who have done very well in life in that distinguished category. One rather

---

1   The figures for France and Germany are calculated from Nickell and Bell, 1995, in References, Table 2b.

familiar name is that of the Beatles genius John Lennon.[1]

An educational expansion always provokes fears about standards.[2] In a sense these are always well-founded. The distribution of academic ability being bell-shaped, if the system is genuinely meritocratic, as it expands, so it necessarily and intentionally educates an increasing proportion of people from further into the 'bell'. But the academic standards of British exams are very high. Concern about falling standards is often expressed by people who would not themselves be able to understand the first line of the question papers.

A summing up

Be these controversies as they may, we can be sure of three things:

(1)   Although the statistics are not entirely comparing like with like they do mean nevertheless that a huge increase in education – quantity adjusted for quality – has taken place.

(2)   The increase in education, intrinsically desirable as it was, also created the conditions for a major increase in meritocracy, of one kind or another, moderate or severe, as the case might be.

The rise of non-employment

Who are the non-employed?

In the outstanding paradox of our time, with the dramatic rise in education has come a sharp rise in what is effectively involuntary non-employment. What does this actually mean? We defined employment, unemployment and non-employment in Chapter 1. All statistically organized countries have methods of measuring these things, either by surveys of firms or households or a mixture of the two. In the UK, however, unemployment is measured from the welfare rolls – people claiming and receiving benefit from state unemployment insurance, or receiving income support by virtue of being unemployed. In the survey method, questions are asked intended to ascertain a person's status by reference to their own opinions or actions. In the US, for example, a person is classed as unemployed if they appear to be

---

1   See Philip Norman, 1981, in References, p. 35.

2   On 3 July 1996, in London, *The Times* carried a front-page story beginning, 'English teenagers are plummeting in the international league in mathematics.... But in science they are the brains of Europe'. Needless to say, the headline over this mentioned only the mathematics.

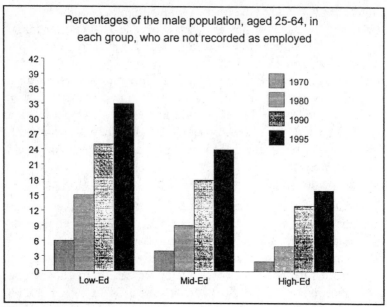

Percentages of the male population, aged 25-64, in each group, who are not recorded as employed

Figure 2.5 Male non-employment and education in the UK, 1970 to 1995.

Source: Estimated from Nickell and Bell, 1995, Tables 2b and 6.

Definitions: – as previous figures.

actively seeking work even if they receive no relief. In the UK, a person who does not apply for unemployment relief, or, having applied, is refused it, is not classed as unemployed.

The non-employed are all those people who are not defined as employed. They are therefore the statistically-defined unemployed plus a residual. Twenty-five years ago, labour-market economists did not think much about the residual. They were either married women or, among men of working age, were, in the UK, less than three per cent of the male working-age population; in the US, less than seven per cent. At that time among American Low-Ed blacks, the Figure 2.6 shows, the total non-employment (including unemployment) percentage was lower than the corresponding figure for whites, a relationship which in the next quarter-century was definitely reversed. In those days, to be a 'residual' non-employed person was likely to be a sign

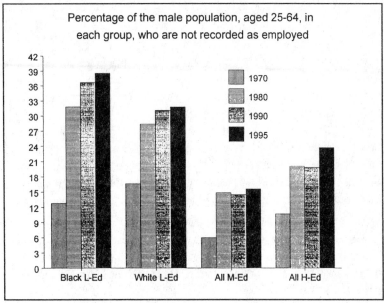

Figure 2.6   Male non-employment and education in the US, 1970 to 1995.

Sources: See Statistical Appendix.
Definitions: – as previous figures.

of affluence.[1] Today it is likely to be a sign of poverty.

If one is non-employed but not unemployed, one is called 'non-participating'. There are a number of reasons why a person may not participate in the labour force. Apart from the case of support by another person with whom one is co-habiting, there are the following:

(1)   private wealth or support by someone with whom one is not co-habiting;

(2)   'early retirement' on an adequate pension;

(3)   invalidity supported by insurance, other persons or public welfare;

(4)   public income-support on account of some factor other than

---

1   I remember a highly-honoured British professional man who married into an upper-crust Boston family. He rather imagined they would regard him as something of a social acquisition. On their side they were rather dismayed to learn that he 'worked'.

direct unemployment, eg a single parent of dependent children or a parent co-habiting with a person who is unemployed, non-employed or earning only low wages.

Twenty-five years ago, although there were a small number of people thriving 'on the road', the above list would have accounted for the great majority of all 'non-participants' in the labour force. Since then, two drastic changes have occurred.

First, there has been a large increase in numbers (2) through (4). Second, there has emerged a large group of males who do not fall into any of those categories from (2) to (4) above, at all, who simply cannot be accounted for. Since they are known to be alive, if not well, they must be receiving income, in money or in kind, from somewhere, but wherever somewhere is, it is not recorded employment.

Early retirement, invalidity and single mothers

'Early retirement' is not a a clear-cut situation because, on the one hand it may be a result of affluence rather than poverty; on the other, of a weak labour market.[1] Be that as it may, on both sides of the Atlantic, in 1995, non-employment rates among the age-group 55-64 are two and a half times as high as among the rest.

'Invalidity' is another foggy problem. Again on both sides of the Atlantic, there has been a sharp increase in the proportion of the population who are not working and receiving insurance or other income support as a result of certified medical incapacity.[2] Undoubtedly one reason is that society, as it has become more affluent, has decided to treat applicants for medical benefit more humanely or some would say more 'leniently'. But the figures are also affected by the general state of the labour market. The reason is not simply that some medically 'marginal' people would, in a more buoyant labour market, prefer to accept economically attractive and medically feasible employment opportunities. It is also because in a weak labour market there is often political pressure to get people off the unemployment books. One way is to allow medically marginal cases to transfer to the invalidity books. A more 'lenient' medical regime might not,

---

1 Atkinson in his 1995 book (in References) already referred to, in Chapter 5 has valuably quantified the structure of the population of non-employed men at the upper end of the age-range along the above lines.

2 See Nickell and Bell, 1995, in References, p 55.

therefore, reduce non-employment; instead it might merely increase statistically-reported unemployment.

When thinking about the effects of 'early retirement' and 'invalidity' on the movement of non-employment rates, the reader may ask himself or herself the following question, 'What would have happened in Western Europe and/or the United States if, since the middle seventies, there had been no increases in early-retirement or invalidity rates?' Maybe the answer would have been, in Europe, 'more unemployment', and, in the US, 'even lower wages'.

Item (4), which includes single parents, is also closely connected with the labour market. Suppose, for the sake of argument, it is true that a some Low-Ed women 'deliberately' breed offspring in order to obtain income support (which of course is precisely what some women do when they marry!). In a weak labour market, this could be a rational individual economic decision, the only alternative being, maybe, insecure employment at low wages or some other form of non-employment.

The missing men

Figures 2.5 and 2.6 show the massive increases in total non-employment, in the UK and the US, in all educational categories. But on both sides of the Atlantic, the increases among Low-Eds have been much the largest.

The other side of the coin is that, as we saw in the previous section, the total proportions of Low-Eds in the population have declined. So, with respect to non-employment among Low-Eds, we have opposing tendencies; we have larger proportions of a declining base. The net result has worked out differently on the two sides of the Atlantic. In the UK, male Low-Ed non-employed, as a proportion of the *total* male working-age population (ie the base includes all three educational categories) has risen from three and a half per cent in 1970 to seven per cent in 1995. In the US, the percentage has remained roughly constant at the even smaller figure of five per cent. These figures contain two important messages: first, that if one believes that the scale of the underclass syndrome is much greater than this, one believes that the underclass, as I defined it in Chapter 1, contains a broader category of people than non-employed Low-Eds. Secondly, given that many people do, in fact, identify the syndrome with non-employment and low education, the problem is not so massive as

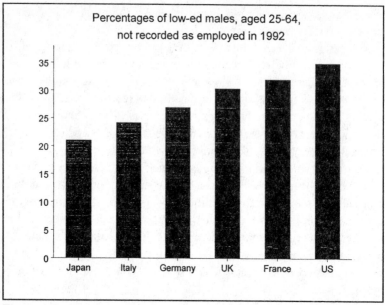

Figure 2.7   Male low-ed non-employment in six countries in 1992.

Source: Calculated from *Education at a Glance*, OECD, 1995, in
               References, Tables C11 and R21.

Definition: Low-Ed   =   OECD bottom category,
                         =   no more than lower secondary education,
                         =   comparable to the definitions used in figures
                             relating to UK and US.

some people think or imply. This does not mean it is socially
insignificant; it means we have a better chance of tackling it. As I
emphasised in the Preface, when a problem is serious, I do not believe
it benefits from exaggeration.

   It is generally accepted that the smaller weight of the increase in
male non-employment in the US, as compared to Europe, is due to the
greater difficulty for able-bodied males in obtaining unemployment
money. Consequently more men accept work at lower wages. The
other side of the coin will therefore be found in the next section,
where wages are examined.

   We do not have corresponding historical figures for other countries, but the high numbers for contemporary Low-Ed non-employ-

ment shown in Figure 2.7 suggest that it is quite possible that in some countries other than Britain the fall in Low-Ed total numbers has been more than offset by a rise in Low-Ed non-employment rates. This Figure also draws attention to the fact that when all ethnic groups are included, the current *level* of the non-employment rate among US male Low-Eds (ie among the residue of 'high-school drop-outs') is, at around one in three, the highest figure among the leading OECD countries.

'Discouraged' workers
Who then are the 'residual', non-*un*employed, non-employed? The general presumption is that they are so-called 'discouraged' workers, ie people who do not qualify as unemployed but do not desire open employment at the wages and conditions available and are finding other means to get by. We do not know their exact numbers, because we do not know how many people fall into categories (1) to (4), and we do not know how many cases in categories (2) to (4) also for the reasons discussed above, conceal discouragement.

A summing up
There have been large increases in non-employment, heavily concentrated among male Low-Eds, in most of the OECD world except Japan. The patterns of the data – especially the comparison between the US and Europe, make it clear that this phenomenon is not due to affluence, and is more likely due to a weak labour market. Typically, at the end of the twentieth century, male Low-Eds have a 25 to 35 per cent non-employment rate, and represent between one in seven and one in fifteen of the total male working-age population.

The rise of inequality
Figure 2.8 tells the final, crucial, part of the story. Real earnings at the bottom end of the distribution stagnate or fall; at the top things go the other way.

The bottom-end fall is most marked in the US, where the purchasing power of men's hourly earnings, corrected both for inflation through time and for UK/US differences in the cost of living, is now significantly lower than in the UK – despite the fact that US GDP per head of population or per worker-hour, is still well above the UK.

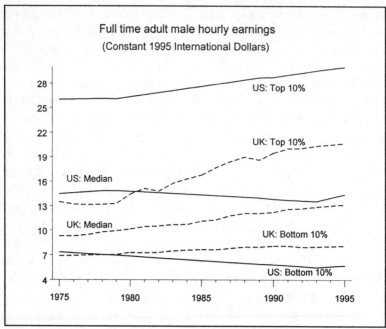

Figure 2.8   Real hourly earnings in UK and US, 1975 to 1995.

Sources: See Statistical Appendix to Chapter 2.

Note: – as explained in the Statistical Appendix these data have been adjusted to correct for bias (first identified by Lawrence and Slaughter, 1993, in References) in cost-of-living adjustments which occurs in periods of rapidly rising housing and other shelter costs: therefore they will not exactly match data from the same sources which have not had this adjustment.

The top-end bonanza is most marked in the UK, entirely taking place after the General Election which brought Lady Thatcher into office in 1979.

The behaviour of the median in the US looks strange. Despite the fact that over the 20 years, US real GDP per worker hour rose, if slowly, nevertheless significantly, median real earnings per worker hour were the same at the end of the period as they were at the beginning. There are two explanations for this. The first is simply that we are looking at the median not the average, and, as was explained in the footnote on page 38, when inequality is increasing, they do not move together.

The second explanation is to be found in the paper by Lawrence and Slaughter, mentioned in the notes to Figure 2.8. It is a statistical effect of sharply above-average rise in housing and shelter costs which not only has the effect, as described in the Statistical Appendix, of understating the increase in inequality, but also separates the path of real output from that of real income. Given the standard method of statistical calculation, rising real shelter costs are not recorded as rising real value added in the business/production economy. In other words, part of the income-distribution shift shown in Figure 2.8 is a shift in favour of those who have a large amount of equity in the property where they live, and those who do not.

The important exception of Germany
We have already seen that West Germany and, increasingly, total Germany, has an exceptionally small proportion of Low-Eds. Figure 2.7 has also shown that at least until recently, total male non-employment in Germany was lower than in both the UK and the US. Much more dramatic is the fact brought out in a vitally important recent paper by Steve Nickell, that during the time when real hourly earnings of the lowest-paid groups were, in the UK and the US, stagnating or declining, those in W. Germany were rising briskly.[1] This discrepancy was so great that these wages, corrected for international cost-of-living differences, are now no less than *twice* as high as in the US. Finally, as we shall see in Chapter 3, Germany has had less de-industrialization than other countries.

How has all this been achieved? Before turning to the carefully researched answers provided by Steve Nickell, it is desirable to consider the international implications of German wages. High as it is, the real output per worker-hour of German manufacturing is still 25 per cent below the US and although the differential in average real wages is almost certainly less than double, it is clear that real unit labour costs in German industry are substantially higher than probably in any other country in the world. Up to mid 1995, however, the currency remained strong and the economy comparatively flourishing. In early 1996 there is some kind of a crisis, including sharply rising official unemployment. Clearly the currency is now overvalued. In

---

1   Nickell, 1996, in References.

fact, it is surprising that international trouble did not come earlier.

But on the longer view, it is not improbable that despite the initial economic dislocations of re-unification, in the territory of old West Germany the sustainable level of total welfare per capita is as high as any in the world. The reason is that the income distribution has remained less unequal and the country displays the signs of a moderate, rather than severe, meritocracy.

The secret, convincingly argued by Steve Nickell, is believed to lie in Germany's century-old system of education and training for the academically *lower* segment of the population. During the period of compulsory education, the German system produces results which, at the top end are no better than other countries, but at the bottom end are quite different. For example, standardized maths tests administered to German children show a distinct international superiority at the lower end. In short, German children, coming into school with a bell-curve of innate ability which is not differently shaped from the corresponding curve in other countries, emerge from compulsory schooling with a bell-curve of academic performance which remains symmetrical but is less spread out.

After ending compulsory education, a high proportion of Germans do not go on to academic higher education. Rather, often while also working, they acquire a variety of vocational and technical qualifications. For example, a person working in the tourist trade might take the full-time equivalent of no less than a three-year course in hotel work. All this kind of training then positively affects the productivity of the whole labour force, eg the productivity of hotel staff is enhanced by the efficiency of supervisors. The system is semi-compulsory (ie if one is in a job without the right formal qualifications, there is a legal obligation on both oneself and one's employer to arrange time off to acquire them) and is essentially Prussian in origin: many suspect that it also partly explains the horrific historical efficiency of the German army.

The system is also the product of the culture.[1] Culture generates law, law generates culture. Some people (maybe from sour grapes or wishful thinking) are beginning to suggest that the famous German system of 'training' is too narrowly technical and lacking in broader educational content to be likely to perform so well in the new-technology age as it has done in the past. Others with practical knowledge of the system say that German non-higher, post-compulsory education and training contains major non-technical, mind-broadening elements.

One could probably tell a partly similar story about the other high-performing ex-war-guilt economy, ie Japan. But in her case fast economic growth persisted after 1973 to such an extent that it would be difficult to distinguish the effects of education from the effects of growth. The pattern is there, however. There is a historically high performance in low-end education. There is a historically low dispersion of wages. And there is great industrial and unfortunately, also military, success.

A summing up

As this chapter ends, we sum it up as having provided the factual frame for a picture of an emerging severe, in contrast to moderate meritocracy on both sides of the Atlantic, with a major exception in Germany. Education has greatly increased, but, on account of increased inequality, total welfare most likely has not. '*SM*', as manifested in the pages above, apppears as a combination of increased education with increased inequality, and inequality manifests itself in non-employment among the remaining Low-Eds, and/or low real wages at the bottom end of the earnings distribution. The total paradox is excellently illustrated by quoting selectively from an article published in March 1996 in *The Times* in London, written by the government's chief inspector of schools, Chris Woodhead:

---

1 In a recent interesting much-discussed book, *Capitalisme contre Capitalisme*, Michel Albert, French ex-civil servant, businessman and political commentator, distinguishes two business cultures, 'Alpine-Rhenish' (Switzerland, Germany, W. Europe north of the Rhine and also partially Japan) and 'neo-American'; the latter based on individualism and short term planning, the former on mediation and long term planning. According to Michel Albert, the latter is the more seductive, the former the more productive.

> The failure of boys, in particular white working-class boys, is one of the most disturbing problems we face within the whole education system. ....Theories of course abound ... Is it that employment prospects are bleaker for girls and that there is no motivation, therefore, for boys to work? Or, in areas where unemployment is not as high, that white working-class boys are more confident than their peers from ethnic minorities that they will secure jobs without qualifications?[1]

There is not enough work for boys because there is not enough work in the whole economy. Further, as a result of the progress of '*SM*', the remaining pool of white working-class boys with no qualifications is probably not only somewhat further below the general population average of innate ability than was the case 25 years earlier, but is almost certainly less well endowed in that respect than many ethnic minority groups and girls. Ethnic minority groups certainly do not face a pure meritocracy. Like girls not much more than a decade ago, to compete successfully for jobs, they need superior, rather than average, qualifications. A boot has changed feet, and we have a potential white male underclass.

How serious that is depends on one's view of the figures. We have seen (Figure 2.2) that in the UK, in 1995, Low-Ed males as a whole constitute a fifth of the working-age population, one-third of whom (Figure 2.5) as a whole, right up to those who left school fifty years ago, are currently non-employed, so that the total group represents seven per cent of the total male working-age population. But the non-employment rate among those under 55 is much lower, so much so that it could be the case that if we remove cases of 'genuine' invalidity and early retirement, economic non-employment of Low-Ed males between the ages of 25 and 54 represents, perhaps, less than five per cent of the total 25-54-aged population when males of all educational

---

1   Chris Woodhead, 'Boys who learn to be losers', p 18, *The Times*, London, 6 March 1996. The reader should know that my long first break (indicated by '....') represents a jump of nearly half a column, and that after the end of the quotation, the article continues for three or four hundreds words. But I do not think I have misrepresented the general sense of Mr Woodhead's words. I should also point out that Mr. Woodhead has become a politically controversial figure accused of exaggerating statistics of educational failure in the UK. Without access to the original data, that is a matter I cannot judge. But the remarks quoted above are not, I think controversial, in that they represent a picture seen as accurate across the political spectrum.

categories in that age range are included in the base. As I have already suggested, I think this is a socially significant figure, but I do not believe it signifies a problem so huge as to seem insoluble.

Statistical Appendix

(1)   SOURCES FOR DATA ON US NON-EMPLOYMENT BY EDUCATIONAL CATEGORIES

General secondary sources:
   Statistical Abstract of the United States, 1994.
   Employment Trends, US Bureau of Labor Statistics, Sept 1995.
Detailed sources:
   Population:
   All years to 1990; Abstract, Table 13.
   1995; *Employment Trends*, Table A-13 with educational details extrapolated using *Abstract*, Table 618.
   Participation Rates:
   Total males, total females and total black, by educational categories:
      All years to 1990; *Abstract*, Table 617.
      1995; *Employment Trends*, Table A-13.
      Note: Sources do not give full detail of participation rates by sex, race and educational categories. Rate for black Low-Ed males is estimated as participation rate for all black Low-Ed persons, raised by the ratio of the participation rate of all black male persons to the participation rate of all black persons.
                  Other detailed rates obtained by subtraction.
   Unemployment Rates:
   Corresponding sources, substituting Table 616 and with the addition of Tables 650 and 651 from 1993 volume of *Abstract*. Mid-Ed male unemployment rate assumed equal to all-male.
      Note: Sources do not give full detail of unemployment rates by sex, race and educational categories. Rate for black Low-Ed males is the unemployment rate for all black males multiplied by the unemployment factor which is the ratio between the unemployment rate for all Low-Ed persons and the corresponding total unemployment rate (estimated from *Abstract*, 1993, Table 650 and trend for corresponding ratio among all Low-Eds).
   1995 Details:
      Note: source does not give full details.
                  Participation rates and unemployment rates by sex, race and educational categories estimated from 1990 by assuming that sub-categories move in proportion to total categories.

(2)   SOURCES FOR DATA ON UK AND US REAL EARNINGS

General secondary sources:
> Data supplied by Amanda Gosling, Institute of Fiscal Studies and Angela
> Nugent, Department of Education and Employment, London
> Gosling, Machin and Meghir, 1994; Lawrence and Slaughter, 1993; Machin,
> 1996; Mishel and Bernstein, 1994, in References
> *International Financial Statistics*, International Monetary Fund; *Penn World
> Tables*, in References
> Robert Lawrence, 1995, in References.

Primary sources:
> Gosling; personal earnings returns in *Family Expenditure Survey* ; Nugent, *New
> Earnings Survey*, based on tax returns.

Detailed Sources:

UK D-10 Index:

Gosling source plus cumulative .13% pa 73-93 to compromise with Nugent.

UK D-10 in dollars:

Nugent 1993 = nominal gross weekly earnings 1993/4 (= £178.03) /40
(= weekly hours, Gosling) x 1.05 (RPI inflation 93-95) x .99 (reduce to
calendar 1993) x 1.61 (market exchange rate) x 1.05 (= PPP factor £/$ 1995
from *Penn Tables* and *Int. Fin. Stats*).

1978 = 1993 adjusted by Gosling index; 1973 = 1978 x $149.63 (= Nugent real
gross weekly 73/4) /£154.10; 1994, 1995, growth at 1% pa from 1993.

UK D-50:

1995 = D-10[1995] x 1.65 (= ratio extrapolated from 1.570 = 1990 ratio given
in Gosling, Machin and Meghir, Tbl 1.1).

Other years through 1992 in proportion to D-10 movements; 1993, 1994
interpolated.

US D-10:

1995 = Mishel and Bernstein Tbl 3.7 1993 at 1993 prices, D-20, all males
= $6.66, reduced $1.5 (half [D-40 minus D-20] x 1.05 to 1995 prices x 1.04
for real growth with GDP x 1.10 for total to adult (one third of 30%) =
$6.23.

1991,89,79,73 = D-50 adjusted by D-10/D-50 ratio given in source Figure 3c.
Other years linearly interpolated.

US median

1995 = Mishel and Bernstein, Tbl 3.7, 1993 at 1993 prices = $11.24 x 1.05 to
1995 prices x 1.05 for real growth x 1.07 total to adult (smaller than d-10)
= $13.25.

1993 = 1995/1.05; 1991, 1989, 1979, 1973, in proportion to Mishel and
Bernstein, Table 3.7, median, real hourly earnings all males. Other years
linearly interpolated.

[Appendix continues on next page]

US Median/D-10 and D-90/Median
   Mishel and Bernstein, Figure 3c.
Adjustment for cost-of-living bias
   Lawrence and Slaughter show that in the 1980s the index of housing and other shelter costs in the general US retail price index rose faster than other items to such an extent that without this effect the rise in the total index would have been on average less by about one-half of one per cent per annum. Apart from helping explain the notable discrepancy between the path of average real earnings and the path of real GDP per worker hour, this phenomenon would also, they point out, bias the deflator upwards in relation to households who own the major equity in their properties and, by implication, downward in relation to renters. Since the former will tend to be concentrated among earners on the top end of the distribution and the latter among those at the bottom, another effect of the phenomenon is to understate the increase in inequality. A similar effect would occur in the UK, although, owing to the much greater prevalence of renting in the first part of the period, plus a degree of insulation of lower-earning households from the effect of the rise in property prices, it would be weaker.
   The numbers estimated from the sources and by the methods described above were therefore adjusted by multiplication by 'Lawrence-adjustment factors' (numbers close to 1, eg 1.015 or .990) defined as follows:

Factor(year t) = Factor(year o) x $(1 + c)$ ^ (year t - year o)

where year t is current year, year o beginning of period and c is the adjustment coefficient. The coefficients employed for different periods, earnings groups and the two countries were as follows:

	US			UK		
	Lowest 10%	Med-ian	Top 10%	Lowest 10%	Med-ian	Top 10%
1975-78	-2.50e-03	0	3.75e-03	0	0	0
1979-89	5.00e-03	0	5.00e-03	3.00e-03	0	0
1990-95	0	0	5.00e-03	-2.50e-03	0	-2.50e-03

3. The Truth about the Growth Slow-down

To understand the growth slow-down we need a theory. The economy has to maintain successive changes from one satisfactory short term situation to another: both demand and capacity must expand repeatedly and in balance. The government is responsible for expanding demand, the private sector for expanding capacity. For that, the private sector needs confidence in the government.

If actual growth is slower than required to sustain the labour market, a slow-down in productivity may be _induced_. If so, in place of a growing physical gap between the supply of and demand for labour, there may be growing employment at low wages.

Slow growth may induce low productivity in a number of ways: direct and indirect, temporary and wage-related. Low wages may reduce productivity by imparting a labour-intensive bias to new investment, or by attracting workers into low-value-added sectors of the economy.

It follows that to answer the question of whether the growth slow-down was or was not demand-related we need to look for statistical evidence of induced productivity slow-down. One way to begin is to separate the statistical record of manufacturing from non-manufacturing. It is also necessary to consider the potential influence of other events or factors which have affected historical productivity, including so-called 'catch-up' effects and the effects of 'exogenous' shocks such as the energy-price shocks of the nineteen-seventies.

The chapter follows this trail in four countries for which good data are available – France, Germany, the UK and the US – first looking at the general background of actual GDP growth rates, working hours and manufacturing productivity, then moving to the crucial comparison between productivity trends in manufacturing and non-manufacturing. Given that (as seen in Chapter 2) real wages fared markedly worse in the US than in the UK, and that in the UK they did less well than in France and Germany, I expected to find strongest evidence for induced productivity slow-down in the US, weakest in France and Germany, with the UK in between. In a series of figures, the prediction is confirmed.

Why did it happen? Why did actual growth slow down? The general answer is fear of inflation provoked by the traumas of the seventies and early *eighties. But maybe inflation was already accelerating in the nineteen-sixties? The question cannot be answered conclusively, but it is likely that if the shocks had not occurred, inflation could have been brought down without the heavy cost in lost growth that we eventually suffered.*

The shocks caused an adverse shift in the relationship between demand pressure and inflation (making more inflation for given pressure), persisting into the middle eighties. Then came a more more benign relationship, which should have encouraged governments to promote growth with less fear of inflation. But slow growth continued. The basic cause was low priority attached to growth by governments. The result was reinforced on the demand side by high long term real interest rates, perverse expectations in the money markets and, on the supply side, by excessive take-over activity. In turn, the high interest rates and perverse expectations were the combined outcome of, among governments, a 'monetarist' view of the inflationary role of the money supply, public-sector deficits partly caused by slow growth itself and by the desire to rely heavily on short term interest rates for the purpose of macroeconomic management. This last had the effect of destabilizing bond markets and raising long term interest rates relatively to expected future short rates. It also turned good news for the real economy into bad news for the markets, creating potentially chronic pessimism among real-economy businesses.

The logical framework

Growth and Keynes

I have already noted that the economic theory of long term growth was a consequence of, but not an immediate part of the 'Keynesian revolution' in economics. Keynes's original theory was essentially concerned with slumps. More precisely it was a theory to explain how an economy containing a given amount of human and material capital could have a low-level equilibrium where both were underutilized. Starting perhaps from a position of high production, something happens to depress the flow of monetary demand, causing producers to reduce output, causing their incomes to decline, causing a further decline in demand. The downward spiral continues until some built-in opposing factor, of one kind or another, halts it. Government intervention, however (of one kind or another) should in principle be able to correct or forestall the process and maintain a continuous regime of good utilization and relatively weak cycles.

At the cost of some oversimplification one can say that the theory of growth begins where the theory of cycles ends. Suppose we do succeed in stabilizing output at high level, what then? Next year, either because the effective labour supply has increased, or because productivity has increased, in order to maintain the same utilization of *labour*, we require an *increase* in output. The previous situation is no longer good enough.

For increased macro output, in turn, we need two things: more demand *and* more capacity, ie more demand and more of the things that combine with labour to produce goods and services – consumer markets, physical capacity and business organization. If both are forthcoming, the economy can move benignly from the first 'full employment' condition to the second, the latter having higher capacity, higher demand and probably higher productivity and total welfare, than the former. The labour market will also be stable, ie the balance between employment and effective labour supply will remain unchanged and real wages will be able to increase by no less and no more than the rise in productivity, thus in turn sustaining the rate of profit in business.

The fundamental policy challenge to government and society (nobody pretends it is easy) is to maintain the repeated process of benign transitions from one 'Keynesian' condition to the next. It is a task where success literarily breeds success, and failure, failure. The government may stimulate demand, but the private sector must organize and finance the growth of capacity. It is more likely to do so if it has confidence in the growth of demand. That confidence will be strongly influenced by the past record.

There are traps in either direction. If the government stimulates demand, but capacity does not follow, there will be inflation. If capacity grows faster than demand, the economy will slip into a Keynesian recession, with likely further de-stabilizing consequences.

The macroeconomic challenge is matched by a general challenge at the micro level. In the business sector,[1] the growth of the individual firm is a microcosm of the growth of the economy. The firm has a range of products and markets, plus productive capacity in the form

---

1 The following argument is based on Marris 1964 and 1987 and Marris and Mueller, 1980, in References. For a quantitative description of the process, see the valuable paper of Alessandro Sembenelli and Laura Rondi, 'The growth of firms and the growth of the economy', 1991, in References.

of a labour force and plant. From these assets it earns profits, a proportion of which are ploughed back into various activities, including, as well as plant investment, production research and market research, that create opportunities for the firm to grow. Growth, for the firm, requires a balanced expansion of market demand on the one hand and capacity to meet demand, on the other. Given balance, sales growth will be matched by profits growth, so return on capital is sustained.

The growth efforts of firms thus combine to make up the private-sector contribution to the actual growth of the whole economy. In consequence, anything that affects the general propensity of firms to want to grow, also affects macro growth.

Two kinds of unemployment
This interaction between growth and cycles creates quite a problem for economics terminology. If there is underutilization of existing capacity and labour supply, we usually speak of 'Keynesian' under-employment. If demand is adequate in relation to existing capacity, but capacity is growing too slowly to absorb the labour supply, we describe the resulting under-employment of labour as 'classical'.[1] So how do we describe a situation (in my opinion chronic since the mid-70s) where neither demand nor capacity are growing at the required rate? If capacity had grown sufficiently, but demand had not, the additional capacity would not have been utilized; both labour and capacity would have become under-employed – a dynamic form of Keynesian unemployment, caused, not by a decline in demand, but by a lack of growth of demand. Alternatively, if demand had grown but capacity had not, not only would there have been, as already mentioned, inflation, but also classical unemployment – a possible, but not the only possible, explanation of 'stagflation'.[2] Finally there is the crucial point that a *reason* why capacity may grow slowly is that business feels demand is growing slowly. So we can have dynamic

---

1 A much more thorough analysis of this distinction can be found in the elegant work of the great French economist and econometrician, Edmond Malinvaud. See Malinvaud, 1977, 1984, 1985, 1994 in References.
2 Meaning a state of affairs with stagnating output, high or rising unemployment and high or rising inflation. It is an economic pathology that had never been seen before the early 1970s.

Keynesian unemployment leading to classical unemployment.

We tend to think of 'Keynesian' problems as 'demand-side', ie we think that Keynesian unemployment is intrinsically caused by demand deficiency. Conversely, we think of classical unemployment as a 'supply-side' problem, because its immediate cause is insufficient capacity. The reality is both more complex and more relevant. Long term demand deficiency can cause long term supply deficiency, which then feeds back into the story by making it more difficult to encourage the growth of demand without inflation.[1]

Pelion on Ossa

The gods of economic creation have then piled Pelion on Ossa (ie one problem on another – in the Greek myths they first put the mountain called Pelion on another called Ossa, then Ossa, with Pelion on its back, was put on top of Olympus) by adding yet another vital causal loop: it is possible to have a balanced growth of demand, labour employment and capacity, and yet be disappointed in the results. Why? Because the resulting growth of output per worker-hour may in fact turn out to be sluggish. This has two adverse consequences, the first the obvious one that slow productivity means slow real wages and/or disappointing profits. The second is more subtle and results directly from the equation of balanced growth I first explained in Chapter 1, namely,

$$Gr(required) = Gr(ELPC) + Gr(productivity)$$

Reminder: in words this said that the growth rate of per capita GDP required to keep labour demand in balance with labour supply on the left hand side is mathematically equal to the sum of two things on the right hand side, namely (i) the growth of per capita effective labour supply and (ii) the growth of productivity: productivity growth displaces labour, which must be re-employed.

As night follows day, slow productivity growth on the right hand side of the equation reduces the required growth rate on the left hand

---

1   The reader can appreciate that a theoretical model of the macroeconomic system which takes proper account of these causal loops must necessarily be mathematically complex. For the type of work that has been done, see the work of the world's leading researcher in the field, the distinguished economic theorist, Richard Goodwin, 1967 and 1984, in References.

side.[1] This is a kind of adjustment mechanism. The productivity slow-down helps the labour market to *accommodate* the adverse situation. But it does more than accommodate, it also conceals.

Suppose we had an economy – maybe one country, maybe the whole OECD world – that happened to be happily travelling the benign path which Joan Robinson christened a 'Golden Age':[2] productivity is growing briskly, also maybe the labour supply, so the required growth rate is quite high. But due to good luck and/or good guidance, the actual growth rate is also high – so high, in fact, that our equation balances. Now suppose things go wrong and there is a general slow-down. Policy makers badly need to know whether the prime cause is on the demand side or the supply side. If they see that productivity appears to have slowed they may infer that the answer is 'supply-side' – something technical has gone wrong with the production system or maybe all the workers have become lazy. But suppose in reality the prime cause was a slowing down of demand growth producing the adverse chain of causes such as has just been described. Included in that chain will be an *induced* (or 'endogenous') productivity slow-down. If that is what has actually happened, the 'supply-side' interpretation will represent a dangerous mis-diagnosis – dangerous because it conceals the true pathology.

The situation also creates another terminology problem. If unemployment is removed by means of lowered productivity, it is no longer unemployment. Jobs have been found, albeit inferior ones. How should we name this situation or these jobs? The term 'disguised unemployment' is no longer appropriate because the jobs in question may be fully reported. At the time of writing, no recognised term exists. As often happens in economics, terminology (or in this case, lack of it) conceals a political problem.

How productivity is induced [3]

How then are productivity changes induced by macro economic

---

1 We already saw in Chapter 1 how this relationship lay at the heart of Robert Solow's Nobel-prize-winning model.

2 In Robinson, 1956, in References.

3 By 'productivity' I mean no more and no less than actual physical output per worker-hour, whether caused by better work, harder work, more capital, more knowledge, or alternatively by 'residual' or apparently unexplained factors.

conditions?[1] There are four overlapping answers: *direct, indirect, temporary* and *wage-related*. The direct answer is that a general scarcity of labour encourages economical use of labour, and vice versa. That applies to any kind of economic activity – industry, trade, services or whatever – where there is some choice in the way of doing things, some choice, that is, of labour intensity. Labour scarcity also encourages employers to help employees of lesser innate ability to become more productive. In a weak labour market, less able workers are simply not hired and therefore not upgraded. They lose the opportunity to learn by doing.

By an *indirect* answer I mean that economic conditions affecting the labour market also go with other conditions affecting production efficiency. For example, it was long ago discovered that if the demand for *output* is expanding rapidly, productivity is also likely to accelerate because, in order to respond to the demand, firms must accelerate their rate of investment. The average age of their physical capital stock is thus reduced, implying a greater proportion of more recently designed equipment embodying the latest technology. The average worker finds herself using equipment which is capable of a greater hourly output for given hourly labour input. In addition, if demand and output are expanding rapidly, both individual industries and the economy as a whole are more frequently enjoying economies of scale or 'increasing returns'.[2]

---

1   The technical term for economic growth that results from induced productivity growth is 'endogenous growth'. This is a large recently re-discovered topic with a research literature actually going back the best part of 30 years. (I believe I was in fact the first person to publish – in Marris, 1964, p 299 – a sentence in which the two words appeared literally in sequence, but first credit for the general idea undoubtedly belongs to Nicholas Kaldor in an article co-authored with James Mirrlees in 1962, in References.) In recent years there have been symposiums in the *Economic Journal* (1992, vol 102, no 2, May), the *Oxford Review of Economic Policy* (1992, vol 8, Winter) and, in 1994, a major survey by Paul Romer, in References. For an excellent survey of surveys, see the June 1995 article by J. P. Marney in the *British Review of Economic Issues*, in References.

2   The substantial research on this subject is often referred to as the literature of 'Verdoorn's Law', after one of its discoverers, P. J. Verdoorn., who published his main article in 1949. He had been partly preceded by Allyn Young, twenty years still earlier. Later important writers in alphabetical order were John Cornwall, Nicholas Kaldor, and W.E.G. Salter, 1977, 1966 and 1960, in References.

There are two questions to be raised here, both of great importance to the interpretation of OECD macroeconomic history (most especially British) since the late seventies. First, is the process a general one or does it mainly apply to manufacturing industry? Second, is it reversible? The answer to the first question is generally thought to be that it applies mainly to manufacturing. The answer to the second is more complex. It is generally agreed that if the growth of manufacturing output slows down, there may be a corresponding slow-down in the growth of productivity. But what happens if manufacturing output actually declines? There may be some losses of so-called 'static' economies of scale, but there can be no reversal of the average age of the capital stock. On the contrary, if, as would be expected, the least efficient activities are shut down first, the opposite will occur, a result which is known as *rationalization*. After that immediate adjustment, however, the story becomes fuzzy. If there is no new investment at all, the capital stock will atrophy. In practice there is usually continued investment in some firms and sub-sectors. The total result will be a rather complex time path in the first stages of which productivity averaged over the surviving activities may be quite sharply boosted. Unless there is then a sharp recovery in the rate of growth of demand, however, even with some new investment, productivity could again slow down. As we shall see shortly, a scenario of this type would be consistent with what has actually happened in recent years to British manufacturing.

Temporary effects

Finally (before turning to wages) there is the effect known as 'labour hoarding'. If there is a short term slump in the demand for goods in an era when long term business expectations are buoyant (ie business is optimistic about the actual rate of growth), firms may hold on to workers, especially skilled workers, because they fear it will be difficult to get them back. Some but not all of the temporary excess of actual over required labour may be adjusted by shorter hours. The remainder will appear, statistically, as an apparent decline in output per worker hour.The phenomenon was very noticeable in cyclical fluctuations in manufacturing industry in the fifties and sixties[1] but

---

1 For a classic study, see Robert Nield, *Pricing and Employment in the Trade Cycle*, 1963, in References.

has not entirely gone away and is still important in interpreting data.

The role of wages

By 'wages-induced productivity' I mean productivity changes that are induced by changes in the macroeconomic real wage, ie the average money wage deflated by prices. The individual business producer of goods and services pays the money wage. If this falls relatively to the price at which the firm can sell a given amount of product, and if the same is happening to most firms, logic says that firms are in fact experiencing the result of an economy-wide decline in the real wage.

The first point to make is that wage-induced productivity decline is a possible consequence of classical unemployment but an unlikely consequence of Keynesian unemployment. The reason is that real wages have no primary role in the Keynesian theory. This in my opinion[1] is still inadequately understood by contemporary economists and was also the subject of confusing statements by Keynes himself. Keynesian unemployment occurs because a decline in monetary demand for business firms mainly induces them to reduce output rather than prices. Given productivity, the real wage depends on the average mark-up of prices over costs. Assuming that firms are generally trying to set their mark-ups at levels calculated to yield good total profits,[2] it follows that the average real wage will change in a recession only if the recession makes the profitable mark-up change.

In a recession, businesses cannot avoid lower total profits. They can, however, try to minimize loss. A fairly simple piece of mathematics[3] shows that the first approximation to that end is to hold margins and let the brunt of adjustment fall on sales volume and employment. This conclusion is qualified if there is labour hoarding and/or if margins are reduced mainly to unload stocks. But these are not qualifications that affect the general prediction (which is supported by the data) that real wages do not move much, either way, in the business cycle. In short, Keynesian unemployment does not have a primary effect on the real wage, and the real wage cannot correct

---

1 Marris, 1991, 1992 and 1996, in References.

2 Excessive mark-up depresses demand, inadequate mark-up depresses unit profits.

3 For details, see Marris references 1991-6 cited above. The theory goes back to the middle nineteen-thirties.

Keynesian unemployment.

In what ways then may wage adjustment function in the case of classical unemployment? And how is open classical *un*employment converted into 'demand-deficiency' (see above) *em*ployment? In Chapter 1, I suggested two ways, the first connected with the Robert Solow neo-classical growth model, the second connected with services. Both need some further discussion.

Wages in the neo-classical model

Solow's argument starts from the situation of a firm considering a new investment to produce a specific amount of output for a specific market at a specific expected selling price. The lower the money wage, relative to the nominal selling price, the greater the forecast total profit and the more attractive the investment.

If the forecast total profit is to be converted into a *rate of return* on capital, it is then necessary to feed the calculation with information concerning the cost of the plant. But technology may offer alternatives. Capital-intensive packages will offer benefits in greater output per worker-hour, while cheaper more labour-intensive systems will pay the opposing penalty. A little calculus will show that the lower the ruling wage, relative to product selling price, the more likely it is that a labour-intensive alternative will give the highest return. Consequently, Solow, and most economists since, have argued that if a long term deficiency in the labour market does in fact push down the macroeconomic real wage, microeconomic investment decisions of firms will take on a labour-intensive bias, so inducing reduced productivity and tending to correct the demand for labour.

This theory was developed in times that were very different from today; in those times we had never heard of 'de-industrialization' and were not expecting a growth slow-down. The theory is obviously most appropriate for an economy where a major part of output comes from capital-intensive industry and it has a problem if there is an actual demand slow-down. In face of a slow-down, the adjustment process requires time for alternative labour-intensive technologies to be introduced into the capital stock. But if growth is slow, so also the capital replacement rate. Hence the process of adjustment to a demand slow-down will itself be slow.

Subject to these qualifications, we shall be wanting to look at the behaviour, since 1973, of actual labour productivity in manufacturing.

Wages and services

In Chapter 1 I suggested that if there is inadequate general demand for labour, employment can transfer from industry to services only if employees accept low wages and thus permit low prices. Low prices, however, mean low valued-added per worker. Hence the process creates an apparent productivity slow-down.

There are however three significant qualifications to this hypothesis. The first is that it seems to fly in the face of another important idea concerning the services trades that has been familiar to economists for some time but was given new and elegant clothing in more recent years by the highly distinguished Princeton economist, William Baumol.[1] Baumol argued that there were numerous kinds of services activities whose intrinsic character was such that their productivity could never increase: for example, it always requires four people to perform a string quartet.[2] If real wages in such activities are to keep pace with real wages generated by productivity growth in other sectors, their relative price must inexorably rise. Baumol also noted that the share of total services activity taken by these sectors had a long term upward trend. Hence Baumol made two predictions, both statistically supported; the relative selling prices of services will historically rise, and the growth rate of apparent productivity in the whole services sector will historically decline.

This contradicts my implied prediction of relatively falling services prices after the growth slow-down and provides an alternative reason for a slow-down. But I think we can be reconciled. If the macro demand for labour is deficient, in the absence of Baumol-effect, some labour can be soaked up in, among other services sectors, the constant-productivity sectors. The Baumol effect tends to restrain this process, however, by making the services in question expensive for consumers. But, and it is a big one, the way out is lower wages.

---

1 See Baumol, Blackman and Wolff, 1989, in References.

2 If we define the input of the whole music industry as all the musicians, recordists, broadcasting units and etc, and if we define the output as the number of person-hours of music enjoyed each year, the productivity of this entity, in the present century, has multiplied very greatly. But Baumol can still argue that the specific input activity represented by the playing (and may be recording, maybe not) of a quartet retains its 'fixed coefficient', ie the number four.

Turning the Baumol argument around, one could cite it as a *reason* for downward pressure on wages. The result will be strongest among less-educated services workers, who have less monopoly power than services professionals: we all know that the top professionals – doctors, accountants and the like – have continued to earn very good money.

If we combine this argument with Baumol's second prediction – the long term downward trend of average services productivity – we face a rather complex situation. What happens to *national* apparent labour productivity when labour migrates in the manner described? If wages in the constant-productivity sub-sectors fall while prices stay constant or moderately rise, what happens to national average value-added per worker? We know its future growth will slow down, but any change in current level will depend on whether, before the transfer, value-added per head in the constant-productivity subsectors, as recorded by the statisticians, was above or below the national average. That difference, according to Baumol, depends on the passage of time.[1] What actually happens, therefore, depends partly on when it happens. Interestingly, as we shall shortly see, the curves of productivity in US manufacturing and non-manufacturing crossed over (the latter falling, for the first time, below the former) in the early nineteen-seventies.

The second qualification to my general hypothesis is statistical. In principle, the indicators used by statisticians to assess changes in outputs and inputs in services sectors, whatever precise form they take, are inherently physical. For example, as input one might measure musician-hours; as output, person-concert-attendances. Therefore in principle it appears impossible that a change in wages and prices could affect the statisticians' measurements of the productivity movement of a single sector. My hypothesis, however, relates to the whole sector. If there is movement between high-wage, high-price

---

1 Constant productivity does not necessarily mean low productivity. The chief executive of a large corporation has, according to the argument, constant productivity (more precisely, it is no easier to measure his increase, if any, than that of the viola player in a string quartet) and yet, being paid millions of dollars a year, his value-added is of the order of thousands of dollars an hour.

services sub-sectors towards low-wage, low-price subsectors, my effect will occur and be statistically recorded.

The third qualification concerns the effect on total welfare. If on account of general demand deficiency, labour moves towards low-wage, low-price services (strictly we should simply say that these services become cheaper than they would otherwise have been), the workers in question are worse off than they would have been if the demand deficiency had not occurred. But that is not so for the *consumers* of these services. Obviously however the biggest demand comes from people with good jobs and earnings. Therefore there is a change in the distribution of income. Therefore the effect on total welfare is uncertain.[1]

Non-induced productivity

So there are several processes – scale economies, rationalization, labour hoarding, neo-classical wage effects and services-related wage effects – that may cause direct, indirect and wage-related induced productivity decline. But when we study the data we must not confine ourselves to these. We must also consider the possibility that the data are influenced by other factors: we may see a productivity slowdown, but perhaps the explanation lies elsewhere. Perhaps, indeed, the explanation is supply-side.

It is impossible to do anything with non-specific arguments, such as, 'Something happened; we don't exactly know what, but surely it was supply-side'. One can however take account of known historical events of a supply-side character which *prime facie* could have caused productivity slow-downs. In fact, in international economic history since 1950, there are two of these, the so-called 'catch-up' phenomenon, possibly covering the whole period, and the physical effects of oil-price shocks of the middle and late seventies. There is also one obvious example applying to a particular country, namely the re-

---

1 In 1995, while visiting to the state of Montana, I found myself drinking espresso coffee from a paper cup served by a young Italian-American woman working at the side of the road in a tiny wooden kiosk. The coffee was good. The business was newly established. My economic welfare gained. The young person's welfare was sustained. Nevertheless, if that little bit of economic activity is eventually officially measured, it will show up in the macro data as an addition to low-wage, 'low-productivity' non-manufacturing, probably with inadequate adjustment for quality.

unification of Germany which took place in the late eighties. Although all our data will relate to the old West Germany, it is possible that the absorption of a large additional backward territory had a significant negative effect on the old West.

The *catch-up* story has a major literature which, like so many interesting ideas in economics, begins with Nicholas Kaldor (although whether he actually thought of it first is unclear) as long ago as 1966. For various historical reasons the average productivity levels of different countries diverge, so much so that there comes a time when the level of technology and general economic organization in the leading country is seriously higher than in other countries. If there are significant barriers to the international spread of knowledge of and/or to the *application* of good practice, the situation can persist for substantial lengths of time. Then, however, something happens which reduces the previous barriers and so, in contrast to the previous divergence, a process of convergence, or 'catch-up' begins. In our century that 'something' was the new general state of the world that emerged from World War II.[1]

The theory can be converted into a statistical model[2] for helping to

---

1 Kaldor, 1966; Rowthorn, 1975; Cornwall, 1977; Baumol, 1986; Romer, 1986; Marris, Mathews, 1982; Gomulka, 1990; Maddison, 1991, 1995; Barro, 1991; in References. A major factor affecting the general development of this research has been the general development of data, most especially of data which can accurately compare internationally levels as well as rates of change of productivity. Thus the earliest comparisons were based on GDP per head of population converted into dollars at market exchange rates, and were thus full of statistical noise due to international differences in employment levels relative to population levels, and to deviations between market exchange rates and purchasing-power parities. The latest work is based either on GDP per worker-hour, converted into dollars at carefully researched final-demand PPPs, or on real manufacturing value-added per worker hour converted at rates based on detailed studies of unit values derived from trade statistics.

2 The economics profession owes a vast debt to the various research groups who have made more accurate calculations possible. Among these I single out first and foremost, Irving Kravis, of the University of Pennsylvania who has devoted a lifetime to outstanding research leadership in the work, and then Professor Bart van Ark, of the University of Groeningen, who is substantially responsible for the recent appearance of 'hard' data for manufacturing. Then come the late and lamented Hugo Krijne-Locker of the EC Statistical Office; Mary O'Mahony of the UK NIESR, who has crucially carried further the work on manufacturing; Alan

explain international differences in growth rates by assuming that the leading country, which was always the United States, was a rather steadily growing moving target, always still ahead of the rest but always, on account of being ahead, growing least fast. Then one assumes that among the 'follower' countries, the strength of the 'pull' (towards convergence with the US) on any one country in any given past year would depend on how far she had already converged. With other factors constant, the growth rate expected from a follower country in a given past year would be greater the greater the remaining gap between her level of productivity and the level achieved in the same year by the US.

The theory has been remarkably successful in explaining historical differences in growth rates, both among developed OECD countries, among intermediate countries and also when data for both these kinds of countries are pooled. It does not apply to very poor countries, where, for good reason the relationship is reversed (ie the poorest of the poor also have the slowest growth[1]). Angus Maddison has shown[2] that the theory can be effectively combined with theories concerning other factors which affect national growth rates of GDP per worker hour.

The point about catch-up is that it also leads to slowdown. If the US slows down, then, in principle the follower countries should also slow down. But even if the US growth rate stays constant, as countries catch her up, the theory predicts they will slow down. That is a kind of supply-side effect – albeit a rather special one – which must certainly be considered when interpretating historical data for countries other than the US.

The *oil-price shocks* came in two waves, the first lasting from late 1973 until around 1976, during which time the price of crude oil, outside the United States, quadrupled; the second from 1979 to

---

Heston and Robert Summers, Kravis's close associates at Pennsylvania and Milton Gilbert who, with Kravis, pioneered the work at the OECD in the 1950's. (See all listings under these names in References.) Great credit is also due to the World Bank, the Price Comparisons Unit of the Statistical Office of the EU, the PPP Unit of the of the OECD and to the United Nations.

1   See Gomulka, 1990, in References.

2   Maddison, 1995b, pp 65 et seq.

around 1981, when it again doubled. During the first period, the US economy was sheltered from the world oil price, and US oil imports and energy consumption continued to rise. In the rest of the world, however, industry was changing its technology to save energy, at a cost, possibly, in labour productivity. After the second oil shock the US government removed the protection from her domestic market, and in the subsequent years US energy consumption, relative to GDP, fell quite significantly. We may therefore look out for possible adverse US productivity results any time after 1980.

In the case of *German unification*, we are looking out for possible adverse effects after 1990.

The statistical background
We are now ready to study the data. What are we looking for? We are looking for evidence for and against my hypothesis that since the mid-seventies the shortage of jobs has been caused by a shortage of growth. I then said that in a country such as the US, where the jobs shortage has appeared as much in the form of low wages as in male non-employment,[1] I expect to see an apparent productivity slow-down in *non*-manufacturing which is not a technical phenomenon, but rather an artificial statistical consequence of the low wages.

It must be understood that I am not implying that the US economy has created *only* low-wage jobs. It is known that it has in fact, under the Clinton Administration in the middle nineties, created many high wage jobs. What we are concerned about is the macroeconomic explanation of the economic situation of people at the lower end of the US labour market. In other words people who, for the kinds of reasons discussed in Chapter 2, may have been left out of the 'Clinton boom'.

---

1   But remember in Chapter 2 we found that non-employment among Low-Ed US males is still comparatively high. See Figure 2.6.

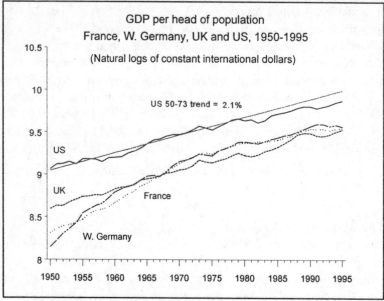

Figure 3.1 GDP per capita in four countries over 45 years.

Source: Calculated from *Penn World Tables*, Heston and Summers, 1991, in References.

Definitions: See corresponding figure for manufacturing. Trend line is 'best fit' (least-squares).

Because the induction effect is intrinsically less likely in manufacturing than in non-manufacturing, we must be particularly interested, therefore, to compare the historical performance of these two broad sectors. This is done on pages 85 and 86 below in two key charts for the UK with US, and France with Germany, the four countries being the main ones for which the hard Van-Ark/O'Mahony data for manufacturing are available.[1] First, however, we need to look at the general trend of GDP per capita – the actual growth rate, the demand side of the balance equation – and also data to give us clues on de-industrialization and catch-up/slow-down.

---

1   Van Ark, 1990 and 1995; O'Mahony, 1995, in References.

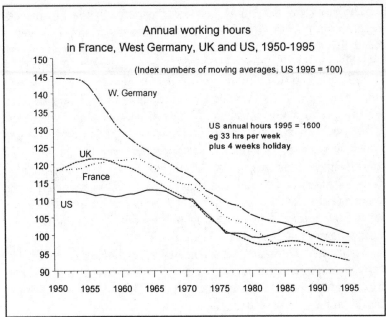

Figure 3.2   The general increase in leisure: all-sector working hours in four countries, 1950-1995.

Sources: Calculated from Maddison, *Monitoring the World Economy*, 1995, Table J-4, and O'Mahony, data base, in References..

Methods: The Maddison data relates to all GDP but is available only for selected years. The O'Mahony data is available for all years but relates to manufacturing. The O'Mahony data have been used to interpolate the missing years in the Maddison data.

The actual growth rate

Figure 3.1 shows the story of actual per capita GDP per in the four countries. The US slowdown is very marked, and is worth in fact more than three-quarters of a percentage point, enough, if it was entirely caused on the demand side, to create, over a quarter of a century, a huge deficit in the demand for labour. When account is also taken of the sharp US rise in effective labour supply relative to population (see Chapter 1), we can see that if we are really looking at a demand effect we are looking at an effect which could be strong enough to account for the whole of, if not more than, the stagnation of US wages.

The story for the UK is less easy to pick out than in the US because, since 1973, British growth has been very erratic. This makes trend lines dubious. However, if, in place of a statistical trend line we take average growth from 1950 to 1973, and compare that with 1973 to 1995, we find that in both periods the UK was growing at about a third of a point faster than the US (ie catching up, but very slowly). So the UK slow-down appears to have been about the same as the US's, and so is also quite sufficient to explain the large adverse gap which, as we saw in Chapter 1, developed between UK employment and effective labour supply. By the same token, my general hypothesis does not expect much 'induced' productivity decline in the UK. The wage incentive has not been strong, and therefore I expect that surplus labour, rather than being soaked up in low productivity non-manufacturing, has simply become non-employed.

France and Germany, who had had spectacular growth earlier, certainly experienced a massive post-1973 slow-down, so marked, in fact, that they began to 'converge' with the UK. Discussion of this is best momentarily postponed.

Working hours

Figure 3.2 is designed to show what has happened, this past half century, to the average employed person's annual working hours. There was a sharp decline in the first of the two quarter-centuries, which tailed off in the second. Differences between the countries are not very significant. We all average about 30-35 hours a week with the equivalent of about four weeks annual holiday. The Germans used to work longer hours than others, but not today. If hours had not declined, the jobs problem would obviously have been all the greater. But this is too negative a way of looking at the matter. Clearly the decline in working hours has signified a major increase in desired and desirable leisure, an unmeasured supplement to the growth of total welfare. It is nevertheless significant that the decline slowed down at around the same time that measured GDP growth slowed down. In other words, when society's capacity to consume goods is rising rapidly, people may decide to take part of the gain in increased leisure, (which in principle means the same thing as shorter working hours). If the cause fades, so does the effect. The slow-down in hours reduction may well be part and part of the general slow down.

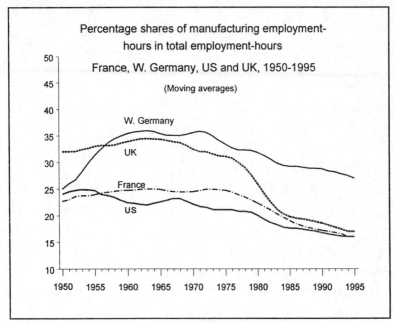

Figure 3.3 The progress of de-industrialization as measured by employment, four countries, 1950-1995.
Sources: Calculated from O'Mahony, 1995, data base, and *Penn World Tables*, Heston and Summers, 1991, in References.

De-industrialization

Figures 3.3 and 3.4 tell the story of de-industrialization. If, as has happened, manufacturing productivity rises faster than apparent non-manufacturing productivity, the *employment share* of manufacturing can move in the opposite direction from manufacturing output. The manufacturing employment-share in Germany rose dramatically in the great phase of her post-war recovery and has since declined on balance less than in the other countries. So as of today, the (West) German figure, at nearly 30 per cent, is very much above the other countries' figures which are typically around 20 per cent.

International comparisons of the *production level* of manufacturing tell another story. Even in the UK, manufacturing output is higher than it was at the end of, and certainly higher than it was at the beginning of, World War II. But Germany and the US have now

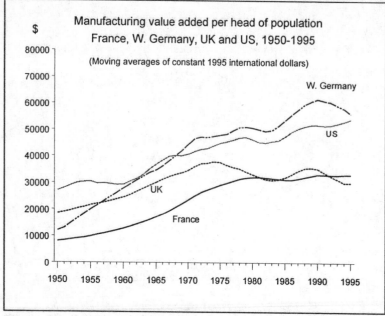

Figure 3.4 De-industrialization measured by output in four countries, 1950-95.

Source: O'Mahoney, 1995, data base, in References.

reached double the figure of the UK and France. (The US production level is comparatively high, despite a comparatively low employment share, because the US still has comparatively high manufacturing productivity.)

Since the late seventies British manufacturers have taken a beating. Two beatings, to be more precise. The first began in 1979 and lasted for five years. There followed a brisk recovery lasting unfortunately only half a decade until put into sharp reverse by the 1990 economic crash, and not yet, as far as can be seen, restored. Few doubt that the sole cause of the earlier disaster was the overvaluation of the pound sterling after it had become a petro currency. Mary O'Mahony's figures show that during the first adverse UK period, the pound typically stood 15 per cent higher than the rate that would have

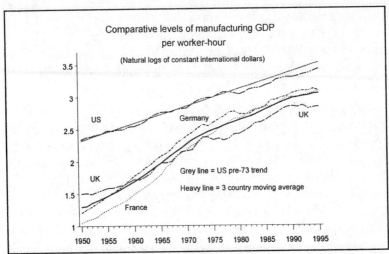

Figure 3.5 Manufacturing productivity in Europe and the US, 1950 to 1995.

Sources: 1950-1970, Van Ark, 1990, in References.

1971-1993, O'Mahony, 1995, data base, in References.

1994-1995, estimated from current news.

Definitions: Value-added per employee-hour in national currency is converted into dollars at rates reflecting unit values for manufactured products. The conversion into logarithms 'linearizes' paths of constant percentage growth. All along the left hand scale, a change of 0.01 on the scale reflects a change of approximately one per cent in the original data. For larger differences, the scale creates a compromise between percentage differences measured in one direction or the other. For example, in 1995 on the grey line, the original number was $34 per hour (= exp[3.525], see chart) and on the heavy line, $21, a difference of $13, which is 64 per cent of $21 or 39 per cent of $34. The average of these two percentages is just over 50 per cent, which corresponds to the log difference (3.5 - 3.0 = .5) on the left scale.

Note on the UK: Previous figures on UK pre-1973 performance failed to allow for the decline in working hours. In reality, British manufacturing productivity in the period grew quite fast but not as fast as on the Continent. Mancur Olson, of the University of Maryland, argues that the explanation was that the UK was not totally disrupted by World War II, and in consequence her established micro-social-economic institutions survived as conservative forces. Olson's theory is founded on his earlier work on social action. (See Olson, 1982 and 1965, in References.) For a critique, see Chapter 3 of Angus Maddison's book, 1995, in References.

equalized the dollar cost of British and German exports, and 10 per cent higher than the rate that would have done the same thing in relation to the US.[1] Thus the British manufacturing production movements in Figure 3.4 will help to explain the productivity movements to be shown in Figure 3.6.

The productivity of manufacturing

Figure 3.5 compares the long term trends of manufacturing productivity among all four countries. The main purpose here is to study the west European catch-up/slow-down process. The heavy moving-average line tells quite a surprising story. In the run-up to the 1973 debacle, west Europe, even with the comparatively slow UK (actually growing, 1950-73 at nearly 4 per cent per year) included was converging on the US at not a decelerating, but an accelerating rate.

Had the region continued in that fashion, it might well have caught up the US by the end of the century. After 1973, although the catching-up process did continue, it had become not only slower but, on the evidence of recent years, also decelerating. I think this new perspective, made possible by the new statistics, does suggest a major disturbance, not only in the UK, whose case and reasons have already been touched on, but also most distinctively for France and Germany.

Supply side, or demand side? Was this 'Eurosclerosis' or was it, as I believe, the result of a disunited Europe paying a higher price for the world-wide economic disruptions that began in the middle seventies than did the United States. By virtue of the size and strength of her economy, the US was able to absorb the oil shocks more gently. The French and German post-1973 historical record does not refute, and can, for those who so wish, be used to support the idea that a distinct deterioration in continental west Europe's 'supply-side' performance did occur, and did affect both actual manufacturing technical productivity and general growth performance. Nevertheless, it is not an easy idea. In effect, the so-called 'Eurosclerosis' thesis boils down to saying that although west Europe grew fast, she did not grow as fast as she might have done.

---

1   O'Mahony, 1995, in References.

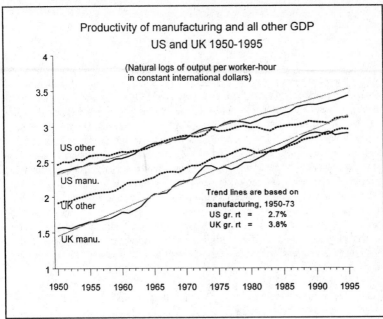

Productivity of manufacturing and all other GDP
US and UK 1950-1995

(Natural logs of output per worker-hour in constant international dollars)

US other

US manu.

UK other

UK manu.

Trend lines are based on manufacturing, 1950-73
US gr. rt = 2.7%
UK gr. rt = 3.8%

Figure 3.6   Productivity of manufacturing and non-manufacturing in the US and the UK, 1950 to 1995.

Sources: – as Figure 3.3.

The crucial comparison: manufacturing v non-manufacturing

We are now ready for the main test, the national and international comparison of the behaviour of manufacturing productivity with non-manufacturing.

The UK and the US

Figure 3.6 tells this story for the UK and the US. The result is quite dramatic. From 1950 to 1973, US non-manufacturing productivity grew only slightly less slowly than her manufacturing productivity and also, throughout this period, the *levels* of productivity in the two sectors, contrary to conventional wisdom, did not differ greatly. Then both things changed overnight. The downwards break of non-manufacturing productivity, as shown in the chart, was historically unprecedented in statistics of this type.

Also notice that there is little evidence of a major long term technical slow-down in US manufacturing productivity. A displace-

The Measurement Hypothesis

In the past few years American economists have begun to sense that there was a question mark over the productivity slow down. In 1993, Robert Lawrence and Mathew Slaughter, of MIT, published an important paper* (which is also referred to in the context of trade, in Chapter 4) containing figures showing, among other things, the same basic story shown in for the latter part of the period. Then, in 1994, Zvi Grilliches, of Harvard, and a particularly distinguished applied economist published an article** containing a chart for the US identical in every respect to Figure 3.6 except for one crucial difference: in place of the division between manufacturing and non-manufacturing, he provided a division between 'measurable' and 'unmeasurable' sectors of the GDP. 'Measurables' are manufacturing plus agriculture, mining, transportation, communications and public utilities. 'Unmeasurables' are construction, distribution, finance, government and general private services. The result is a picture similar to, but stronger, than the one shown in Figure 3.6.

Grilliches therefore argues along similar lines to Baumol that there is a fundamental measurement error which is failing to pick up output from the 'unmeasurables' because productivity increases in those sectors mainly appear in the form of intangible improvements in quality. He concludes his article with a strong plea for better measurement. In that he has my very strong support. In the middle eighties I wrote a report for the Statistical Office of the European Community suggesting a programme for obtaining more meaningful data on services outputs, and published some resulting thoughts in an article about international measurements.*** Unfortunately the project died for lack of support from governments.

My hypothesis that the spurious slow down is due to services labour shifting into low-wage/low-value added subsectors is also a kind of measurement hypothesis, but a different one. Both hypotheses imply that in the US the 'required' (or 'natural') GDP growth rate did not slow down, and consequently both hypotheses, in my book, imply that some form of demand-side factor must have been responsible for the weak performance of wages. In addition, we need to think about reasons why the US history is not mirrored in other countries. Do other countries have less of a measurement problem? The question is not entirely rhetorical, as at least one major non-US country is reported to add an arbitrary two-and-a-half per cent per annum to the productivity of the whole public sector on the ground that the standard method of measurement in this sector (which basically assumes output = input) is inadequate!

---

* Lawrence, 1995, in References. ** Grilliches, 1994, in References.
*** Marris, 1984, in References.

ment did occur, coinciding, as expected, with the beginning of US internal adjustment to the energy situation, after which a reasonably steady new path seems to have been established, along which it could be said that the long term growth rate was at the very most two-tenths of one per cent slower than the old trend.[1]Taking these two points together, I feel that the chart provides strong support for my hypothesis. Not only is there almost no evidence of a technical slow-down in US manufacturing, the same is also true for supply-side explanations in non-manufacturing.

The contrast with the UK case is also dramatic. After a displacement, UK non-manufacturing apparent productivity followed almost the same path as manufacturing. I suggest this confirms my contention set out in the previous pages that the explanation is to be found in the better performance of wages, and weaker performance of employment, in the UK than in the US.

France and Germany

Because it is possible that these two countries did suffer a supply-side disturbance of manufacturing productivity, there is also the possibility of a similar factor at work in their non-manufacturing sectors. This makes interpretation more difficult. Nevertheless, Figure 3.7 is also startling. After 1973, all four lines break away from their previous trends and converge! We know that both countries have had a better wage performance, especially for the lowest paid people, than either the US or the UK. Germany in particular, as we saw in Chapter 2, has a special record of sustaining the productivity and earnings of the less-academically-educated worker. We also know that both countries have had substantial increases in male non-employment. But low wages are clearly not the explanation of the non-manufacturing apparent slow-down. It is important to appreciate however that the slower growth rate of French and German manufacturing after 1973 was still markedly faster than the corresponding rate in the US.

---

1   Edward Denison has shown that incorrect treatment of the computer industry exaggerated the US manufacturing productivity performance in the years leading up to 1989. Fortunately his corrected results give the same growth rates for corresponding periods as the rates derived from the Van Ark data I use here. See Denison, 1989, and Van Ark, 1990, in References.

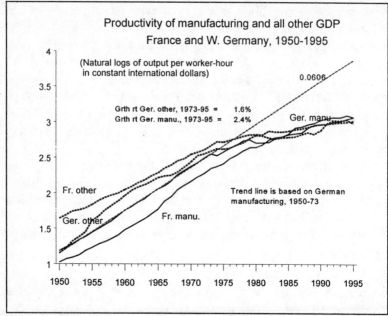

Figure 3.7 **Productivity of manufacturing and non-manufacturing in France and Germany.**

Sources: – as for UK and US.

A summing up

Our hypothesis of a low-wage induced services-sector productivity slow-down in the US has been statistically supported by the evidence of a major divergence in the paths of manufacturing and non-manufacturing productivity after 1973. The prediction that in France and Germany, where wages are known to have held up, the corresponding convergence would not be observed, has also stood up, together with the prediction that the UK would fall in between.

Therefore I can claim that my general thesis, though, of course, not 'proved', is supported.

Why did it happen?

In 1970, the OECD world could look back on nearly a quarter of a century of unprecedented prosperity. In the slowest growing countries – the Anglo-Saxon war-winners – the real income of the least-advantaged economic groups had been growing at a rate to double

Annual percentage inflation rates, 1950-1995
Unweighted average of France, W. Germany, UK and US

Figure 3.8   Inflation in the US and Western Europe, 1950-1995.
   Sources: *Penn World Tables,* Heston and Summers,1991, and *OECD Economic Outlook*, Dec 1995, in References. The data are GDP deflators.

every thirty years, while inflation had averaged under 3 per cent. Unemployment rates in most countries were typically under 5 per cent.

Within five years this golden age lay in ruins. Some economists think that the 'super-Keynesian' regime was inherently non-sustainable. Others, such as myself, believe that most of the blame for the turn-round can be laid at the door of the series of severe shocks which soon occurred. In turn, the other side may retort that the shocks, if not provoked, were certainly facilitated by the previous environment.

Figure 3.8 can be used by both sides in the debate. If one ignores everything to the right of 1970, one can, if one wishes, see a persistent acceleration of inflation after 1965. Alternatively, one could say that the data of the period 1965-70 represented no more than the upswing of a cycle. A factor in the argument is that the years 1950-52 were disturbed by the war in Korea. At the other end of the story, after 1965, the United States, in Viet Nam, was now fighting a major war with a peacetime economy. The British did this in the early stages of World War I and found it a perfect recipe for inflation. By contrast, in World War II, both Britain and the US fought total war with a totally regulated economy and experienced remarkably low inflation.[1] In the late sixties the US situation triggered a wage explosion which spread quickly around the world culminating the famous *évènements* in Paris in 1968.

I personally believe, however, that with good international government and economic cooperation, in the absence of the shocks, the problem would have been corrected without any significant cost in real growth, and certainly without any cost that compares to the actual losses the world did, in fact, subsequently suffer.

The shocks

There was a world-wide commodity-price boom in 1972, which is variously attributed to the war, to a somewhat injudicious collective international fiscal and monetary expansion and/or to the knock-on effect of US government purchases of wheat for sale to the Soviets.

After that came oil.

Before 1968 the United States was a not a net oil importer. She had a large population, high GDP and high energy consumption per real GDP dollar. Thus she was responsible for a very large share of total world energy consumption. But she produced all this energy herself. Historically, as the US economy grew, so did her domestic energy production. Then something mysterious happened to halt the growth of domestic oil output and for the next ten years the whole weight of the energy requirement for US growth was thrown onto the world market, with a consequent very large effect on the world balance of crude-oil demand and supply. Then another war, between Israel and some Arab states, added to the brew, provoking the Organization of Petroleum Exporting Countries to raise the price of crude oil by four times inside a few weeks. For domestic political reasons, the US economy was for some years insulated from the new world energy price, and both per capita energy consumption and oil imports

---

1   In Britain, one of the leading administrators of rationing was my father; in the US, one of the leading administrators of price control was John Kenneth Galbraith.

continued to rise. The result was the so-called 'second' oil shock in 1979: this time oil prices merely doubled.

The consequences

Figure 3.8 graphically illustrates the world inflationary consequences. Reasonable conditions were not restored until the mid-eighties. While the storm was raging, two things were inevitable. First that governments, and especially the Federal Reserve Board under Paul Volcker, would attempt to restrain inflation by restricting the money supply. Second that the money cost of public expenditure would rise faster than tax receipts. The purchasing power of the money balances held by people and business, reduced by inflation, could not easily be restored. Government money deficits increased, but the real value of public spending was if anything reduced.

The secondary consequences of these primary events were extremely adverse both to business expectations of the stable growth of real consumer demand, and to the general business incentive to expand production capacity. Central banks' attempts to hold money tight and the increased public deficits permanently raised real interest rates to double the levels which had prevailed on average in the hundred years preceding 1970, with adverse effects on investment.[1]

In a fascinating, fast-selling, book, Paul Ormerod[2] has shown that the

---

1   Actually, the factual-causal chain concerning private investment is somewhat elusive. Tease et al, 1991 (OECD, in References), Table 1, compare the ratio of private investment to GDP in the 1980s with the 1960s in a group of ten countries which did not include France or the Netherlands. In six countries (one of which was the US) such change as occurred was of the order of a percentage point or less. In the UK there was a modest increase. The remaining countries, all of which did show marked decreases, were Japan, W. Germany and Italy. These were all countries with a strong catch-up/slow-down history (one suspects if data for France existed she would be included), which would inevitably imply lower investment rates.

2   Paul Ormerod, *The Death of Economics*, 1994, in References. As well as his theory about the Phillips curve, Paul Ormerod's book contains an interesting theory of growth. The growth of capacity is largely driven by reinvested profits. Since higher wages mean lower profits, he predicts a negative relationship between wages and growth. This appears diametrically opposed to the theory used in this book. Ormerod is saying that higher wages cause slower growth; I am saying that slower growth causes lower wages. But we both agree that anything that encourages reinvestment of profits encourages growth. We also both agree

basic underlying relationship in the economics of inflation is not, as has always previously been supposed, a relation between the inflation rate and the *level* of the unemployment rate, but between the inflation rate and the *speed of change* of the unemployment rate. If unemployment falls fast, wages rise fast. If unemployment is at a high level which has been reached slowly, the effect on wages is minimal. This is a major re-interpretation of the famous 'Phillips-curve'. That relationship remains as a mathematical by-product of the new relationship, but is now unstable. More precisely it is liable to be displaced by shocks. Before a shock, maybe a five per cent unemployment rate would generate no more than a two and a half per cent inflation rate. After the shock, the same unemployment rate could generate an inflation rate that could easily be three times worse. Turning the problem around, this means that after the shock, in order to maintain a socially acceptable inflation rate of eg five per cent, it may now be necessary to restrict demand and growth in the economy to an extent that will be reflected in a current official unemployment rate that could be anything up to ten per cent.

In short, the whole economic system becomes impossible to manage within the ranges of real demand and inflation that were previously regarded as acceptable. Ormerod provides strong evidence[1] that just such a malignant situation developed after 1974 and persisted for the next ten years. This long persistence is consistent with the dynamic implications of his theory, and does not require additional explanations.

Why did the trouble continue?

An under-employed market economy is stable but not at all nice. A fully-employed economy *can* be stable, but is vulnerable to shocks. If it receives big shocks, the adverse dynamic effects may stay around for a long time. That said, it is clear that the effects of events that took place nearly a quarter of a century ago, have now, at the time of writing, stayed around for much too long. Why has that happened? I

---

that reinvestment will be encouraged not only by supply-side factors (in which I would include a reduction in the the threat of take-overs) but also by business optimism over the long term growth of demand.

1   Ormerod, 1994, p. 129.

would pick on five particular factors, among a number, that go to answer that question: failure on the *demand side*; high *real interest rates*; *perverse 'expectations'* in the money markets, *'globalization'* of money markets and trouble on the supply side caused by *excessive take-over activity.*

Slow real-demand growth
Ormerod shows that between 1983 and 1985, the 'Phillips' relationship did eventually jerk back into a position that although less favourable than in the 1960s, was markedly improved as compared to that of the period 1973-83. More generally it seems reasonable to say that in the labour market the primary dynamic effects of the shock events of the mid-70s were by now no longer around. Yet, in the previous part of the present chapter, we have seen powerful evidence of inadequate economic growth that must always have 'demand-side' explanations. *By that I do not necessarily mean that current real demand is under-utilizing current capacity, but rather that, due to inadequate expectation of steady long term **growth** of demand, the business sector is not sufficiently succeeding in expanding commercial organization, markets and physical capacity.* (And I have suggested, it will be remembered, that the effects are particularly manifest in non-manufacturing.)

Nationally and internationally, public macro policy has continued to be dedicated not to real growth or economic welfare, but to what is called 'stability', meaning, in fact, low and stable inflation. Alternatively, it has been devoted to 'supply-side' or 'intermediate' targets – such as reducing government regulation and increasing the efficiency of markets. These general tendencies have taken different historical forms in different countries and international organizations. Among the latter, the prevailing attitudes of governments have been reflected in the orientation of staff economists: for example, the OECD staff, who in earlier years were noted as conventional Keynesians, today emerge as the authors of the very supply-side-oriented Jobs Study.[1] The European Union, while constantly worrying about increasing unemployment, has shown little evidence that its collective intellect really understands the problem. Consequently the Union members, in

---

1 OECD, 1994, in References.

planning to form a single currency, created so-called 'convergence' conditions for admission to membership which made no direct reference to economic growth or economic welfare. The conditions were in fact adopted to meet German fears that the new currency would suffer inflation at the highest of the previous rates among the members. As a result, it is now widely accepted that the plan had a built-in in deflationary bias which has exacerbated the growth slow down in Continental Western Europe – thus politically endangering the project itself. Yet as recently as February 1996, Hans-Dietrich Genscher, the distinguished ex-Foreign Minister of Germany, wrote,

> A fully-fledged monetary union will....provide the market economy in Europe with a powerful boost for growth.....[But] this assumes that monetary union will be a genuine 'community of stability'. A central task .... will, therefore, be to ensure that .... the participating countries continue to pursue stability-oriented budgetary policies...[1]

The significance of the wording lies in the emphasis. Growth indeed is mentioned, but stability has priority.

In the UK, at the time I am writing, we have a chief economic Minister (Chancellor of the Exchequer), Kenneth Clarke, who is reputed to make, on convivial occasions, remarks that sound remarkably Keynesian.[2] He will also be remembered with gratitude for consistently trying to press down real interest rates, against the persistent opposition of his central bank. But when, to help write this book, I wrote to Mr. Clarke to enquire about his views on growth, he declined to be committed. And when faced with meetings of the economic ministers of other countries, such as the Group of Seven, or when defending his record in domestic political circles, he mentions only performance on inflation, never growth.

The foregoing critique does not apply in full force to the conduct of the US central bank (Federal Reserve Board) after 1984 under Paul Volcker. He felt with some justification that he was achieving low inflation, falling unemployment and reasonable growth. With hindsight we can see that the long-run growth rate was inadequate to prevent the decline, documented above, in the apparent productivity of the non-manufacturing sector and the sad associated story of wages

---

1   Quoted from an article by Herr Genscher in *The Guardian,* London, Feb 19, 1996.

2   See for example an article by William Keegan, 'Hark, hark to Clarke! But is he to the left of Tony Blair?', *The Observer,* London, 4 Feb 1996, p. 2.

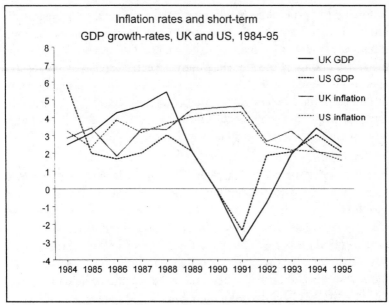

Figure 3.9   The Anglo-Saxon disturbances of the late eighties.
Sources: – as corresponding previous figures.
Definitions:
　　GDP:　　GDP at constant prices per head of population
　　Inflation: GDP deflators.

and family incomes. In effect, it could be said, the problem was caused by looking too hard at an intermediate target, the official unemployment rate, rather than at what should be the primary target, total welfare.[1]

At the end of the eighties both the US and the UK experienced unhealthy inflationary boomlets followed by quite severe (in the UK very severe) slumps that adversely affected the ten-year economic growth records of both countries. The data of these boomlets is shown in Figure 3.9. Measured by inflation, they appear like storms in teacups. Measured by output fluctuations, they were more serious. The authorities in both countries were surprised by the speed of the expansion – which was essentially transitory and debt-financed,

---

1   This line of thought is entirely due to my brother, Stephen Marris, ex-chief economist of the OECD.

following the general de-regulation of financial markets (causing all kinds of institutions to chase around persuading people to borrow money for spending) – and surprised again by the severe response of the real economy to the monetary corrective measures. The net result, apart from the loss of several years' growth, was a long term reduction in consumer and business confidence, the effects of which are still with us. Many households got into debt and they, as well as others who did not, have become cautious about the future.

The problem of interest rates[1]

It is also widely believed that from 1980 onwards high 'real' interest rates have added to the problem. The 'real' rate is the actual (or 'nominal') rate adjusted for inflation. In the case of short rates (ie rates for short term loans), the concept is quite hard. If I am a person or institution thinking of buying a three-month Treasury Bill (which pays no interest) at a time when the going rate on these kinds of transactions is eight per cent per annum, I expect to be able to buy the bill at a two per cent discount on its redemption value, so as to earn a net return equivalent to a quarter of a year's interest at eight per cent. In deciding whether to do the deal, however, since the Bill is not index-linked, I must also allow for rising prices: my real annual return, rather than eight per cent, will be eight per cent *less* the annual inflation rate.

In transactions as short as three months, it is not unreasonable to regard inflation rates of the recent past as good forecasts of near-future inflation rates. But when we think about long term interest rates, for example the rates on ten-year, twenty-year or perpetual bonds, the picture is much less clear. If inflation ran around four per cent for five years but had recently, as a result of some shock, increased to ten per cent, what am I to think about the 15-20 year prospect? Has the inflationary environment changed permanently, or

---

1 The argument following owes much to extremely helpful discussions with Professor Dr. Wilhelm Nölling, distinguished author of *Monetary Policy in Europe since Maastricht* (1993, in References, especially pp 244-5), but he has of course no responsibility for what I actually say.

has it not?[1] The question is as crucial to borrower as to lender. If I borrow money at 13 per cent on an inflation forecast of nine per cent, and actual inflation turns out at four per cent, even though my business plan was sound, I may not earn enough to pay the interest. Consequently, any economist attempting, as I have done in Figure 3.11 below, to present historical data on long-term real rates, is compelled to make highly subjective estimates of past relationships between historical actual inflation and historical expected inflation.

Subject to this conceptual problem, what does economic theory say about the forces determining interest rates? In the case of short rates, it is widely held that these are very much the creatures of governments and central banks. The manipulation is done by the setting of central-bank lending rates[2] and/or by open market operations that affect the liquidity of the banking system and hence the general money supply. In effect, the governments of major countries can move short rates in their own money markets over wide ranges provided they are content with the required corresponding money-supply variations in accordance with time, place and circumstances. Consequently, in the international arena, the direct collective power of the Group-of-Seven governments over global short rates is strong indeed.

One concern of individual governments in relation to local-currency short term interest rates derives from their concern with the currency's foreign-exchange rate. If they want to keep the local exchange rate up, they can encourage people to hold the currency by keeping local interest rates up, and vice versa if they want to drive the exchange rate down. We return to that subject shortly. Leaving it aside for the moment, the most outstanding monetary phenomenon of the late twentieth century has been government reliance on *nominal* short rates as a general weapon of macro economic management and a particular weapon of inflation control. What this means in effect is that when governments' fears of inflation increase, they tend to raise

---

1 Before World War II, prices as often fell as rose. A rise in prices, such as occurred in World War I, could create an expectation of a future fall in prices. The correlation between current inflation and expected future inflation could be negative.

2 Ie the rate at which the central bank undertakes to lend to other banks or recognised money-market operators.

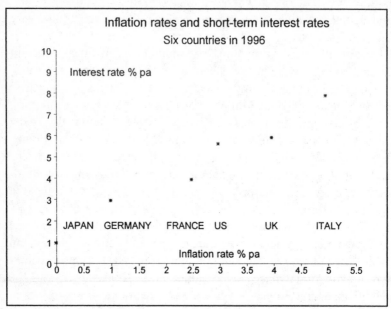

Figure 3.10   The international dimension of short term interest rates in the middle nineteen nineties.

Definitions:

Interest rate   =   September 1996 forecast of nominal three-month rate on secure loans denominated in local currency (eg central bank rediscount rate or base rate).

Inflation rate =   September 1996 forecast annual rate of increase of consumer price index.

STR (short-term real interest rate)

(1)   STR for an individual country is the value on the y-axis minus the value on the x-axis.

(2)   The fact that the data fall rather close to a straight line indicates that despite differences in inflation rates, STRs are all much the same.

(3)   The typical STR is indicated by the point where a line through the data would intercept the y-axis, ie is about *two per cent*.

Source: *UBS Global Research*, UBS (Unions de Banques Suisses), London, 6 June, 1996.

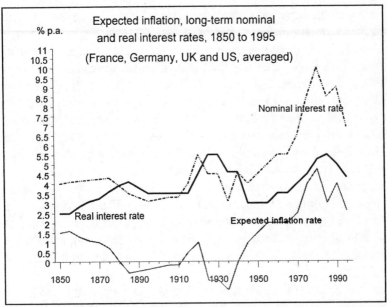

Figure 3.11 A century and a half of real interest rates.

Definitions:

Nominal interest rate   = Total return to maturity of a representative long term government bond.

Expected inflation rate = The subjectively expected future long term inflation rate for goods and services implicitly applied by willing borrowers and lenders to transactions in representative bonds.

Real interest rate   = Nominal rate less expected inflation rate.

Sources: Nominal interest rates from Homer and Sylla, 1991 and OECD 1992, in References. Expected inflation estimated by the author from actual inflation rates (from OECD and from Mitchell, 1991, 1993 in References) on the assumptions that adjustments to changes in the current inflation rate are slow and that extreme rates, especially those associated with war or similar disturbance, are heavily discounted.

nominal rates by an amount sufficient to raise *real* rates. Consequently, if governments believe that actual inflation is actually accelerating, they must raise nominal rates by *more* than the increase in the inflation rate.

Statistically speaking, if governments do tend to forecast short term future inflation on the basis of current inflation, we shall expect to see that in data relating to a number of countries, the national figures for short term nominal interest rates converge towards the corresponding figures for local current inflation rates *plus* whatever must be added to get from the nominal rate to the *desired* real rate. If it should happen that most governments are aiming at much the same real rate, we shall expect to see a correlation between current short term local-currency nominal interest rates and current local-currency inflation rates. The common international real rate would be suggested by the level where a straight line drawn through the points in an appropriate scatter diagram intercepts the y-axis. This idea is supported quite strongly by Figure 3.10, with a suggested target real short interest rate among G-7 countries in 1996 around two per cent.

It is however the long term (real) rate that is most likely to affect private investment and economic growth. Figure 3.11 shows that although in the nineteen eighties and early nineties this has certainly been very high as compared with the golden age of the nineteen sixties (for example 5.5 in 1985 compared to 3.5 in 1965) it has only moderately exceeded the worst pre-World War II levels for periods, such as the nineteen thirties or eighteen nineties, that were free from the effects of World War I.[1] The eighteen nineties and nineteen thirties were periods of economic depression with falling prices. By contrast, the nineteen eighties had economic depression (in the sense described in this chapter) with *rising* prices. The argument that high real long term interest rates have significantly contributed to the continuing trouble is therefore convincing.

So what is the cause of the cause? What is the economic theory of long term interest rates? The economics profession has devoted

---

1   As a result of highly effective government policy carried out, much under the influence of Keynes, on both sides of the Atlantic, World War II on the Allied side was fought with the aid of relatively moderate inflation and remarkably low interest rates.

millions of words, many equations and many thousands of statistical observations to the study of this question and, in consequence, there are a number of respectable theories. At the end of the day, however, there are few economists who would disagree with the proposition that at any moment of time the nominal long term rate will tend to equal average of future short term rates expected at that time, *plus* a premium for extra risk. For example, suppose the current short term rate is six per cent and I believe that on average this will be constant in the future, but subject to oscillation. If I am offered a ten-year bond that currently shows a redemption yield no greater than six per cent I will refuse it: I will prefer eg a three month Treasury Bill yielding six per cent. Why? Because, with the bond, if, say, five years ahead I need to sell, I may find that at that particular moment the general level of interest rates is above or below the long term average. Consequently on selling the bond I may make a capital gain or a capital loss. Being, to some extent averse to risk, I do not like this prospect. Consequently, in order to be persuaded to buy the bond, rather than the Treasury Bill, I must be offered an average expected yield of *better* than six per cent.

This is a theory that is strong on logic and weak on measurability. The average *expected* future short term rate is by no means necessarily the same as the current actual rate and cannot therefore be directly observed. This being the case, we lack a firm statistical basis for historical measurement of the risk premium.[1] What we can say, however, is that anything which tends to increase the *expected variability* of future short rates must increase the premium. The most powerful force to that effect one could imagine would be the markets'

---

1   In a careful study of data from the second half of the twentieth century, John Campbell and Robert Shiller (1989, in References) pursue the hypothesis that in any past year, say 1960, the average short-term rate expected from 1960 to 1987 tended to be equal to the historical rate actually subsequently experienced in the same period – ie markets are assumed on average to be perfect forecasters. This is a modelling technique that has been described as characterised by 'consistent' expectations, although also (improperly, in my view) sometimes described as embodying 'rational' expectations. Campbell and Shiller show that the hypothesis fails in what they describe as their 'sample period', implying to my mind that having failed over a long period during which markets became increasingly sophisticated, it is likely to fail in any other period for which data are likely to become available.

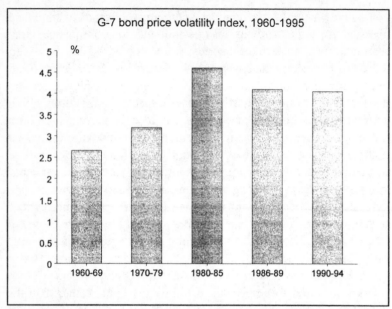

Figure 3.12 The riskiness of bond holding, 1960 to 1995.

Definition:

The index is the standard deviation of monthly changes in long-term bond yields averaged over Canada, France, Germany, Italy, Japan, the UK and the US expressed as a percentage of the average nominal yield on long term bonds in those countries during the corresponding period. It may roughly be interpreted as follows:

Consider a bond bought on the first of a month. If the index reads 2.5 there is approximately a one in three chance that the market price of the bond will have changed, in either direction, by two and a half per cent or more by the end of the month. If the index reads 5, there is the same probability (ie one in three) that the price will have changed by at least five per cent.

Sources:

The variance of monthly changes is an unweighted average of the figures given by Edey and Hviding, 1995, in References. The nominal rates are from the same sources as Figure 3.11.

---

perceiving that governments are increasingly relying on short term interest rates as a weapon of macroeconomic management.

In these circumstances we cannot use the historical variability of short term rates as a guide to their subjectively expected future variability. We can however reasonably assume that an increase in the expected variability of future short rates is likely to be paralleled by an increase in the historical variation of expected future average rates. If the latter occurs, the historical variation of *actual* long rates will also increase. This last we can measure, as in Figure 3.12, and the result is that the riskiness of long term lending did sharply increase between 1970 and 1985, has since fallen back, but was still, in 1995, substantially greater than before. It is difficult to believe that we are not seeing here a major explanation of the persistence of high long term real rates with correspondingly adverse implications for the real economy.

But this is not the end of the story. One cannot assume that increased risk is the whole explanation for high long term interest rates. It is possible, if not likely, that governments have also been holding short term rates at levels calculated to create expectations of future rates high enough to cause in turn high long rates. We have seen that the power of governments over short rates presumes a willingness to assent to required associated changes in the money supply. How much 'macro' money needs to be created to support a given interest rate depends on the total volume of debt, long and short, already in existence, needing to be funded. There is a belief, held especially strongly among bankers and monetary experts, that persistent government deficits both in the G-7 and in many other countries, including Third World countries, have greatly added to the world stock of debt requiring funding. The money supply required to support given short rates has therefore, according to this argument, also been increased.

Governments, however, may well be unwilling to create the larger amounts of money they may believe are needed for lower real interest rates because they believe that money creation, as such, is *ipso facto* inflationary. This is based on the 'monetarist' story that even in an economy where all other inflationary signs are weak, money creation will tend to push up prices rather than real demand. In the opposing Keynesian view, money creation may accommodate, but cannot cause inflation.[1]

---

1 As many readers will recognise, these two sentences attempt to summarize a huge controversy which is now sixty years old. In the monetarist view, if people and institutions are supplied with more liquid assets (such as money) than they need, they will unload the excess by buying goods of various kinds and especially

It is not necessary to resolve the issue in order to see its significance. The fact that the 'monetarist' view is widely held in policy-making circles is sufficient to produce an effect. If the monetarist view is held in central-bank circles, and also condoned by governments, operational decisions aimed at reducing current short rates, in the hope in turn of reducing current long rates, will not be taken. Alternatively, even if some governments and bankers do not hold the monetarist view, but it is still held by the markets, governments will find long rates refusing to respond to lower short rates.

The above-described syndrome – a mixture of theories, beliefs, illusions and realities – almost certainly represents a major element in the explanation of high long term real interest rates in the final decade of the twentieth century. To the extent that its causes include the government deficits that have actually occurred, the deficits are part of the syndrome. But what caused the deficits? The answer, in part at least, was slow macro economic growth. That is the vicious circle first mentioned in Chapter 1.[1]

Irrational expectations

To make matters worse, the syndrome has become associated with another closely associated syndrome which not only reinforces the tendency to excessive real interest rates but also adversely affects the real economy directly. It is illustrated by the press cuttings presented in the box on page 105. They are only a selection; one could find hundreds of others similar.Their common message has two elements. The first is an unpleasant paradox that what is good news for the real economy is bad news for the money markets. The second point is that these paradoxical 'expectations' (economic jargon for forecasting assumptions) are not only perverse but highly unstable. Any statistical whiff of change can reverse the values of billions of dollars of

---

physical assets, such as property and real estate. The prices of these things rise, yielding capital gains, which are inherently inflationary. In the Keynesian view, the decline in short-term interest rates, which is part and parcel of the operation, will be sufficient to persuade asset holders to accept increased liquidity. But also in the Keynesian view, in times of genuine underlying inflation, the total demand for money will increase. If this demand is frustrated by a tight-money policy, not only will interest rates rise, but expenditure generally will become rationed, and, as a result, a desirable inflation-restraining effect achieved.

1   Page 15.

Strange Headlines*

JANUARY
'Consumer spending surge could trigger 8% base rates'
– London, *The Times,* Jan 9, 1996.

JULY
'Output rise may stall new rate cut'
'Britain's strengthening consumer sector helped to produce the first rise in manufacturing for six months. The news is likely to make Kenneth Clarke cautious about calling for a rate cut when he meets the Governor of the Bank of England tomorrow.'
– London, *The Times,* Jul 2, 1996.

'Jobs surge causes Wall St. pandemonium'
'There was pandemonium on Wall Street yesterday when share and bond prices plummeted after figures showing a surge in new jobs took US unemployment to a six-year low last month. Average hourly earnings surged by 9 cents, the biggest monthly increase on record.'
– London, *The Independent,* Jul 2, 1996.

ONE WEEK LATER!
'Easing of inflation lifts rate cut hope'
'A dramatic fall in inflation pressure in industry and continuing stagnation in the manufacturing sector could tempt Kenneth Clarke into another base rate cut later this month say City analysts.'
– London, *The Times,* July 9, 1996.

---

* The box title is intended to parody that of the book *Strange Fruit* by Caryl Phillips (1981, in References). In the book a narrator is travelling on the eastern side of the Chesapeake Bay in southern Maryland, today a couple of hours drive from Washington, DC. In the distance he sees a tree with something hanging in it, which on closer inspection turns out to be the body of a black man who has been lynched. 'Strange fruit', he muses.

funds.

The reader who has followed the preceding discussion can easily see how this has come about. Governments have created in the minds of markets the 'rational' expectation that they are very nervous of inflation and that they regard brisk increases in real output as storm warnings. So, if and when brisk output increases occur, the markets believe governments will believe the economy needs a touch of brake. Unfortunately, the only kind of brake the governments seem to know is the short term interest rate. If that is raised, even by a small amount, for the reasons given above there is likely to be some fall in bond prices. This might be an event of no great significance for long term personal or institutional holders of bonds, but to those whose chosen profession is the making of money by working with money, it is very important indeed. It is important to the managers of pension funds, for example, if they are employed in conditions where they are expected to take credit or blame for short term movements in the total market value of the managed assets. So, on the successful anticipation of small rate changes, hang personal fortunes, bonuses and career prospects. The markets are therefore very sensitive to 'news' and who can blame them?[1]

The effect has spread from the bond market to the stock market. News that the real economy is improving should create an expectation of rising profits and dividends. This however is inevitably nebulous. Share prices in real life react much more strongly to actual dividends than to expectations of dividends. When equity shares, are, as is the case today, widely held in widely-spread funds, they take on some of the economic characteristics of bonds, and fluctuate accordingly. An expected rise in interest rates, even if resulting from events that have optimistic implications for dividends, can therefore actually cause share prices to fall, as they did for example on Wall Street on July 2 1996.

Given the traumas of the seventies and eighties, one cannot blame governments for being cautious about inflation. One can blame them however for relying excessively on a single instrument of policy, namely the interest rates, when others, such as fiscal changes, are readily available. Be that as it may, the total effect on the business people whose chosen profession is to operate the real economy must be dispiriting. The harder they work to create profits, employment and growth, the greater the danger, it must seem to them, they will be

---

1   Even in media terms it is news of a peculiar kind. Basically this kind of news is what the people operating in the financial markets of the City of London, Wall Street, Tokyo or Hong Kong, regard as news, and is not necessarily convergent with the economic concerns of the general population. As a result, journalists working in the fields of finance and economics are subjected to a kind of schizophrenia – the style in which they write in one context may differ significantly from the style adopted in another. For example, all the *Times* quotations in the box came under the by-line of Janet Bush, the paper's excellent Economics Correspondent. But in the paper's 'Economic View' section, the same writer has on several occasions discussed exactly the paradox we are discussing, and in fact on 7 March 1996 forcefully argued that Kenneth Clarke should be bolder in reducing interest rates.

clobbered by adverse monetary movements. The total result is a diabolic macroeconomic *ménage a trois* inhabited by government, the markets and the real economy, with the last-named always at the bottom of the heap. The consequences of rational expectations in the markets are thus acutely irrational for society.

Irrationality globalised

The irrational situation in national money markets has also been internationalised. As is well known, in the past quarter century both exchange rates and international movements of money have been freed from controls and a vast global money market, supported by the new technology, has grown up. In the early seventies the world's various governments held total foreign reserves (ie stocks of foreign currency available for market intervention) equivalent to about five hours total turnover of the world's foreign-exchange markets. Today, that figure is down to 15 minutes.[1]

The professional dealers who operate these markets are absolute short-termists. Four-fifths of their transactions involve movements into and out of one currency within seven days. Many boast that their idea of the 'long term' is ten minutes.[2] In consequence their perceptions of the future have little relation to and are often diametrically opposed to the long term aspirations of governments. The objective realism of government aspirations has only small influence on the markets' evaluations. If dealers think that other dealers think that a government's policy is unrealistic, that is the view, irrespective of genuine facts, that will drive the markets' transactions in that country's currency. This situation, combined with the already-mentioned paper-thinness of the currency reserves, means that governments cannot easily 'buck the markets', irrespective of the consequences for national or global total economic welfare.

As a result, the practical potential of a policy of reducing local short term interest rates in order to encourage (via long term rates) long term economic growth is severely constrained by fears of exchange crises. A national economy could be in a situation where, in

---

1 Calculated from the statistical appendix to *The Tobin Tax,* conference report edited by Mahbub al Haq and others (1996, in References).

2 Paraphrased from James Tobin's introduction to *The Tobin Tax* (Haq, ed, 1996, in References), p xii.

the absence of this fear, the government, if it reduced current local short term interest rates, would succeed in creating the desired expectation of reduced future short rates, and hence succeed, in the manner already described, in reducing current local long rates. But if the foreign-exchange dealers choose to take a different view, they will tend to move out of the currency, putting downward pressure on the exchange rate. From the government's point of view, a mild devaluation might be desirable. A mild devaluation is not, however, what necessarily occurs. The initial fall in the foreign value of the currency creates (in dealers' minds) expectations of further devaluation, causing large additional movements out of the currency, leading to the familiar unstable spiral of decline and heavy 'overshooting' of the exchange rate compared to the economically rational level. Domestic inflation may be stimulated (prejudicing the real effectiveness of the devaluation) and the government may also suffer major political loss of face. Thus the British 1992 devaluation did lasting good to the British economy, yet did lasting damage to the prestige of the administration. It is a type of lesson other politicians are unlikely to forget and as such, inevitably, a constraint on growth.

Trouble on the supply side

Finally, there has been, since the early 1980s a major adverse influence on economic growth deriving from key features of the process, already described, by which business firms themselves grow and thus contribute to the growth of the economy.[1]

When firms retain profits for the purpose of growth they remove

---

1   The argument which follows is based on a theory of my own, propagated over the past thirty years, which I originally called the theory of 'managerial' capitalism. A short reading list could be Marris, R., 1964, 1980 and 1987, in References. It is a sad sign of recent times, that able economists such as Oliver Hart of MIT and John Moore, of the LSE (see Hart and Moore, 1993, 1995 in References) publish elegant mathematical theories supporting corporate financial structures designed to reduce management incentives for growth. When I argue with them about this they reply that their theory is not intended to have macro implications. They are concerned to improve microeconomic allocation of resources by preventing self-serving managements from squandering money that could more profitably be invested elsewhere. I retort that in aiming to divert investment towards 'better' management, they also inevitably reduce aggregate investment. The debate illustrates precisely the emphasis that I believe has underpinned adverse public policy towards growth since the mid eighties.

income from shareholders today in return for prospects of increased income in the future. If the future prospects are attractive, there need be no adverse effect on share prices. But inevitably, the greater the proportion of profits retained, the more likely, for a given firm with given prospects, that the market will begin to prefer a larger dividend distribution; failing that they will mark down the shares. There is consequently an explicit theoretical relationship between the long-term growth rate a management desires to pursue, on the one hand, and the firm's stock market value on the other. Up to a point, faster growth prospects may raise current market value; beyond that point the curve must turn over, so that yet stronger growth-favouring policies (with their cost in current dividends) now mean weaker and weaker stock prices. It can be shown that this 'law' still holds when allowance is made for the financing of growth by either new stock issues or by bond issues or other forms of debt financing.

The result is clearly a constraint on management growth efforts. Of many adverse effects on management of low stock prices, the most obvious and important is the threat of take-over. Take-over is always possible, but it is *more likely* if share prices are low (this is a well-known statistical result). But take-over is also more likely in some institutional environments than others. Japanese firms, for example grow fast and pay low dividends, but are virtually never involuntarily taken over because of legal and cultural barriers in Japanese economic society. Generally the greatest ease of take-overs is found in the Anglo-Saxon countries. In these two countries, take-overs run in waves or 'fevers'. When a fever is rampant, take-over of a given firm, with given dividends and growth prospects, is more likely than would otherwise be the case. In short, time and place affect the general risk of take-over.

It is obvious that the incumbent managements of large corporations do not like the risk of take-over. The greater it is, the more cautious they will be about lowering dividends to promote growth. High take-over risk therefore discourages the growth of firms, and hence the growth of the economy. Low risk, as in Japan, has the opposite effect with macro consequences that are obvious for all to see.

There was major take-over fever in both Anglo-Saxon countries throughout the 1980s and early 1990s.[1] There was also a large increase in corporate debt (more precisely, in the burden of debt relatively to assets). Both factors almost certainly slowed down the corporate sector's contribution to the growth of the economy.

Governments did not create the take-over boom, but they did little to discourage it and in some respects – a by-product of financial deregulation – effectively encouraged it.

A summing up

The short answer to the question, 'why did the growth slow-down continue into the nineties?', is that, in practice, growth remained low in government priorities: other targets took precedence. Thus a miscellaneous collection of policies, both 'demand-side' and 'supply-side,' effectively retarded growth, with the negative results on total welfare already described.

---

1 On this and other aspects of mergers there is a large literature. My own favourite author in the field is Dennis Mueller, University of Vienna. See Mueller, 1988, 1989 and 1992 in References.

4. The Role of Trade

There has been a 'second phase' of trade between developed countries and developing countries. In place of relying on primary products, the developing countries now export low-skill manufactures. But although this has benefited the average person, it has hurt unskilled workers in developed countries and contributed to the growth of 'SM'.[1]

That is the proposition. What is the theory behind it? What is the evidence for it? The theory is based on a modern version of the classical economic theory of **comparative advantage**: if two countries specialize in products where they are least inefficient, it is possible for the citizens of both countries to be better off than if no trade had occurred. The key word is 'possible'. Developing countries have a comparative advantage in unskilled-labour-intensive goods because their populations, at the present time, contain large proportions of unskilled people. Therefore in these countries unskilled wages are comparatively low. Therefore exports of the corresponding products are competitive.

But in exporting goods containing the results of comparatively low unskilled wages, the South also 'exports' her own wage structure. Unskilled wages in the North will come down and/or there will be more unskilled non-employment. So although skilled workers in the North gain from both higher wages and cheaper imports, unskilled workers may gain nothing at all, or in fact may be absolutely worse off.

To understand the process fully, it is also necessary to understand the role of exchange rates. The labour of one country is not 'cheap' in another just because, in the first country, real wages are lower than in the other. The comparison of hourly unit labour costs in a common currency also depends on the exchange rate. The theory of comparative advantage assumes that trade is balanced and the balancing of trade is achieved by exchange-rate adjustments. Before the second phase of trade, developed countries' exchange rates are much lower than their PPPs.[2] As the trade and develop-

---

1 'Severe meritocracy', see Chapter 1.
2 Purchasing-power parities.

ment process unfolds, they must converge.

The theory is cast-iron. Owing to statistical problems, however, the evidence is controversial. American economists have tended to find that the effect on the US labour market has been small. Adrian Wood, in Britain, gives reasons for thinking that those calculations are seriously biased downwards. He claims that the trade effect has in fact reduced the demand for unskilled labour in the whole OECD by as much as a fifth. I believe that he is more likely to be right than wrong, and that the effect has also probably been quite significant in the UK. But I do not believe it has occurred in Germany and also have doubts about France.

The theory of trade

'Comparative advantage'

The idea that opening up of 'North-South' trade – through better communications, reduced tariffs and quotas and improved manufacturing ability in developing countries – will hurt unskilled workers in the North, is based ultimately on the fundamental theory of international trade created by the one of the founding fathers of economics, David Ricardo, and was first published in the year 1817.[1] It is another of those laws of economics which cannot be wrong. Suppose two countries who do not trade, produce two goods. One country for some reason has higher productivity in producing both of them, but the difference is greater in one case than the other. For example, if the country is three times as efficient as the other country in producing cars, maybe it is only twice as efficient in producing shoes. In that case the country is said to have a *comparative advantage* in cars. The *inferior* country, disadvantaged all round, has a *comparative* advantage in producing shoes. Now, if the two countries trade, with each tending to specialize in the goods where they have comparative advantage, it is possible to find terms of trade which permit a *balanced* exchange (no trade deficit or surplus on either side) as a result of which *all* the citizens of *both* countries *could* be better off.

Today, in the way the theory is working out, the key word is 'could'. Some people have good jobs and enjoy the cheaper goods. Others, less well placed, may not have money to buy them.

Comparative advantage is not the only reason for trade. Among

---

1   David Ricardo, *Principles of Political Economy*, ch. 7, p. 135, vol. 1, Sraffa and Dobb, Ricardo's collected works, in References.

countries at similar states of economic development, for example the countries of the European Union, much international trade has the same cause as intra-national trade, ie the general movement of goods from one place to another. It is possible for a single plant to produce the whole of a large country's needs of electric light bulbs. The plant has to be located somewhere. If somewhere happens to be South Wales, then South Wales is a 'net exporter' of light bulbs and a net importer of other things. If the whole European demand for long-life light bulbs can be made in one plant in the Netherlands, the Netherlands is likely to be a net exporter of long-life bulbs and a net importer of regular bulbs.

Comparative advantage, however, is undoubtedly a major factor in trade between developed and developing countries.[1]

The effect on wages

In Ricardo's description of his theory, he implicitly assumed that international differences of comparative advantage were entirely due to technical productivity. In his famous example he assumed that the two goods were wine and textiles and that the two countries were Portugal and Britain. Britain had the comparative advantage in textiles and Portugal in wine (A relationship which, two centuries later, has almost been reversed!). The theorem means that it would pay Portugal to trade with Britain even in the unlikely event that she was absolutely disadvantaged not only in producing textiles but also in wine. He did not discuss the problem of 'distribution' (eg what happens to Portuguese weavers).

That problem arises in the context of a later (about 100 years) development of the Ricardo theory which is generally known as the

---

1 In the first phase of trade, however, the terms of trade tend to settle near the end of the range where most, if not all of the benefit, falls to the developed countries. When account is taken of side effects, developing countries may even lose out absolutely during this phase. In the early 19th century when Ricardo, as described above, published his example based on Britain and Portugal, the per capita real GDP in the latter country was about two thirds of the former's. In the best part of two hundred years since, vigorous trade between the two countries, helped by an early free-trade agreement, has been well known. Unfortunately, over the same period, the gap between their respective development levels has actually increased, and stands, in 1995, at two to one. (See Maddison, 1995b, in References, Tables B-10a and B-10b.)

'factor-price-equalization' theorem and is associated with some equally great names in modern economics.[1] In turn, the application of the fundamental theory to the contemporary problem – the problem of a trade-related increase of inequality *among* workers, ie between the skilled and the unskilled – has been worked out by Adrian Wood.[2]

Imagine a country which has been cut in half by a concrete barrier preventing all trade and all migration. Call the two areas North and South. Suppose that politics, economics, sociology and maybe other things then lead the two regions to diverge in such a way that although the two populations are the same size, in the North, as compared to the South, there is a much higher proportion of skilled labour. Now imagine the consequences with very extreme assumptions. There are only two kinds of labour, skilled and unskilled, and only two kinds of products, goods and services. The skilled labour can produce only goods, the unskilled only services. In each region the strength of demand for each kind of product depends on relative prices and consumer incomes, but, for any given set-up of prices and incomes, in each region demand would be the same.

On the macro side assume that in each region the government guarantees conditions where both kinds of labour are always fully employed. Within each region the two kinds of producers can trade with each other so that each can consume the other's product. But given full employment, the amounts of each product (goods or services) produced in each region are totally decided by the labour supplies.

On those assumptions, the prices in the internal markets will have to adjust until the pattern of demand is matched to the fixed supplies. Obviously, because the supply of unskilled labour is relatively high in the South, the market prices of the product made with this labour, ie 'services' will be relatively low. But low price, inevitably, means low wages. So, so long as the concrete barrier remains in place, unskilled wages in the South, relative to skilled wages in the South, will be low

---

1   Eg Bertil Ohlin and Paul Samuelson. For a full discussion see the book by Adrian Wood already mentioned in Chapter 1 (Wood, 1994, in References) especially pp 27-9 and 32-42, or for a shorter version, his subsequent article in the *Journal of Economic Perspectives* (Wood, 1995, in References).

2   See preceding note.

as compared to the North.

There is no difficulty in seeing what happens if the concrete barrier were modified to permit free migration without free trade: unskilled workers would migrate from South to North and change the supply situation, the market situation and the wage situation. In the North, the relative price of services would fall and unskilled wages correspondingly.

Not quite so easy to see is the result if trade barriers were removed but not migration barriers, rather as to some extent is happening today. As well as trading with each other internally, the two kinds of producers are now able to trade across the barrier. The consequences are far reaching. For example, in the North, 'services' were previously (relatively) scarce because unskilled labour was (relatively) scarce. Now however the supply of 'services' in the North can be augmented by trading with the South. So, in the North, the relative price of services, and the relative wage of unskilled labour, must come down. On the other side of the coin, in the South, the relative wage of the skilled (goods producers) must come down.

This semi-simple story is the nub of the whole argument about trade.[1] In theory and in practice there are many variations and ramifications. Of course, real-life countries do not produce only two kinds of goods, and of course, the removal of simple things like tariffs and quotas does not take away all the constraints on trade: there remains the basic barrier, for example, of transport costs. Some things are more expensive to transport, per unit of value, than others. Consequently, some things are more 'tradeable' than others. This particularly applies to real-life services, which are often traditionally described as 'non-traded'. But it is not impossible – merely expensive – for a famous coiffeur to fly from London to New York to do the hair of a rich client.

It is generally believed that, as well as reduced tariffs and quotas, increased tradeability, not only for goods but also for services, due to technical and social change, has been a major feature of the general

---

1   For simplicity I have left out a major element in the economic theory of 'factor-price equalization', namely that within given industries, trade also induces changes in the balance between labour-intensive and capital-intensive, and/or between 'skill intensive' and 'non-skill-intensive' methods of production.

process of 'globalization'. The model with only two products needs the addition of at least another commodity, eg we should consider two kinds of manufactured goods, one mainly requiring skilled and the other mainly requiring unskilled labour, plus a third product, actual services, which mainly uses unskilled labour. Adrian Wood then neatly summarized the way in which this model[1] can be used to light up recent history.[2]

> I argue that reduction of trade barriers [ie 'globalization'] has shifted developed countries from 'manufacturing autarky', in which they produced all the manufactures they consumed (skill-intensive and labour-intensive), to specialization in the production of skill-intensive manufactures and reliance on imports from developing countries to supply their needs for labour-intensive manufactures[3].

How do developed countries (the 'North', the OECD) pay for their new imports of unskilled-labour-intensive manufactures? By exporting larger amounts of skill-intensive manufactures. So, not only is demand for unskilled workers in the North reduced, but the demand for skilled workers is increased.

De-industrialization and de-unionization
The theory of factor price equalization is described as if the economic systems of the developing countries were highly competitive. In real life many industries are 'oligopolistic'[4] and in real life some industries persistently pay higher wages for work of given quality than others. When these factors are taken into account, an additional adverse effect on Low-Ed wages in developed countries leaps out.

---

1   The original creator of the model was Edward Leamer. See Leamer, 1993, in References.

2   An extremely elegant mathematical model on similar assumptions can be found in a short paper presented at the annual meeting of the American Economic Association in 1993, by George Johnson and Frank Stafford (Johnson and Stafford, 1993, in References).

3   Wood, 1995, p 61.

4   In economics jargon, 'monopoly' means only one seller, 'oligopoly' means a smaller number of sellers. 'Oligopolistic' industries are identified in practice as 'concentrated' industries where a large total market share is held by a small number of firms. Even without collusion, selling prices, although lower than in monopoly, will be higher than in 'competitive' industries (meaning industries where the product is highly standardised and no firm holds a large market share).

In a rich and extremely interesting paper,[1] George Borjas and Valerie Ramey undertook a statistical test of an additional route by which increased exports of industrial goods from developing to developed countries adversely affect the wages of blue-collar workers in developing countries. Using a sophisticated 'recursive'[2] statistical model applied to the United States they successfully tested a theory based on the following chain of hypotheses:

(1) trade penetration from developing countries into developed countries has been quantitatively strongest into the most 'oligopolistic' industries (such as cars and other similar consumer goods),

(2) in these industries, profits were above average,

(3) these industries also employed a disproportionate amount of less educated labour,

(4) being profitable, in these industries it was also possible for unions to ask for good wages,

(5) above-average wages were in fact paid to all workers in these industries,

(6) therefore in these industries the relative wages of less educated workers (precisely, of 'Low-Eds' as defined in Chapter 2) had been, before trade opened up, higher than in other sectors of the economy,

(7) increased trade, therefore, by reducing the weight of these industries in the national economy, reduced the average relative wages of Low-Eds in the national economy.

The positive results were impressive, and I would be very surprised if a similar study made in the UK did not produce similar ones. The total hypothesis is a distinct element in the general story – in effect, an additional cause of de-industrialization and a more explicit model of the effects of de-industrialization.

---

1 Borjas and Ramey, 1995, in References.

2 A recursive model is structured in a causal hierarchy of sub-models. The results of the first sub-model form the input into the second, and so on. Consequently it is not possible to compute the results for a sub-model until those for all the preceding sub-models have been computed.

The role of exchange rates

The fact that one is assuming *balanced* trade is crucial to any argument based on the theory of comparative advantage. In effect, the theory is not concerned with the utilization of total resources (in either country) but (in both countries) with the *allocation* of resources between sectors. Before trade opens up, each country has a separate allocation pattern. After, there is, in effect, only one allocation, ie the 'global' balance of production among a common list of goods. The theory predicts that in this common allocation, as compared with the two previous sub-allocations, the citizens of both countries have the *possibility* of doing the same amount of work (albeit differently distributed between employments) and yet, as compared with the previous situation, of consuming more of each and every commodity

What happens if trade does not balance? And why *should* it necessarily balance? What if the general price level in one country is much lower than in the other, so that the opening of trade, rather than creating increases in both directions, causes instead a general flood of goods in one direction?

If trade does not balance, one country goes into deficit, the other into an equal surplus. Imports kill jobs, exports create them. The deficit country will suffer a net decline in the demand for labour, the surplus country the opposite. Each government may correct its respective internal macroeconomic distortions by internal expansionary or deflationary internal policies, but both, and especially the deficit country, will suffer various national and international monetary problems. In the deficit country, if nothing else is done, there may have to be a painful deflation of internal prices – a process that in practice is likely to be accompanied by increased unemployment. On the other side, the surplus country may be compelled (as Japan has done with dollars) to accumulate quantities of the other country's currency.

Precisely the foregoing type of scenario features strongly in the public mind when international trade is discussed. That is hardly surprising because things often turn out that way. Most especially at the present time, while people do not so much fear opening trade with countries where the general standard of living is similar to their own, they fear trade with less-developed countries whose exports will be founded on 'cheap labour'.

What do we mean by 'cheap labour'? Are we we referring to the *real* efficiency-earnings (ie purchasing power of the hourly wage adjusted for productivity) of the foreign workers or to their hourly unit labour cost *expressed in our own currency?* The answer is fundamental, because it is the latter, not the former, that indicates whether there is a danger of unbalanced trade. And what decides the conversion of the one number into the other? The answer of course is the exchange rate. If real efficiency wages in one country are lower than in another, there must nevertheless exist some value of the exchange rate that will equalize their unit labour costs expressed in either currency. In other words, the exchange rate plays a crucial role in deciding whether, after opening more trade, the result is or is not internationally balanced.

Exchange rates and PPPs

In fact, the critical number is not the exchange rate itself, but the numerical relationship between the countries' exchange rates and their *PPPs* or *purchasing-power parities*. A PPP is that particular value of an exchange rate, eg between pounds and dollars, which makes the price level in the two countries, whether measured in dollars or in pounds, the same. For example, a Britisher goes to America at a time when the exchange rate is for simplicity, say, $2 to the £. He finds America cheap. He means that when he converts prices back into pounds he finds things cheaper than they would be at home. How much cheaper? 'Well, maybe 25 per cent.' If we take 25 per cent off $2 we arrive at $1.50. In other words, if the exchange rate the Britisher had actually paid had been not $2 but $1.50, he would have found America neither cheap nor dear. This rate – the $1.50 – is called the PPP.

If we divide the PPP by the exchange rate or vice versa and multiply the result by 100, we get an index which, because it compares apparent 'cheapness' or 'dearness' as the case may be, is sometimes called the *'international price level'* in one country compared to another. 1.5 divided by two = .75, multiplied by 100 = 75, implying, as already indicated, that *at that exchange rate* America is 25 per cent cheaper than Britain. 2 divided by 1.5 = 1.33, implying (because, when seen that way round, the base of the percentage is smaller) that Britain is 33 per cent dearer than America – both statements, of course, mean the same thing. If we decided to use America as 100, then we say that while her international price level is 100, Britain's is 133.

Roughly speaking, then, we say that what is required for trade to balance is that the *actual* exchange rate converge to the PPP; in other words, to a state of affairs where the international price level in both countries is 100. Why? Because if the international price level in both countries is 100, it is more than likely that hourly unit labour costs in the two countries will also be close.

Exchange rates and development

All of this is familiar to economists; less widely familiar is the practical nature of the exchange-rate adjustment process which should occur in the process of world economic development. In that process there are two elements: the under-developed countries become less under-developed, and trade between developed and under-developed countries increases. The first element means that the absolute disadvantage of the developing countries should be declining, the second that international price levels, as seen from either side, must go through a continuous related adjustment.

In the first phase the great mass of unskilled labour in the developing countries is isolated from trade and works at an internal price level which, calculated at the market exchange rate rather than the PPP, looks, from an international standpoint, ridiculously low. For example, as Table 4.1 shows, the real per capita GDP of India (a country which has only recently begun to open up trade) calculated at the current PPP, is about seven per cent or about one fifteenth of the United States – low enough but not impossible. Calculated at the actual exchange rate, however, the seven per cent becomes nearer to one per cent, or one hundredth of the US, which if it were true would mean that everyone in India was dead.

In the next phase, the trade base is broadened and developing countries can now export manufactures, as well as materials, to developed countries. Initially, on account of the low exchange rate, the international price level in the developing country is low and so also, as discussed above, is the international unit cost of industrial labour. If developing country exchange rates did not change in the direction of raising their international price levels, the developed countries would have huge trade deficits and unemployment. But if exchange rates and international price levels do adjust, trade can re-

Table 4.1 Exchange-rates, PPPs and GDPs per capita, 1995

Country	Exchange rate per $	PPP per $	Price level	GDP per capita
US	1.000	1.000	100.0	100.0
Germany	1.372	2.264	165.0	80.5
Sweden	7.355	11.195	152.2	79.2
Japan	86.160	193.524	224.6	78.4
France	4.805	7.031	146.3	76.5
Netherlands	1.536	2.088	135.9	70.3
UK	0.621	0.690	111.1	68.0
Italy	1722	1888	109.7	67.7
Spain	126.580	138.315	109.3	52.5
Brazil	6.258	0.872	13.9	21.2
Turkey	50344	15646	31.1	21.1
Egypt	3.528	1.274	36.1	9.8
China	12.750	2.007	15.7	9.8
India	50.500	6.285	12.4	7.2
Kenya	50.668	12.733	25.1	5.1

Definitions See text – 'Price level' means 'international price level' as defined in text, ie second col / first col x 100.

Sources For 1950, *Penn World Tables*, Heston and Summers, 1991, in References; for 1995, data from the same source carried forward using current indicators from IMF and OECD.

balance. As countries develop, therefore, there is a tendency for their international price indexes to rise. Table 4.1 illustrates this. Fifteen countries are arranged in order of real GDP per capita, with the highest, the US, at the top, and the lowest, Kenya, at the bottom.The first column gives the country's early-April 1995 exchange rate, the second the corresponding PPP and the third, her international price index on base US, as just described. Our theory predicts that, as the countries are ordered in terms of GDP so they will also be ordered in terms of price level,[1] and by and large that is so. At the top of the table there are exceptions caused by Japan and the US, the former partly because of the high quality of her manufactured exports but mainly because of a major disparity between her export prices and the prices of goods and services produced for the internal market; the latter, the US, because she has been running a huge trade deficit, which could be seen as the counterpart both of the Japanese trade surplus and of the the US Federal government deficit. In the lower part of the table, and in the comparison between the lower part and the upper part, where our theory is really intended to bite (ie it is a theory about comparisons of countries who are widely apart in development), the correlation is not perfect (useful correlations never are) but it is strong.

The fundamental prediction of the Adrian Wood story can now be re-stated. As trade opens up between 'North' and 'South', exchange rates will adjust so that by and large the trade balances. The higher

---

1   The proposition that in countries with less high GDP, less-tradeable goods will tend to be less expensive, and vice versa, I have called the 'Ricardo-Balassa' effect, after (1), David Ricardo, who, in the same part of his *Principles* (ie Chapter 7, see References) in which he discovered comparative advantage also nearly discovered this and (2), Bela Balassa, the distinguished American trade economist who, a century and a half later, undoubtedly did. See Marris, 1984, in References. At the top end of Table 4.1, however, the correlation breaks down. Other international forces, such as special factors causing the contemporary 'soft' dollar, as discussed in the text, have affected the data. That qualification also applies to developing countries. In an earlier paper (Wood, 1991, in References) Adrian Wood showed that after taking account of certain specific factors such as the oil-price booms, the historical trend of the international prices for Asian and African countries as a whole was in the wrong direction. One reason he suggests (and I suspect it is the main one) is that increased trade works both ways, throwing open previously protected markets within the developing countries to greater competition.

level of trade will embody the results of the theory of comparative advantage. But it will embody the theory in its contemporary, Adrian Wood, version. The changing *general* international price levels will also embrace changes in the *relative* prices of goods containing skilled and unskilled labour and, with these, changes in the relative wages of skilled and unskilled workers, to the disadvantage of the latter.

The evidence

The sixty-four trillion dollar question is how important has all the foregoing theory been in practice? There is no simple way of quantifying the impact of increased trade. Actual imports into the OECD from the rest of the world have, over the quarter-century, been increasing about three and a half times faster than the growth rate of aggregate real OECD GDP. But they began from a tiny level so even with this rapid relative growth, in 1995 they still accounted for *less than a thirtieth* of total amount of OECD GDP. Could such a small tail wag such a large dog?

The answer is, in principle, 'yes', for two reasons. First, because the South-North exports are especially unskilled-labour intensive, the simple ratio of value to GDP is not an appropriate measure of, as it were, the waggability factor. Second, producers and their wages in the North are affected not only by actual trade, but also by potential competition. Neither is easy to measure, and that is the origin of substantial current discussion, if not outright controversy, within the economics profession.

'Factor-content' calculations

The best-known method of attacking the statistical problem starts from the basic theoretical prediction that even though, in the second phase of North-South trade development, manufactures are being swapped for manufactures, the commodity break-down of trade will be different on the two sides. (If that were not the case, comparative advantage would not be happening.) If the commodity pattern of a given volume of trade varies, because different commodities use different production processes and different production processes use different relative amounts of skilled and unskilled labour, so also, we expect, will vary the relative skill content of the two volumes. We expect from the theory that the commodity pattern of exports from the developed countries will be on average more skill-intensive than their imports from the developing countries. If we could calculate the actual effect of the difference, we could calculate the apparent quantitative effect of trade on the markets for skilled and unskilled labour within the developed countries.[1]

In order to do this calculation, we need, therefore, physical coefficients indicating the quantities of the two kinds of labour required to produce a dollar of exports or imports of all the different commodities. Where could such data be found? Answer, possibly, in already existing US internal data on the proportions of 'production' and 'non-production' workers employed in different industries. If 'non-production' activity is a kind of statistical proxy for 'skilled' activity we may then make the further large assumption that coefficients thus calculated for particular commodities in US export statistics are also valid for the corresponding commodity groups when they appear in the import statistics. In other words, the assumption is that given commodities use the same skill-related technology wherever they are produced. (In other words it is only the difference in commodity pattern between imports and exports that creates the possible effects of trade on internal labour markets.)

Calculations made by American economists using the above method, culminating in a well-known paper by Sachs and Shatz[2] have tended to find a definite negative net effect on the US unskilled labour market, but a small one. But for two very important reasons, Adrian Wood believes those calculations were severely downward biased. First, the procedure of employing export data to estimate the import coefficients overestimates the relative skill content of imports, because the inevitably broad statistical commodity categories conceal the information that in some categories numerous sub-products of low skill intensity are no longer produced in the US. Thus the broad commodity categories for imports include low-skill-intensive sub-products which

---

1   Suppose total exports and total imports are both 100, but exports contain 70 units of skilled labour, plus 30 unskilled, while for imports the numbers are reversed. Then if trade were eliminated, the demand for unskilled labour would rise and the demand for skilled labour fall, by 40 units. Trade has therefore made a 40 unit negative impact on the unskilled labour market. If trade represents a fifth of the economy, then the unskilled labour market has declined by 8 per cent.

2   'Trade and jobs in US Manufacturing', Brookings, Washington DC, 1994, in References.

are not included in the corresponding broad categories of exports, with obvious resulting bias. Using alternative data sources, Wood attempts corrections by methods described in his book.[1] He then adjusts for some further effects, the most important of which (whose size can, in truth, only be guessed) flows from the proposition that as trade expands, developed-country manufacturers will be provoked to find new technology which *further* economizes unskilled labour over the whole range of commodities.[2]

Without his second effect, Wood estimates that in the absence of trade with developed countries, the demand for unskilled labour in the United States today would be no less than *ten per cent* higher than it actually is. His second effect doubles the first, producing, at *20 per cent*, a result which is certainly large enough to account for a significant part of the troubles of the underclass.

Relative price calculations
Another method of calculation is to first, as above, break down imports into categories according to skilled-unskilled intensity and then attempt to estimate what has happened to the relative prices of the two categories, the prediction being, of course, that import prices of unskilled-intensive goods into developed countries will prove to have historically fallen relative to those of skill-intensive categories. The various different studies[3] along these lines seem to show rather murky results, although Adrian Wood argues that one of them,[4] at least, can be interpreted as showing an effect on prices that could have gone a significant distance to explaining what has happened to US wages.

Conclusion
The theory of comparative advantage predicts that as developing countries improve their ability to export manufactures, they will

---

1   Wood, 1994, already quoted, in References, Ch 4.

2   The implication is that although these technologies could have been found and profitably applied before, firms needed the spur of competition to overcome research apathy.

3   For example, Lawrence and Slaughter, 1995, Sachs and Shatz, 1994, and Rowthorn, 1994, 1995 in References.

4   See Wood, 1995, discussing Sachs and Shatz, 1994. The statistical problems are considerably due to the absence of data for sufficiently fine commodity and industry categories.

specialize where they have a comparative advantage, namely in products whose production techniques are inherently unskilled-intensive – the reason being that developing countries, as compared with developed countries, have greater supplies of un-skilled as compared to skilled labour.

On account of this theory we *expect* statistical calculations to show there has been a significant adverse effect on the unskilled labour market in the 'North' as a result of the second phase (where manufactures are swapped for manufactures) of increased trade. Unfortunately, the several enterprising studies that have actually been made are clouded by data problems, and, as they disagree in the weight, if not the direction of the calculated effects, the result is controversy. I myself personally suspect that American liberal-minded economists may be especially cautious of uncertain results that could give ammunition to 'populist' politicians advocating a return to trading protectionism.

Given the *a priori* expectation that there will be a 'result' (as the Cockney expression goes) – and given that his work is based on careful research and scholarship – particular attention, in my opinion, should be paid to Adrian Wood. He has certainly convinced me, for one, of the likelihood that there has indeed been, interacting with the growth-effect, a significant trade-effect, contributing to the rise of severe meritocracy, not only in the US, but also in the UK. I do not believe there has been a significant effect in Germany, and I also have doubts about France.

5. Meritocracy, Intelligence and Welfare

Why should the 'overclass' care about the underclass? The fact that a significant part of human ability is inherited puts society in a bind. We cannot redistribute intelligence and it is difficult to redistribute income without affecting incentives. Therefore it is vitally important to know how much ability is inherited, how much can be changed by education and what are the effects of inequality on economic welfare. These questions are the task of this chapter.

How much can we understand if we treat the brain as a 'black box' only studied from outside? What is IQ? How valid are statistical results relating a person's early IQ to their subsequent place in the meritocracy? How strong is the hereditary factor in the final statistical distribution of earnings?

Some answers to these questions can be gleaned from the 'shape' of the earnings distribution. It appears to be roughly bell-shaped at the bottom, moderately skewed in the middle and highly skewed at the top. Fairly straightforward economics can explain this.

What are the implications of these findings for the measurement of welfare? There is a controversy in economics, originally set going by V. Pareto, as to whether welfare is a measurable quantity. I strongly believe that it is. Otherwise economics is politically impotent. For example if one is not allowed to conceive of quantifiable welfare one cannot even discuss whether it is better to have low wages and low unemployment, as in the US, or higher wages and more unemployment, as in Europe.

The 'overclass' should care about the underclass because economic policies are chosen and carried out by elected governments. Unfortunately the mathematics of the trusted system of majority voting is not designed to ensure the choice of policies aimed at maximum welfare. As a result, some people get their ideas on the subject from morality. Where do morals come from? Some people's morals come from religion. There is an interesting conformity between some religious pronouncements on economics, and views, such as the author's, which are based on the principle of maximizing welfare.

The roots of meritocracy

Meritocracy occurs because people have different abilities. Unfortunately there is rather strong evidence that differences in personal ability are partly innate and difficult to change. In Chapter 1 we saw they were likely to be distributed on a bell curve. The market system, however, converts this into a J-curve, thus inevitably creating at least a moderate meritocracy. We saw how it was then possible for adverse historical circumstances to stretch out the *J*, convert moderate into severe meritocracy and probably reduce total welfare. So we seem to be in a bind. In order to modify the income distribution we need somehow to interfere with the system, but the interference itself may have adverse economic consequences and/or be politically unpopular.

The concept of 'endowments'

Even today, I think many economists do not fully appreciate the potential gravity of this 'bind'. There is a familiar argument that runs as follows. 'The distribution of income that actually occurs results from two factors – an initial distribution of "endowments" and the working-out of market forces. If we feel that the actual distribution of income is unsatisfactory, rather than interfering with the market process, it is more effective to redistribute the endowments. Why? Because interfering with market forces adversely affects incentives and reduces general efficiency. In contrast, endowments can be redistributed by "lump-sum" transfers[1] which do not affect incentives.'

I believe this argument contains contradictions. If the differences in individual endowments mainly consisted of differences in inherited wealth, the right policy would be inheritance taxes. But as soon as we recognise that much more than inherited *material* capital is involved, there is a grave problem indeed. As well as material capital, there is *human capital'*,[2] ie one's personal stock of skill and ability. If ability is partly the result of genes and parenting (see below) our human capital, like our material capital (if any) is also partly inherited. But

---

1 These are transfers which are designated by referring to who people are, rather than by what they do. For example, a tax which is based on a person's objective ability rather than their actual earnings, to finance a benefit to some other person on the basis of objective disability rather than actual need.

2 See Gary Becker, *Human Capital*, 1964, in References.

<u>Who was Pareto</u> ?

Vilfredo Pareto (1848-1932), a key figure in this chapter, was a native of North Italy who originally trained as a mathematician and engineer. He was a radical-liberal free-trader; anti-government, anti-Marxist, libertarian, humanistic and also originally a pacifist. Towards the end of his life he became more conservative and may have had some sympathy for Mussolini. He had friends across the political spectrum and distrusted professional politicians. Although pursuing a business career, he was by the age of forty already well known for publishing articles and pamphlets criticizing the economic policies of the government of the young state of Italy. In 1893 he was appointed Professor of Political Economy at the University of Lausanne, in French-speaking Switzerland, in succession to the great French theoretical economist, Walras. From then, until he retired 20 years later he produced massive contributions in French and Italian to economics, sociology and politics. Within a few years he had published a book[*] which contains one major idea used in this chapter – 'Pareto's Law' of income distribution (see box on J-curves) – and the seeds of another – the concept of 'Pareto Optimality –[**] whose relevance to today's problems is discussed in a separate section below. The second has had a vast influence on economics, some aspects of which I and others do not agree with. When Pareto died most of his papers were destroyed, and the few surviving original documents are held today in an excellent archive at the Walras-Pareto Centre at Lausanne University. There are no original manuscripts of his main work in economics, but some in sociology.[***] Figure 5.1 gives a sample of the latter. Translated, the extract reads,

> Imagine a chemist saying, "It is a pity that when a certain chemical is exposed to light it should change spontaneously into a virulent poison. I shall therefore look for a chemical theory that will render such a thing impossible." Yet there you would have a widely cultivated type of moral theory.

Eighty years later some contemporary economics reads to me as if it were saying something rather similar, such as,

> It is a pity that the market economy often spontaneously produces unemployment. I shall therefore look for an economic theory that renders such a thing impossible!

As a matter of fact, although Pareto was a passionate believer in scientific objectivity, in my opinion his own work is often open to criticism which, if not exactly the same, is not unlike his criticism of the imaginary chemist.

---

[*]   *Cours D'Économie Politique*, 1897, in References.
[**]   Presented more completely in the famous mathematical appendix to his *Manuale d'Economia Politica*, 1906, in References.
[***] *Trattato di Sociologia Generale*, 1916, in References.

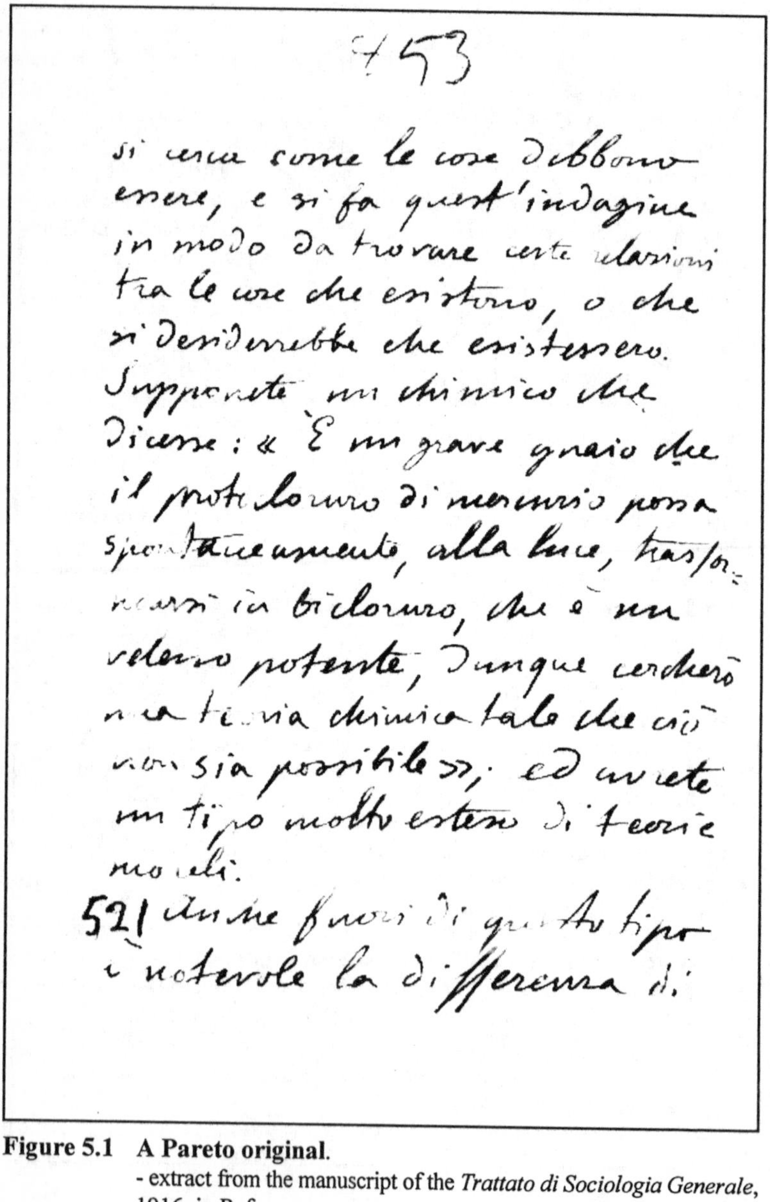

453

si cerca come le cose debbono
essere, e si fa quest'indagine
in modo da trovare certe relazioni
tra le cose che esistono, o che
si desidererebbe che esistessero.
Supponete un chimico che
dicesse: « È un grave guaio che
il protocloruro di mercurio possa
spontaneamente, alla luce, trasfor-
marsi in bicloruro, che è un
veleno potente; Dunque cercherò
una teoria chimica tale che ciò
non sia possibile »; ed avrete
un tipo molto esteso di teorie
modelli.
521 Anche fuori di questo tipo
è notevole la differenza di:

Figure 5.1   A Pareto original.
 - extract from the manuscript of the *Trattato di Sociologia Generale*,
 1916, in References.

how could inherited human capital be re-distributed? How can one make a 'lump-sum transfer' of intelligence, for example, from one person to another? If, instead of transferring intelligence itself, we attempted to transfer cash in lieu, we have to imagine that the brains of infants are inspected at a very young age and the results recorded in a central register. Then around age 25, the intelligent ones (if they have not gone into hiding) are required to begin paying a poll-tax!

In the literature about human capital this conundrum was usually answered by assuming that the most important factor in a person's *eventual* human capital is not inherited ability as such but the amount of education that is applied to it. Then expenditure on education can be seen as a form of investment, partly similar to the processes of acquiring material capital. A business-person borrows money to buy assets to earn revenue to pay the debt and leave herself or himself with a net profit. In the human-capital literature, a young person is seen as borrowing money to finance education as an investment in their own human capital, which will enhance her or his earnings sufficiently to repay the debt and leave a surplus.

The main justification for state-financing of primary and secondary education, and state support for higher education is, according to this argument, to ensure 'equality of access' to the means to finance the investment. In the case of the majority of young children, neither they nor their parents can obtain education loans, so the state is unfortunately compelled to finance education from general taxation which, not in practice being 'lump-sum', does have adverse macroeconomic effects. In the case of higher education, however, so the argument goes, student loans are feasible. Provided these things are done, it is argued, individuals will have the incentives necessary to make 'correct' education decisions, as a result of which the market system will do its business, the resulting income distribution will be satisfactory and all will be for the best in the best of all possible worlds.

You can easily see that the argument depends crucially on the assumption that inherited factors play a small part in the ultimate distribution of earning power. Today, that assumption is increasingly doubted. But if we accepted it, then given the basic paradox of meritocracy (as set out in Chapter 1) the argument has a remarkable implication which as far as I can tell has not been widely discussed.

Total equality?

The problem is as follows. If one could actually have perfect equality of the so-called 'initial distribution' of endowments, and if every young person were perfectly well informed and rational, every young person would undertake an *equal* amount of education, and thus acquire an equal amount of human capital, ie *everyone would become equally skilled*. All the trouble about the problems of unskilled workers in North or South, for example, would not exist.

Would there still be differences in income? The usual answer is, 'yes', because of differences in luck and differences in effort. Morally, we instinctively feel that differences in luck do not 'deserve' to be rewarded, while differences in effort should be. But given the same pay-offs, why does one person make more effort than another? What are the well-springs of motivation? The answer to the latter question *could* be that motivation is a *biological* phenomenon, stemming from the emotional part of the brain, put in place by evolution to ensure that, having used our reasoning power to see the need for an action (like going out to get some food), we are emotionally driven to carry it out. And it could be that a person's genes affect the character of the electro-chemical circuitry doing that job so that one might *inherit* motivation. Indeed it is certain that we all inherit some motivation, in a very complex way, not only directly from our parents' genes, but also indirectly, yet powerfully, from the way we are brought up – more precisely, by all the comings and goings of emotional and practical events that occur during the course of our upbringing.

So it is possible to conclude that if it were really practicable (which it obviously isn't) to achieve a true equality in the 'initial distribution' of personal 'endowments', the end result would be a totally equal distribution of personal earnings. Horror of horrors; bosses would all be paid the same as their subordinates, because every one would know that if bosses demanded more, their places would instantly be taken by other people who could do the job equally well! In other words, in a hypothetical society with truly equal 'initial distribution', meritocracy is impossible. So if, as in real life, inequality does occur, we *know* there must be inequality of endowments.

The structure of the roots

From which it immediately follows that the *causes* of the paradox of meritocracy lie in the realities that inhibit 'initial' equality. If barriers to access to education have been eliminated,[1] these all consist of potential differences in ability and motivation, due to genes, to parenting and to the inevitable interaction of the two. It follows that in order to understand the relation of meritocracy to welfare we need to answer the following:

(1) How much 'ability' is 'inherited' in the broad sense, including not only genes and parenting but also such things as infant nutrition (which is known to affect later mental ability) and also possibly motivation?

(2) How much could the 'inherited' endowment of initial ability perhaps be redistributed by eg special education?

(3) What is the nature of the process by which the differences of broadly defined inherited ability are translated into an income distribution?

(4) How do economists evaluate income distribution?

All these steps are required to trace the roots of meritocracy and the results on total welfare.

The enigma of ability

Ability has many aspects; muscular strength, muscular dexterity, visual perception and visual-muscular co-ordination (eg a gifted artist's ability not only to perceive a subject but to execute the actual painting) musical ability, verbal ability, social ability, 'energy', imagination, creativity, etc, etc and last, but, of course, not least, memory and reasoning power. Virtually every one of the foregoing can be involved in a person's economic performance, but there is a current opinion, held across the political spectrum, that in the modern world the final item – mental reasoning power – has become increasingly important in setting the rungs on the meritocratic ladder.

---

1   Michael Young (1958, in References, already discussed) had a fabulous passage where he satirically predicted that the British movement for 'comprehensive' state education would not last. He wrote this before the movement had got fully under way, and then, when the Labour governments of the mid-sixties to late seventies carried through extensive 'comprehensivization', his prediction was superficially discredited. However, in Britain, in the mid-nineties, right across the political spectrum, the question of possibly restoring a degree of 'selectivity' in the state educational system has become a very live issue.

What is intelligence?

With almost the sole exception of pure muscular strength, every type of ability mentioned above involves the activity of the brain. If people or animals differ in their specific abilities at a specific time, it is mostly because of things that are different inside their heads, some of which will represent processes in the conscious mind, but most of which, at any one time, will be unconscious. In practice, most people, when they speak of mental ability or 'brain power',[1] are referring to the conscious activity called *intelligence*. This can loosely be described as capability in manipulating logical concepts. What is the relationship between intelligence and the actual, physical brain?

Many people feel this is such a difficult question there is no point in even asking it. And there are still many who basically believe that such things are not open to conventional scientific investigation at all. In that view, there is 'brain' and there is 'mind' (or soul). The former can tell us nothing about the latter and the latter is outside science. Consequently most people desiring to discuss problems such as the nature of intelligence, or human psychology or mental disorder, employ the approach which is called 'behaviouristic'. You study the thing entirely by reference to what it does, avoiding discussion of what it is.

'Black-box' theorizing

The behaviouristic approach can also be called a 'black-box' approach. An imaginary scientist is faced with an imaginary box containing a set of mechanical or electrical connections, and there are external knobs, levers or terminals so that when some are stimulated as inputs, the internal mechanism or circuitry responds with outputs. It is physically impossible to open the box. The only experiment is a long study of the outputs obtained from various inputs. If the mechanism inside the box is static and not too complex we may succeed in predicting quite accurately how it will respond to various inputs. In turn this knowledge may enable us to build a 'model' of the internal mechanism. (Freud's theories, and many other psychological theories,

---

1   In the anti-education culture found among contemporary white secondary-school boys, eg as described in the quotation from England's Chief Inspector of Schools at the end of Chapter 2, when one boy wants to disparage another he calls him a 'brain box'.

are examples.) It is by no means sure, however, that if and when we eventually get into the box, our model will be even roughly correct. If the true mechanism really is static, that may not matter much. If a theory works, it works. But the brain (like society) is not static and is profoundly complex. It is a biological learning machine which is changed by every detail of its ongoing experiences, including, for example, experiments that may be conducted on it. As to complexity, its substance is the most complex material in the universe. Billions of electro-chemical cells called neurons, each of which is itself a complex object, are linked together by a system that is both 'parallel', in the sense that each neuron is linked to many others, but also contains many 'local' processing centres where particular activities are conducted. Whenever one applies the black-box technique to a subject of that kind, there is fog and controversy. Research depends on inadequately controlled statistical studies which can 'prove' nothing. 'Behavioural' predictions work for a while and then break down. When, as is often the case, the subject matter is politically or emotionally loaded, he situation is exacerbated.[1]

Of course, the cause of all the trouble is that we cannot get inside the box. In the case of the brain, until recently we could not examine the living brain without creating fear of harming it. In the past ten years, however, this situation has changed dramatically; new machines have been developed making it possible to observe, from *outside,* neuronal activity during mental processes. So I believe the time will come when we shall be able to scan the brains of two people taking an intelligence test, note differences in their neural activity patterns and compare the results with the test scores![2] If I am right, the answer to the question, 'What do we mean by intelligence?' will then be no more and no less than a description of what we have observed.

---

1 For example, one of the most distressing moments in the near half-century history of research on the link between cigarette smoking and disease came when an extremely distinguished academic pioneer of the statistical methods that helped establish the link became a consultant to the tobacco industry.

2 After I wrote those words, I was not surprised to read that an experiment of that kind has, in fact, been successfully carried out comparing brain operations between normal people and people who have symptoms of dyslexia. See *Daily Mail*, London, 26 March, 1996, p. 36. The differences are clear, strong and explicit.

Reading List on the Brain
*(*details in References)

The Brain and Consciousness

Paul Churchland, *The Engine of Reason*, 1995.

A beautifully written, lucid, state-of-the-art critique of the whole field of brain function, consciousness and intelligence.

Francis Crick, *The Astonishing Hypothesis*, 1994.

A brilliant, powerful and deep investigation into the biological basis of consciousness.

Gerald Edleman, *Bright Air, Brilliant Fire*, 1992.

A closely reasoned, research-based, alternative theory of consciousness.

Freeman, William, *Societies of Brains*, 1995.

A an important, original and authoritative discussion of the whole field, with special reference to the problem of intentionality in consciousness.

John Taylor, *When the Clock Struck Zero*, 1993.

An extremely readable and original book on general science, consciousness and neural nets (see also below).

Intelligence

Daniel Goleman, *Emotional Intelligence*, 1966.

An interesting discussion of the interaction between the parts of the brain involved in logical reasoning and the parts involved in the emotions.

Richard Hernstein and Charles Murray, *The Bell Curve*, 1994.

The controversial book, based on a considerable quantity of statistical data, suggesting that IQ does have a strong role in creating meritocracy and also other problems such as crime.

Earl Hunt, The role of intelligence in modern society, 1995.

A scientifically rigorous survey, including a critique of Hernstein and Murray.

Christopher Wills, *The Runaway Brain*, 1993.

A fascinating, deep, detailed yet extremely readable account of human mental evolution.

The Brain and Neural Nets

David Rumelhart et al, *Parallel Distributed Processing*, 1986.

The great book; a rich three-volume collection of theoretical and applied papers on every aspect of this field..

John Taylor, *Towards the Ultimate Intelligent Machine*, 1995.

An important lecture by a leading world authority on neural nets and consciousness (see also above).

The brain as a 'neural net'

There is, however, a major and very difficult question concerning the possible forms of the structure and performance of intelligent reasoning within the human brain, namely that the animal brain did not evolve as a logical, problem-solving machine, but rather as a pattern-recognizing machine. Animals, human and the rest, survive in nature by perceiving subtle patterns in signals from the environment that indicate the presence of food, sex, danger and other essentials.

> **David Rummelhart on Intelligence**
>
> 'If the human information-processing system carries out its computations by "settling" into a solution rather than by applying logical processes, why are humans so intelligent? ... How can we do logic if our basic operations are not logical at all? We suspect the answer comes from our ability to create artifacts; that is our ability to create physical representations that we can manipulate in simple ways to get answers to very difficult and abstract problems.'
> – David Rummelhart, 1986 (see brain-reading-list box above) vol 2, p 44.

Typically action based on these perceptions is, or at least is considered to be, based on associations and/or emotions. With this type of functioning goes an *associative* memory: uniquely, as compared with computers, the animal (including human) brain can retrieve what it wants from its long-term memory without either already knowing how the item has been stored or alternatively searching the whole vast file.

Extremely gripping recent developments, heavily based on computer simulation, have gone a long way to explaining how the trick is done. These developments are based on research into *artificial neural nets*, or *distributed processing* (more or less the same fields). The problem is that although these models have an uncanny ability to mimic mental performance, from their nature they have no obvious capacity for reasoning or intelligence. David Rummelhart, the outstanding and brilliant pioneer in the field (see box), has neatly posed the question, 'Why are people smarter than rats?'[1]

An artificial neural net is a set of memory cells in a computer acting as imaginary neurons, imaginarily wired together in an extensive set of parallel links: not every cell is necessarily wired to every other, but

---

1   Maybe he begged the question: are we sure we *are* smarter than rats? After a recent brush, I began to wonder. The most noticeable thing is that after only one creature has been killed by a new kind of poison, no other rat will take it.

there are likely to be systematic layers of inter-connectedness. Therefore any signal coming out of a given cell is transmitted to many others. By the same token, any given cell will at any given time be receiving potential input - from many other cells. It follows that any signal origi- nating anywhere in the sys- tem is likely to spread out widely and also, possibly, feed back on itself.

However, and it is a very big one, the re-transmission process is not straightfor- ward. In the computer, by means of sub-programmes, and in the real brain, it is believed, by an electro- chemical micro process at

> **John Taylor on Intelligence**
>
> Intelligence is the ability to perceive logical relationships and use knowledge to solve problems and respond to novel situations. This requires *awareness* (consciousness). Conscious processing also involves crucial pre-conscious procedures for evoking past memories that are explicitly relevant to the problem in hand. The human animal, possibly uniquely, also has the crowning glory of *self-awareness*, which must involve the emotional parts of the brain.
>
> – a summary, drafted by the present author, of parts of John Taylor, 1995 (see brain reading-list box, above).

the 'synapses' of the neurons, the initial signals are systematically modified. For example, if one neuron, stimulated by some inputs, sends out on all its 'tentacles' a certain strength of signal, each receiving neuron will have in place a sub-routine which tells it to either decrease or increase, by a specific percentage, all signals from that source, before incorporating them as input. Similarly, when a cell has added up these modified inputs, it will apply a global modification before activating the command for general re-transmission Therefore, at any one time the network has in place a whole basket of modifica- tion sub-routines, which are known as 'connection weights'.

How does such a thing behave? Rephrase the problem. Suppose some of the cells are selected to be output cells and connected to the screen of our computer. Others are selected as input cells and are con- nected to the keyboard. By pressing keys, therefore, we can create inputs. These will spread through the software and quickly arrive, in modified state, at the output cells, and be displayed on the screen. So we can conduct extensive input-output experiments. For example, we could type in names on the keyboard which would eventually generate sets of numbers in the output cells that could represent bit-maps. So, possibly (it has in fact been done), we could type in names and see faces. Of course, there is a way of doing that with a conventional computer. First one stores the data of the bit-maps in specific, 'local' memory address. At the same time, one records in another file the list of names and the memory addresses for the corresponding faces. When I type in a name, the software searches this 'address-book' file sequentially until it lands on the information it needs.

In the 'brain-like' artificial neural net, what determines the relation between the inputs and outputs? How could I design the thing so that if I type in your name I get a bit map of your face, rather than some other face? The answer is that the input-output relation depends in a unique yet complex way on the system subroutines or set of numbers representing the connection strengths. Such is the complexity of the relationship, however, that I cannot personally *design* the set of subsystems to do what I want. In effect I have a black box that I have myself designed. I know what is inside it; yet, in order to find out what it will do, I must still rely on trial and error. Although I am not in a genuine 'black-box situation', it is as if I was.

Consequently one has to ask how mental processes based on neural nets could be intelligent. The network's 'knowledge' is distributed throughout its weights. In very sharp contrast, a human-built electronic computer does just the opposite; it stores specific memories in specific physical locations (addresses). In a neural net, unlike the case when we read the memory of a normal computer, it is not possible to read the memory by directly inspecting the connection weights. The weights contain the information, but we cannot directly unlock it. The only way to find out what it knows is to send in some inputs and read the outputs.

Paul Churchland on Intelligence

'A great diversity of artificial networks has been built to imitate one or other small aspect of human cognition. This diversity illustrates that intelligence is not a one-dimensional commodity. Rather, the intelligence of any human has many dimensions, and in a normal human population the scattered variation in cognitive ability within each of those dimensions will be considerable. One's intelligence cannot be defined except by specifying one's idiosyncratic pattern of abilities across all of its many elemental aspects. This means that intelligence comes in many different flavours.'

– paraphrase by present author of p. 254 of Paul Churchland, 1995 in References.

How then could I 'train' a net so that it behaves as I want, ie knows what I want it to know, ie learns, ie forms memory? If I used unsystematic trial and error, I would lose my lifetime. But it is not difficult to design computer algorithms to do the job systematically and quickly. That is the good news. The bad news (some might not see it as such) is that at the present time we have no reason to believe that the successful algorithms have any analogies in the biological brain, and that we basically, at the present time, have no more than ideas as to how the actual brain might carry out the task. In addition, there is overwhelming evidence that the neural net is only a partial analogy to the architecture of the real brain.

So we are currently a long way from knowing how the brain does its logical-reasoning business. David Rummelhart (see box) has published suggestive ideas concerning how reasoning power might have developed in the course of evolution, and even how it may be simulated but that does not necessarily foretell the eventual explanation. John Taylor (see box) has developed a strong theory, consistent with the neural network, of how the job may actually be done. Among other things he convincingly argues, as does Daniel Goleman (see reading list) for a close connection between the reasoning and *emotional* functions of the brain. Finally, Paul Churchland (see box) has given powerful reasons for expecting *multi-dimensionality* in the cognitive function – a point of great significance in the debate, which we are about to consider, on the social significance of *variations*, between humans, in their mental abilities.

'Black-box' intelligence

In consequence of the practical situation as it actually was, ninety-nine per cent of all previous scientific discussion and investigation of the concept of intelligence has perforce adopted the black-box approach.[1] What is a black-box experiment in the case of general mental ability? The answer, of course, is an intelligence test. And that answer leads in turn to an answer to the original question, 'What is intelligence?'. Intelligence, we now see, is whatever it is that is measured by

---

1   *The Encyclopaedia of Human Intelligence* (Robert Sternberg, ed, 1995, in References) appears to contain not one article directed to the relation between intelligence and the biological brain.

intelligence tests: intelligence *is* 'IQ'.[1] Since, however, you cannot eat or otherwise usefully consume an IQ, this answer is interesting only if IQ can also predict some practical features of mental performance, such as conventional exam results, or ability in the money markets. (Big question, are successful speculators, apart from being lucky, also intelligent? When one is sometimes tempted to answer, 'no', one falls back on the idea of intuition. What is intuitive decision-making? I suggest it is decision-making based on sub-conscious pattern recognition.)

There is the best part of a century-and-a-half old tradition of attempting to measure peoples' intelligence by tests directed to ability rather than knowledge. I personally experienced one such test in my early teens. Following a mediocre academic record, I was entered for a private school which, very unusually for that time, screened applications with an intelligence test. To my parents', to my teachers' and to my own great surprise, I not only passed but was offered a scholarship! So I went to that school and again resumed my only-modest exam performances. By a set of chances, however, I did find my way to Cambridge to study economics. Again there was general amazement when I eventually graduated top of my year. I think I am a mixed-up person intellectually, but as a result of my experiences I am rather convinced that intelligence tests do have a power to predict *academic* performance.

Bell, book and candle

Hernstein and Murray, in the controversial 'Bell-curve' book,[2] go further and claim that the tests measure not only academic ability but general smartness. They also argue that over recent years the structure of US meritocracy has become increasingly closely related to IQ. A selection of specific findings is as follows:[3]

(1)　If a white child from an economically average family has *a moderately below-average IQ*, then;

　　1.1　he or she will have a one in *four* chance of becoming a *high*

1　Intelligence Quotient, ie standardized score in a standard test.

2　1994, in References.

3　For item (1.1) see Hernstein and Murray (1994, in References), p 149; for (1.2), p 134; for (1.3), p 249, for (3), Ch. 7 and for (4) p 183.

school drop out – by contrast, the drop out rate for average IQs is about one in twenty;

1.2   he or she will have a one in *ten* chance of being *below the official poverty line* at the age of 40 – the corresponding figure for average IQs is one in 20 and for moderately above-average IQs, one in 50;

1.3   if he is male, he will have a one in fifteen chance of *doing time in prison* – for average IQs the figure is about one in 50.

(2)   There are similar figures for various indicators of male *non-employment.*

(3)   There are similar figures for various indicators of the probability of never-married *single parenthood.*

H & M describe their statistical methods in appendixes. These enable a person, such as myself, who understands the techniques they have used, to evaluate the ranges of error. I have done this and also read various critiques of the book.[1] I have a major criticism of my own, described in the box, of an important aspect of the logical structure of their statistical model the effect of which is to cast doubt on the value of their results in relation to a vital question for public policy, namely the likely costs and benefits of special efforts to encourage Low-IQs not to drop out. I also have deep suspicions of the political motives of the book. Although the authors show a superficial balance of humanity with realism, there is a tone of social pessimism, of a kind usually associated with political conservatives, that I do not trust.[2]

Having said all this, I suspect that the numbered points (above) where I have summarized H & M, probably do fairly describe the coarse anatomy of US meritocracy today. It is the anatomy of *MM* degenerating into *SM.* Therefore in my view the implications are as much 'liberal' or 'left-wing' as the other way about.

---

1   In particular the article by Earl Hunt, in the Summer 1995 issue of *American Scientist*, in References.

2   Since writing this chapter I have seen Charles Murray interviewed on British television. It is now clear that he holds general political opinions about as far away from my own as it would be possible to imagine. The book, standing alone, partly conceals the extent of the right wing outlook of one of the authors.

An important criticism of Hernstein and Murray

Because, in the statistical calculations, the socio-economic class of parents has been 'held constant', although the parents' genes may be affecting the child's IQ, the possible spurious effect of a correlation between parents' intelligence, parents' class and a further correlation between the latter and economic success has been, in principle, eliminated. But, although H & M thus hold parents' class statistically constant in the study of education, they do not hold education constant in the study of poverty. We know that 25 per cent of Low-IQs drop out of high school and we might expect that among this group the probability of subsequent poverty is markedly higher than for all Low-IQs. But H & M do not give the probability of poverty among Low-IQs from average families who do *not* drop out of high school. So we cannot separate the effects of low IQ from its statistical interaction with education.

In order to get a full a picture of the anatomy of this aspect of meritocracy one should employ a statistical model set out as a tree.* At the top stands Joe. God hands him parents, whose genes hand him an IQ, which is not identical to but is statistically correlated with the parents' IQ. Joe now goes down one or other of two branches, high-school graduate or drop out, according to probabilities statistically influenced by his own IQ. Each branch then divides, into 'poverty' and 'OK', again with statistical probabilities. So at the bottom of the tree we have four final 'destinations' each with an IQ profile and final probability compounded from the preceding data on the tree: high-school graduates who are OK, ditto who are in poverty, drop-outs who are OK, drop-outs in poverty.

By this means we could determine not only the overall chance of low IQ leading ultimately to poverty but also how much of that result is due to the compounding of the trouble by the higher propensity, at the second level of the tree, for Low-IQs to drop out. This knowledge is vital to public policy on the potential of special efforts to discourage Low-IQs from dropping out.

---

*   The technical name is a 'recursive' model. It is the type used by Borjas and Ramey, 1995, in References) in their study, discussed in Chapter 4, of trade, de-industrialization and de-unionization.

If a similar book were written about the UK, there would no doubt be differences, but the tendencies are there. Whether and to what extent the same could be predicted of the various countries of Western Europe, let alone in the educational enigma which is Japan (she has an intensely competitive educational ladder but a less unequal distribution of income), is an interesting question.

The hereditary factor

Subject to controversy, numerous researchers have concluded that IQ is to a considerable extent inherited, meaning that the well-known statistical correlations that we actually see between the IQs of children tested in their early teens and similar tests previously taken at similar ages by their parents, are mainly due to *genetic* factors present at birth, rather than to effects of the various things that happen to a child between birth time and test time. As long ago as the late nineteen-seventies, Tony Atkinson, currently Warden of Nuffield College, Oxford, recently Professor of Political Economy at Cambridge, and an outstandingly distinguished and rigorous scholar in the field of social policy and income distribution, reached the conclusion that hereditary factors in isolation could be responsible for as much as 50 per cent of the degree of income inequality we actually observe in the world.[1]

Notice that all this still basically a black-box kind of discussion: we are not currently (although I believe we will soon be) scanning the infant brain for physical evidence of inherited intelligence. As the question of the heritability of intelligence is even more politically loaded than the question of its existence, the resulting controversy is typical.

I will not go into the detailed evidence. I simply say I believe it. Again, my personal experience predisposes me to do so. I believe I can easily see the seeds of my peculiar intellectual make-up in my parents.[2] Personal stories apart, I do not think that anyone who genuinely knows the qualitative and statistical evidence will, in their heart of hearts, believe the opposing conclusion.

Research is in train in London in the search for genes affecting intelligence. The work is led by Professor Robert Plomin at the London University Institute of Psychiatry and I quote from a letter he kindly wrote me:

> I believe the evidence for genetic influence on cognitive abilities is better than for any other behavioural dimension... For this reason, I decided that an obvious direction for genetic research is to attempt to identify some, of what I am sure are many genes responsible for this influence. My model is that

---

1   Atkinson, 1983, in References, p 87.

2   My mother was imaginative but did not have an especially high logical IQ. Quite unusually for her time, she went to Cambridge, not on a scholarship, and got a Third in first-year economics. My father did get a First in his Cambridge maths finals, but only following three erratic preceding years, and after graduating he never used his maths again.

'Distribution' Technicalities

When statisticians and economists speak of a 'distribution' they are using a technical term. In that sense a 'distribution' is any data – such as data on intelligence or data on incomes – arranged in *groups*. For example the data on personal incomes could be arranged in a table with the first column showing ranges of income (eg £5000 to £6000, £6000 to £7000, £7000 to £8000 etc), the second showing the mid-points of the ranges (eg £5500, £6500 etc) and the third the number of people having incomes within the range of each group. The second and third columns are then plotted on a graph with the former on the x-axis and the latter on the y-axis. The *shape* of the resulting curve defines the *type* of distribution.

If the curve is based on actual data it is called an *empirical* distribution. There are also very important *theoretical* distributions. These are based on imaginary experiments, for example a hundred people tossing pennies many times and adding up their scores. By means of mathematics it is possible to predict that as this game went on the distribution would converge to a precise shape, called the *'normal distribution'*, for which the more popular name is the **'bell curve'** (because the shape is a like a bell).

The peak of a distribution, indicating the group containing the largest number of items, is called the 'mode'. If the shapes of the two halves of the curve on either side of the mode are approximate mirror images, the distribution is *'symmetrical'*.

The normal distribution is symmetrical but not all symmetrical distributions are normal. From the social point of view, it is more important to know whether an distribution is symmetrical than whether it is normal.

there are many genes of varying effect that contribute to genetic variance to general and specific cognitive abilities. Most neuro-scientists have a 'bottom-up' view in which they think that genes specific to elementary cognitive processes drive genetic influences on higher levels of brain function. The genetic evidence, however, tends to support a 'top-down' view in which genetic variation affects some general factor like processing speed. I lean towards a compromise view.

From my own reading and discussions with brain scientists, I am personally slightly sceptical of the idea that the main cause of human variations in intelligence is likely to prove to be variations in processing speed in the sense of the clock speed of a conventional computer. The electro-chemical transmission system mainly used by the normal brain is patently slow, and there may be good reasons why evolution has done this: in some types of artificial neural nets, excessive speed causes instability.

Professor Plomin mentions genetic evidence, but I think there is still some 'black-box' nuance there. I think we must already try and look directly into the brain. If as I have suggested we shall not long from now be able to scan brains while they are carrying out intelligent tasks, what *kinds* of differences would one guess we may see? Professor Christopher Frith, deputy director of the London University Institute of Neurology, an outstanding authority on modelling brain function by means of scanning techniques, has kindly hazarded to me a surmise that the more intelligent person would prove to be the person whose brain showed the *less spread-out* neuronal activity. Professor John Taylor, as already mentioned, predicts a powerful link between reasoning activity and the frontal lobes.

Numerous bits of DNA, yet to be identified, code for development processes in the human embryo which, interacting with subsequent external experiences, eventually produce our mature brain. As a result, like every other human feature, each brain is unique, differing from others, like fingerprints, in a multitude of dimensions. So an accumulation of small variations act together to produce differences in, among many other things, conscious reasoning power. This process will cause general intelligence to tend to be 'normally' distributed, ie for IQ to follow the *bell curve*.

Intelligence and Education

None of the foregoing means that mental ability inherited at birth cannot be modified by subsequent experience and education. Dr Craig Ramey, of the University of Alabama, has recently described[1] a successful intensive educational programme that has proved able to raise the IQs of low-IQ children by a huge amount, sufficient for example to reduce their probability of dropping out of high school, according to my calculations, by as much as a factor of five.

So the conclusion is that although infants inherit significant amounts of IQ from their parents' genes, the *results* are not immutable. Consequently 'liberals' and people of centre-left political disposition should not shy away from the evidence. It provides in fact the fundamental moral case for public intervention in the actual income distribution, as well as, of course, the practical case for intensive education programmes for slower learners.

---

1   Ramey, 1996, in References.

The causes of the J-curve

How do we go from a bell curve of ability to a J-curve of earnings?

In reality the distribution curve of actual earnings, although strongly skewed, can only loosely be called J-shaped.

The distribution actually appears to be made up of *three* distributions, one applying to the lower range of incomes, one to the middle and one to the top ten or 20 per cent.

The bottom distribution is a *'truncated'* normal distribution, ie a cut-off bell curve.

The middle distribution is a *'log-normal'* distribution

The upper distribution is a *'Pareto'* distribution.

The meanings of these terms are described in the boxes.

The bottom distribution

Among this group, representing maybe the lowest-earning 20 per cent of the people, we must accept that average ability for the group is likely to be significantly below the average for the whole population. Within the group, however, there will be some variation in the form of a rather tight bell curve, so that some people will have ability rather nearer to the national average, while others, sadly, will be further disadvantaged in the negative direction. Let us hypothesize further that within the group as a whole earnings will, in practice, correspond more or less proportionately to ability. Inevitably, therefore, the actual earnings of the double-disadvantaged would be pushed low, maybe below subsistence or below what the rest of society regards as acceptable. There may be a legal minimum wage and if not there is likely to be a *de facto* conventional minimum wage. Alternatively people of low ability with low potential earnings may withdraw from the labour force, and become supported by the welfare safety-net (this would include welfare-supported single mothers). Finally in some countries it is possible to receive income support while earning low wages. Only these last remain in the data. The first two categories – minimum wage and income support – both inevitably 'truncate' the distribution. Truncation 'squashes in' the distribution from the left and reduces inequality. The reduction will be greater of course, the higher, relative to average wages, the minimum wage (if there is one) and/or the safety net. If public policy moves in the other

The Pareto Curve

If a distribution is not symmetrical it is called 'skewed'. Income distributions are almost always skewed, with a long tail to the right. As a result, the average income is greater than the income at the mode: the 'typical' person is below average. I loosely call these kinds of curves 'J-curves'.

Income distributions are also 'truncated' – ie cut off to the left – because people with incomes below a certain level either do not exist or do not get into the data. In a welfare society, the point where the truncated curve meets the x-axis indicates the level of the safety net and can also be called the 'poverty line'.

Two particular types of skewed distributions are vital to understanding how it is that although ability is symmetrically distributed, earnings are not. The first of these is the *'log-normal distribution'* and the second is the *'Pareto distribution'*.

A *log-normal distribution* exists if, starting with the skewed data, you convert the x-axis into a log scale and then find that the curve based on the converted scale now appears approximately normal.

A *Pareto distribution* exists if both axes are converted into log scales and the resulting 'curve' is an approximately straight line running downwards from left to right.[*]

In modern times the distribution of all earned incomes often appears like a combination of three subsidiary distributions: in the middle sector, a log-normal distribution; to the left, among lower incomes, a truncated normal distribution; and to the right, a Pareto distribution. Why this should be so (given a normal distribution of ability) is the problem discussed in the text. At the left hand truncation point, the higher the curve, the greater the number of people in the underclass. The further to the left the location of the truncation point on the x-axis, the greater the poverty of the underclass. At the other end, in the 'Pareto' area, the shallower the downward slope of the Pareto curve the greater the inequality of incomes among the top people.[**]

---

[*]   Pareto actually expressed his 'law' (as described in his *Cours D'Économie Politique*, 1897, in References, book 3) as a relation between the logs of income levels and the logs of the numbers of people with incomes above that level, but the concept is the same. He called the gradient of his curve, 'α', and from studies of late-nineteenth-century European income-tax statistics, found values of α between 1.0 and 2.0.

[**] Pareto was confused concerning the relation between his α and the general degree of inequality. He implied that a steeper curve, with higher α, implied greater inequality, but as it means incomes are less spread out, the opposite is obviously the case.

The effects of multiplication

Suppose average earnings are 100, typically made up of, say, 40 units of ability, 20 units of education and 30 units of other factors.

If effects are *additive*, a person with 30, 15 and 35 would have earnings of $30 + 15 + 35 = $ **80.**

If effects are *multiplicative*, the average is $40 \times 20 \times 30 = 24,000$, while $30 \times 15 \times 35 = 15,750$ which, as a percentage of 24,000 is **66.**

So if effects are additive, the example person will earn only a fifth below the average. In the multiplicative case, the same person earns a **third** below the average.

Skewness: because the component numbers are on average larger at the right than at the left hand end of the distribution, the multiplicative effects are larger to right than to left, thus causing skewness.

---

direction, the 'squashing-in' effect will be reduced, and, at this end of the distribution, inequality will increase.

The middle distribution

Here we have a process which may well also apply to some extent in the bottom distribution.[1] It is obvious that genetic ability is only one of numerous factors affecting a person's earning power. Others will be parenting, inherited motivation, education and the supply-and-demand situation in the labour market in the region where one lives or the occupation where one is normally employed. Like ability, one may surmise that these other factors are also approximately normally, or at least symmetrically, distributed. If they operate on individuals *additively* then the combined result will also be a normal (or at least symmetrical) distribution. But for reasons indicated in the box, if they operate *multiplicatively* the result will be a log-normal distribution, or at least a strongly skewed distribution.

It is fairly obvious that the various factors contributing to individual earning power will, in fact, work multiplicatively. Unfortunately, a person of higher IQ will tend to gain more earning power from a given amount of education than a person with low IQ. An industrial worker of higher dexterity paid on piece rates will gain more money

---

1   The process was first identified by Andrew Roy, in Cambridge, and first published by him in 1950. See Roy, 1950, in References. For a later full mathematical treatment, see Aitchison and Brown, 1969, in References.

per hour from an increased rate than a person of lower dexterity, and so on. So we have little difficulty in seeing why the combination of approximately symmetrically distributed ability with other symmetrically distributed factors generates a skewed distribution of earning power, tending to the log-normal.

In Chapter 1, I said that a moderately skewed distribution of earnings was probably not only inevitable but also socially acceptable. Increased skewness, however, implied the danger of unacceptably severe meritocracy. So what determines the *degree* of skewness caused by the multiplicative process? The answer is what is called the *dispersion*, or *spread* of the component distributions.[1] If we combine symmetrical distributions multiplicatively we obtain a skewed distribution. If we increase the *symmetrical* spread of any one of the component distributions, we increase the *skewed* spread of the combined distribution.

The upper distribution

To help understand the reasons for the Pareto distribution of the upper tail of earned incomes it is helpful to begin with a rather simplified picture of what goes on in this area of society. Many of these incomes are earned by people in either upper middle or top management, who work in large organizations with administrative structures that are like pyramids. Except for the chief executive, everyone has a boss, and every boss has a given number of subordinates. Subordinates in turn boss lower subordinates, until we reach the workers at the bottom. The reason for this system is to find a way of controlling and co-ordinating the whole organization without requiring every boss to be in close direct communication with every other. Of course it is an unrealistically simplified picture of the typical contemporary organization, and of course it does not apply in small firms or to independent professionals. But we will come to all that in a moment. What is important here about the simple-pyramid model of organization is that

---

1   A bell curve (normal curve) becomes more dispersed, without becoming skewed, if the two tails are equally pulled out and the peak pulled down. Dispersion is measured by the 'standard deviation', σ, which is the square root of the average value of x^2, where x, for a given item, is the value of that item less the average value of all items.

it is also a model of salary structure.[1] Suppose for the sake of argument that the 'span of control' is constant from top to bottom of the hierarchy, ie that every boss has the same number of subordinates. As shown more fully in Appendix B to this chapter, it then follows that if we know the number of workers we can precisely calculate the numbers at every level above. Now add a similar, 'for the sake of argument' assumption about salaries, namely that the workers are paid a given salary, their immediate bosses are paid x per cent more than they, and that the next layer of bosses is also paid x per cent more than the first layer, and so on all the way up to the CE. Then, given the bottom salary, we can calculate salaries all the way up.

Because we can calculate the salaries at each level and the numbers of managers at each level, given the assumptions – numbers and wages at the bottom level, span of control and salary gradation – *we can also calculate the whole distribution of the salaries of the bosses.* And what will that distribution be? Answer, a Pareto distribution![2] Not only that, but the skewness of this Pareto distribution will be precisely determined by two numerical factors we used in our assumptions. More precisely, instead of the colloquial x to describe the salary gradation, we can better employ a coefficient β, meaning that the salary of a boss is always β times the salary of the immediate subordinate, so if x were 50 per cent β would be 1.5. Then it is shown in the mathematical appendix that if S is the span of control, a single coefficient, $\alpha = \log S / \log \beta$, entirely controls the whole shape of the distribution and thus its skewness. A fall in α means that β has risen relative to S: bosses are being paid more in relation to their responsibility. By the same token, Appendix B shows, a fall in α stretches out the Pareto 'curve' (actually a straight line; see box) to the right. This means an increase in skewness and inequality.

So what determines α? What do bosses do and why are they paid more than their workers? Are bosses more able (more intelligent?)

---

1   The person who first noticed this was Economics Nobel Laureate Herbert Simon in an article first published in 1957 (Simon, 1957, in References).

2   See Appendix B to this chapter. As far as I know the first person to point this out and to see its economic significance was David Grubb, then at the LSE, now at the OECD, in a paper (1982, in References) which has completely inspired both the appendix and the rest of this section.

than workers, or merely better at office politics? The answer, at least in principle, is that bosses, in their organizing capacity, are supposed to contribute to the productivity of their workers. If they do not, the system is failing. In principle, therefore, the value added by a boss includes not only his or her contribution to the productivity of his or her immediate subordinates, but also some part of the productivity of people all the way down the line via the intermediary subordinates. This being the case, the potential gains or losses to the organization from the ability or lack of it of bosses, increase as we go up the ladder. In strictly economic terms it is in theory more important to have an able chief executive than an able middle manager.

The coefficient α, from its definition (see above) measures salary relatively to responsibility as indicated by the span of control. Therefore in principle it should depend on the ability which bosses are believed in fact to possess in the function of enhancing the productivity of others. For the same reasons it depends on the most able people getting the top jobs. The roots of meritocracy among the meritocrats lie in their potentialities, at least, as general productivity-enhancers. Of course, many of us, especially key subordinates, see a very different picture. But it is fair to say that it is widely agreed that an organization containing many high-up duds is an organization which is probably going downhill quite soon unless it has a monopoly or is otherwise free from pressures to be efficient.[1]

As well as the problem of personal inefficiency, the traditional pyramid also contained built-in organizational inefficiency, called 'control-loss'.[2] The larger the base of a pyramid, the greater its height. So the greater the size of an organization, the longer the chain of command, communication and productivity-influence from top to bottom. Given human nature, there will always be errors, accidental or partly deliberate, in the two-way communications of bosses and subordinates. Errors at one level will be passed to the next level, added to and maybe amplified, until the whole system suffers cumulation of misdirection. This problem attenuates the productivity-

---

1   In Japan, it has been observed that failing managers are not dismissed but sidetracked into posts lacking operational responsibility.

2   For an excellent account see Oliver Williamson, 1970, *Corporate Control and Business Behavior*, 1970, in References.

enhancing function of bosses and therefore reduces their value added. It is a factor tending to reduce salaries relative to span of control, raise α and reduce the spread of the Pareto distribution.

So, if the whole economy consisted of large pyramidal organizations, we would have a simple explanation of the Pareto curve. But many people with high incomes do not work in large organizations. Furthermore, at the end of the present century many organizations are 'down-sizing' (a rather ugly term, I think, for getting smaller) and many are 'out-sourcing', ie contracting out functions previously done internally. In addition, the rigid pyramid has always been an over-simplification. Dynamic firms have always employed various forms of greater flexibility and have also developed horizontal as well as vertical channels of co-ordination.

Nevertheless, all these people, professionals, independent small contractors and the like, share with organizational bosses the crucial feature that the quality of their work is supposed to affect the productivity of numerous other workers. Rather than a hierarchy, the picture is a network, which contains, however, some hierarchical elements. An independent contractor who supplies consultancy services to a certain number of other people who influence the productivity of a large number of other people may create more value added than one who serves the same number of people directly, but fewer indirectly. In other words, the simple-pyramid story is a kind of paradigm (ideal model) of what is really happening in the upper economic reaches of society at large.

Why inequality has increased

In Chapter 1, I described the general problem with which this book is concerned as having three parts: the poverty of the underclass; the insecurity of the middle class; and the greater general spread of earnings throughout the social spectrum. The total effect I called Severe Meritocracy, or *SM*. In the following pages I described various forces which contributed to these developments, two of which, slow growth and trade, were discussed in further detail in Chapters 3 and 4. Now, with the benefit of the present chapter, it is possible to both expand and integrate these explanations.

The facts to be explained are:

(1)   The lower and mid-range distributions of employment incomes have moved further apart: average earnings in the mid-range have moderately increased, while those in the low-range distribution have stagnated or declined.

(2)   Within the lower (bottom) distribution there may have been an increase in dispersion (inequality), implying a bell curve whose tails have become longer and peak lower.

(3)   In the mid-range, there may have been no net increase in the dispersion of the distributions of ability, education and earnings, and no obvious tendency for the skewness of the distribution to increase. But it is likely that the 'Pareto' character of the top-range distribution has spread down into the mid-range.[1]

(4)   In the new combined 'Pareto' area, the α-factor has declined, reflecting higher wages for given responsibility and thus greater inequality.

In the preceding chapters we have seen that the main causes of (1) are the effects of the general adverse macroeconomic environment, including the effect of the services shift, plus the effects of increased North-South trade.

The main cause of (2), if it has occurred, could well be found in an interesting recent theory[2] that the new technology, by increasing communications between all members, permits organizations to *de-specialize* the structure of work tasks. In turn this increases the comparative advantage of *versatility* among individual workers: some workers will better adapt to a less specialized working environment than others. If, as seems possible, versatility is a form of inherent ability that is also associated with general intelligence, then the effects

---

1   For example, senior secretaries, properly renamed 'administrators' relieved, by means of the new technology, of much of the worst of the old donkey work are now paid comparatively more than junior secretaries. In my personal opinion, in the 'old days' the relative pay of top secretaries usually failed to match their responsibilities and abilities.

2   Put forward in *The American Economic Review* in May 1996 (in References) by Asa Lindbeck, the highly influential Swedish international economist, and Dennis Snower, specialist in labour market theory, of Birkbeck College, London University, 1996.

of technical changes which increase the comparative advantage of versatility are similar to the effects of an increase in the comparative advantage of general intelligence as such. In the 'old', specialized mode of working, it could be argued, the economic potential of naturally versatile people was suppressed and is now released. If these people, by virtue of general intelligence, were already people of above-average earnings, inequality is increased. Notice that the 'if' is crucial to the conclusion. It is not certain. Therefore the conclusion is not certain. But it is certainly interesting and suggestive.

The explanations of (3) and (4) are likely to include the following:

(a)   Organizations, in the course of becoming more 'competitive,' have tightened the link between pay and apparent ability.

(b)   The new technology has reduced control loss. A major effect of computers is to increase the accuracy of control information and also to permit humans to cope with larger amounts of information. The former reduces communication errors, the latter permits bosses to take on increased spans of control ('de-layering') without loss of efficiency, so that their value added, relative to span of control is enhanced, and with it their salaries (thus reducing α).

(c)   For the same reasons the new technology has encouraged *out-sourcing*, which in turn has two effects,

(i)   Some aspects of out-sourcing work like (b),

(ii)   Out-sourcing, based on short term contracts, also reduces the job security of people who might otherwise have worked in integrated organizations with greater security. Thus out-sourcing explains one feature of the situation (middle class insecurity) and also contributes to the explanation of another (greater middle- and upper-end earnings inequality).

A summing up

As the reader knows, the very considerable concern that exists today about the economy and society, with its different nuances in the US, the UK and Western Europe, has, to the great credit of all concerned, already resulted in a substantial literature. Some of the most interesting of these works such as those of Robert Reich[1] and Will Hutton,[2] represent 'qualitative' descriptions. The foregoing sections in the present chapter are more quantitative and theoretical. Both are basically telling the same story.

As a result of the genetic process and the character of our biological brains, humans are born with mental variations that, subject to nutrition and some effects of education and upbringing, mature into definite differences of intelligence and general ability. These variations are, however, quite moderate and are more or less symmetrically distributed. But at the upper end of society, where Robert Reich's 'symbolic analysts' do their business, the organization of interdependent productivity converts the symmetrical distribution of ability into a highly skewed, 'Pareto-shaped', distribution of earnings. Because the Information Technology revolution has made interdependent productivity more efficient, earnings for given responsibility have increased, and the 'Pareto' effect correspondingly strengthened, causing more inequality. This effect has spread into the old mid-range, while, in the lowest group, the adverse forces discussed in my preceding chapters have reduced this group's average earning power relative to the general average and thus the underclass problem. In addition, among the lowest group (and maybe among the mid group also) there may be increased inequality due to increased comparative advantage for a form of innate ability related to versatility.

The general result, including the macroeconomic failure, is a move towards severe meritocracy with adverse consequences for total welfare.

Meritocracy and welfare

It is therefore time to give more discussion to the whole concept of total welfare.[3] Before Pareto, economists, although using different language, had no problems with the basic idea. They thought of

---

1   Reich, 1991, in References.

2   Hutton, 1995, in References.

3   For the previous brief discussion see the box entitled 'Welfare and welfare' in Chapter 1, p 9.

economic satisfaction as a quantity called 'utility'.[1] If one had more sugar, and no less of anything else, one had gained utility. The gain, per ounce, was, 'the marginal utility of sugar'. The total utility of one individual, as derived from all of her or his consumptions, later came to be called his or her 'welfare'.

The gain in welfare from having more income was called 'the marginal utility of money'. The 'law of diminishing marginal utility of money', as already mentioned in Chapter 1 was based on the widely accepted belief that an extra dollar means less to a rich person than to a poor one.

Welfare as a quantity

If personal welfare is a quantity so is total welfare, the one being obtained from the other by adding up. If one had a scale for converting income into welfare one could convert any income distribution into a welfare distribution, and from that calculate the total welfare of the society.

Even though we know that in the present state of science the relevant scales cannot be measured, these concepts have major political significance arising from the following implications:

(1) The inequality of the distribution of welfare will always be less than the inequality of the distribution of income. On account of diminishing marginal utility of money, the welfare of the rich, however much we may envy them, is not as extreme as their wealth. Despite the skewness of the distribution of income, the distribution of welfare, could in fact, be symmetrical.

(2) In the case of an income distribution which is log-normal and is represented with a log scale on the x-axis, we can imagine economic changes which moved the whole curve to the right without a change in shape. It is then more than likely total welfare will have increased.

---

1 Based on the ideas of Jeremy Bentham (1748-1832). His starting point was that public policy should be based on its practical consequences for living humans, rather than on religious or other moral precepts. The only valid system of morality was usefulness. Policy should try to create 'the greatest good for the greatest number'. When applied to economics, this can be interpreted as meaning, although it does not necessarily mean, that utility is a quantity that can be added up over all the citizens and hopefully made as large as possible.

(3)   Alternatively, with the same assumptions as in (2) we can imagine the log-normal distribution being reduced in dispersion (squeezed-in from the tails) without changing its location, ie with no movement of mode or average. Then it is also more than likely that total welfare will increase.

For obvious reasons, conclusion (1) is not often mentioned in 'left' or 'liberal' literature, while (3) is highly unpopular on the 'right' because it means that any transfer from rich to poor will increase total welfare provided only that average income is not reduced.

Pareto's bombshell

Almost exactly a hundred years ago, Pareto threw a bombshell into these ideas, whose effects spread only slowly among Anglophone economists because the original words, being based on lectures given in French (the language of the Canton of Vaud, where Lausanne is situated) have never been translated. A third of a century later, Lionel Robbins, a highly influential professor at the London School of Economics, reached the same conclusions as Pareto, although, as far as we know, he had not read him. By one route or another the bombshell has been strongly influencing economics, for better or for worse, ever since.

Pareto said that welfare was not a quantity. Consequently all conclusions, such as (2) and (3) above, based on the assumption that it was, were nonsense. Freely translated by myself, his momentous pronouncement read as follows:

> It is logically impossible to make any comparisons of utility[1] between different individuals. The proposition that one human being has more utility than another, makes no sense: for how can one say one thing is bigger than another if the two things cannot be compared? How could one say that pre-historic man was more, or less, happy than modern man? Pushing the argument further, could one say that an ant is happier than a man, or a lion than a gazelle?

Although Pareto repeated the assertion in later writings he never repeated the arguments. The reader will see that the arguments although persuasive, are hardly deep. Lionel Robbins' words were

---

1   Pareto felt that Bentham's use of the term utility had broader connotations than strictly personal economic satisfactions, and coined another term, 'ophelimity' (from a Greek root), which has not however caught on. What Pareto called ophelimity is precisely what a modern economist means by utility.

similar:

> There is no way of comparing the satisfactions of different people. Of course, in daily life we do continually assume that such distinctions can be made...But although it may be convenient to do this, ...*it cannot be justified by appeal to any kind of positive science.* [emphasis added][1]

Unlike the case with Pareto, to save space I have had to make huge cuts in Robbins's elegant prose but the reader who looks up the original will see that I have extracted the main thrust. To me Robbins's most significant contribution to the debate was contained in his assertion that inter-personal comparisons of welfare are inherently 'non-scientific'. The question I asked myself when I first read the original Pareto text was, 'Is this meant to be a scientific statement or a philosophical one?' What would Pareto, Robbins and all the thousands of economists who have followed them say if I could report an experiment comparing the firing rates of neurons in the pleasure centres of the two animals when a lion is eating a gazelle?

The answer is that they will say that there is no knowing that the two observations are comparable. This is a proposition similar to a familiar debate in brain-science concerning what are known as 'qualia', for example some quality in the mental process which interprets the redness of the colour red. How can I ever know that what you perceive when you see red, is the same as what I perceive when I see red? (The pun is deliberate, because obviously the question is emotional.)

I happen to hold the view that all of this makes mountains out of molehills. Red light comes into my eyes and then, as in the case of music coming into my ears, I apply complex processes, beautifully described by Francis Crick,[2] to create meaningful images. To that end I will use some code to record the fact that part of the story consisted of light (or sounds) at certain frequencies. The redness of red is nothing more than that coding. I do not think the issue is very important. What is important, I suggest, is the extent to which the experience in question stimulates the brain processes which have

---

1 Robbins, 1932, in References, p 124-5. It cannot be proved that Robbins had not read, or heard about, Pareto's arguments; what is certain is that his text contains no references to Pareto.

2 Crick, 1994, in References and brain-readings box.

I.G. Patel on inter-personal comparisons

Dr. I. G. Patel, who graduated in Economics one year ahead of me at King's College, Cambridge and subsequently became, among many other high distinctions, Governor of the Reserve Bank of India and Director of the London School of Economics, recently gave a remarkable lecture in a series celebrating the centenary of that outstanding institution.* Among numerous rich passages, he made a particularly eloquent attack on those who deny the validity of interpersonal comparisons of welfare.

> In my younger days, I was repelled by the argument then so fashionable at the LSE that interpersonal comparisons of utility are not possible and, as such, utilities cannot be aggregated into some social whole. As I have grown older I have come to be more amused than annoyed by the pretence of such pristine purity. The argument invalidates any discussion of what may be construed as a better distribution of income or wealth. At a certain level it is, of course, undeniable that you cannot compare my satisfaction from eating ice-cream with yours from eating an identical scoop from the same can. But at a more significant level, we know that an extra dollar in the pocket of a poor peasant in Malawi means much more than a dollar in my pocket or yours. We instinctively accept this, even if we cannot prove it. Is it not incumbent upon us, then, to lay out all distributional changes resulting from a particular policy?

Notice that Patel, in the piece about ice-cream (he is asking, in effect, 'how can we evaluate the sweetness of sweet or the coldness of cold?') does buy the argument discussed in the text, about 'qualia', which I do not. Otherwise we agree a hundred per cent.

---

*   See Patel, 1995, in References

evolved to provide me with pleasure, pain and hence motivation. If one day we are able to observe *quantities* of dopomine moving about in response to positive economic stimuli, maybe *that* is what I will define as utility. Why? Because that is what the process is for. Evolution has provided us with a motivating system originally designed to keep us alive, but now exploited to do much better than that; so if and when we could see the system in operation, and could measure the strength of the motivational impulse, why any further mystery?

These questions I raise are only partly rhetorical. Maybe one day we shall have biological evidence that whatever 'pleasure' is, it is for some insurmountable *practical* reason inter-personally non-comparable. Although I personally doubt that, I concede the possibility. What I object to are assertions unsupported by experiment presented in the name of science. Why do I feel so strongly? First, because such statements do not permit argument. Second, because they have the effect of denying any social usefulness to economics. There cannot be an 'underclass problem' because the problem cannot be defined.

Many economists escape that dilemma by saying that although it is not possible to judge income distributions by reference to the concept of total welfare, it is possible to make 'value judgements' about them. One could 'value' the situation of the underclass as undesirable. To which I reply that the whole idea of 'value' is nothing if not quantitative. Where, if not from some basis of a calculus of human happiness, could economic value judgements come from?[1]

Pareto Optimality

Having said all this it must be recognized that from the starting-point of denying 'inter-personal comparisons' Pareto laid the foundations for a powerful logical structure that increasingly influenced economics from around half a century after he first published it. In the process, more than one Nobel Prize has been gained.

This logic can be illustrated by thinking about what has been going on, in the past twenty years, on the two sides of the Atlantic. On the west side, people with good ability have done well in two ways; their relative earnings have increased and they have had access to cheap services provided by the less advantaged. On the east side, the change in relative earnings has been less marked, but there has been more non-employment. So as between the two situations, some people are better off and some worse off. Pareto says that the comparison cannot be evaluated.

But *then* he says that other circumstances may occur when an economic change would make some people better off and others no worse off. If, so, you do not need a value judgment, he implies, to infer that the change is desirable. The second situation is 'obviously' superior to the first. I personally consider that if one really believes welfare is not quantifiable that conclusion is not obvious at all. Either it implies that quantitative welfare exists, but merely happens to be difficult to measure, or, again, we are talking philosophy rather than economics.

But if we follow Pareto we say that if in situation A everyone is

---

1 The Pareto-Robbins position has come under attack from many quarters. See I.G. Patel in the box and the writings of Brian Barry and Amartya Sen in References.

better off, whereas in situation B, some are worse off, then situation A *dominates* situation B. If there was a vote, everyone would vote for A, but only some would vote for B. 'Domination' in this sense has proved a very useful logical concept for economists because if you accept Pareto's axioms you can try to concentrate attention on a 'short list' of results that dominate all other results and are not themselves dominated by any other results. Results on the short list are called 'Pareto optimal'.

From here comes the crucial theorem in support of the market economy and the whole idea of a benevolent 'invisible hand'. Pareto partly, and later economic theorists – particularly Nobel Prize winners, Kenneth Arrow and Gerard Debreu[1] – rigorously proved that *given* a set of initial endowments, the outcome of the operation of free competitive markets, with no government intervention, no income taxes and no sales taxes or VAT, is a *unique* Pareto optimum, dominating all other results, and dominated by none.

What does this mean in a discussion of the relative demerits of the situations on the two sides of the Atlantic? In a recent discussion with Professor Patrick Minford, of Liverpool University, and a very noted supporter of free markets, when I pointed to the inferior situation of less advantaged people in the US, he replied to the effect that although one could not claim the US situation was Pareto optimal, the US economy was better because it was more competitive.

What could this mean? Suppose we agree that the European system is less 'competitive' than the US system, in the sense of having less 'flexible' labour markets. But the disadvantaged may be less well off in the US. How then do they benefit from competition? The answer is the one we have seen before, namely they *could* benefit *if* we could redistribute the initial endowments. But since we cannot re-distribute ability, we would have to make 'lump-sum' cash transfers from 'ability-haves' to 'ability-have-nots'. So, starting in 'Europe' we should institute measures to make the labour market more 'flexible', ie more like the US. This will increase productivity so much that 'haves' will benefit even if we transfer enough of their gain to 'have-nots' to ensure that the latter are at least no worse off.

As far as I am concerned, it is all cloud cuckoo land, because, for

---

1   Arrow, 1951, and Debreu, 1959, in References.

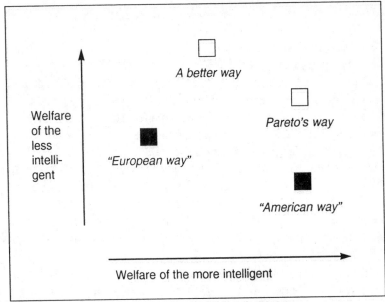

Figure 5.2 **Pareto optimality in the modern situation**.

the reasons given in the previous section, the transfers required by this story never happen because they are not feasible. Of course governments transfer large amounts from rich to poor by means of taxation, but not by 'lump-sum' taxation, because it is not feasible. What is interesting about the argument is the light it throws on the true nature of the perennial debate about the pros and cons of unrestricted markets. The ideology of the 'hands-off', 'laissez faire' 'governments always foul-up' school of politics is founded on the idea of potential, rather than feasible, efficiency. If its assumptions were correct, its conclusions would be correct, but they never are.

The case for total welfare

I therefore come down to my own version of the modern situation as described in Figure 5.2. Although I do not show the origins of the scales, I represent welfare as something that is in principle quantifiable and comparable between individuals and groups. In addition I assume that 'lump-sum' transfers, related to intelligence, are impossible. The figure does take account, however, of normal transfers. For example, the comparative welfare of the less intelligent on the two sides of the Atlantic takes account of the differences in the scale and conditions of unemployment pay and other social benefits. Correspondingly, the welfare of the more intelligent takes account of the taxes they pay to support those benefits.

The two small filled squares are actual situations on the east and west sides of the Atlantic respectively. The unfilled squares are hypothetical situations. Now imagine two alternative programmes for improving the welfare of the less advantaged on both sides of the Atlantic. The programme whose result is labelled 'Pareto's way' is the more moderate of the two, producing, in the comparison with 'America', a medium improvement for the less intelligent, and no loss of welfare for the more intelligent. The programme resulting in a 'better way' is more radical. The improvement of welfare for 'less-intelligents' is greater, and American 'more-intelligents' suffer an absolute loss.

According to Pareto, his 'way' dominates both the existing 'European' and 'US' situations and is not dominated by my 'better way'. But nor does it dominate the better way. Neither situation dominates the other. Pareto says this means the choice of programme, if it must be made, could only be a 'value judgement'. The general result of this type of thinking is usually conservative and will tend to favour 'Pareto's way' or worse.

What do I say? I say that we should add up the welfare along the two axes (remembering that I have not shown their origins) for each of the alternative situations, and ascertain which has the greatest total welfare. Suppose the answer is, in fact, 'a better way'. If Pareto and his modern followers deny the meaningfulness of my calculation, and say we should consequently choose 'his' way instead – thereby, according to my supposed calculation, losing a potential gain in total welfare – there is, I suggest, something wrong at the heart of their philosophy.

The politics of welfare

Economic policies affecting total welfare are carried out by governments. Governments should reflect the interests of the people. The people however are not one but many, and, owing to differences in abilities and other endowments not only have different interests but also different capacities to understand things. Furthermore, the choice and execution of economic policies is not a simple matter, like being presented with a fully worked out version of Figure 5.2, holding a meeting, and saying, 'We'll have that one, please'. Apart from the fact that we cannot, as yet, measure total welfare unambiguously there is also huge uncertainty about the relations between cause and effect.

All this would be hard enough were it not for two further crucial problems. The first is that politicians have to win elections and the second is that the system of voting by majorities, excellent as it is as a general method of democracy, is not designed to resolve the problem of conflicting economic interests.

The voting dilemma

If Figure 5.2 represented a true account of a situation, and all the people on both sides of the Atlantic were asked to vote between the two hypothetical situations, and they all completely understood their own prospects in each (which means they all know their own IQ), the result would simply depend on which group had the greatest numbers. So majority voting might produce maximum total welfare or it might not. In a less simplified story, alternative economic policies would be set out as likely to lead to alternative *distributions* of welfare, in which case the resulting choice would depend arbitrarily on the shape of each income distribution in combination with the distribution of intelligence. Again, there is no guarantee that the resulting choice would be the maximum-welfare one.

It follows that even if people are perfectly informed, which they are not and can never be, there is a very serious problem here. Some commentators have pointed out that the change in the distribution of earnings which has occurred in the Anglo-Saxon countries was strongly supported by the so-called 'Reagan-Thatcher' policies of the elected governments on both sides of the water *and* that the long run of election successes of these governments was made possible by votes from citizens who, in the event, suffered losses of welfare from the results. If they had known what was going to happen, would they have voted the same way? We do not know. So many emotional and other factors are involved that we can by no means be sure that the answer is, 'no'.

The American Nobel-winning political economist James Buchanan, noticing that in a democracy policies are selected by voting procedures that can produce arbitrary results, and himself believing very strongly in the Paretian denial of inter-personal comparisons, reached the startling and in my opinion ridiculous conclusion that nothing in society should ever be changed without *unanimous* consent. In Appendix A, I deconstruct Buchanan and give my reasons for saying that in today's situation his principle would mean we should do nothing for the underclass.

The contribution of John Rawls

There are no Nobel awards for philosophy. If there were, John Rawls would surely have deserved one. As long ago as 1971[1] he pointed out that once people know who they are, the voting dilemma is inevitable. Once you know who you are, *and* you are completely well-informed, you will tend to vote for your own interests. Therefore it follows that voting by people who already know who they are will not necessarily increase welfare.

Rawls therefore conceived an imaginary experiment in which people were asked to choose between alternative societies *before* they knew who they were. This is obviously not an easy thing to imagine. What it means in the light of all that has gone before in this chapter is that in theory people should choose their favoured economic systems *before* learning the results of the genetic lottery which determines their IQ. At the time of choice, they are all equally intelligent, and intelligent enough to understand what they are doing, but after the choice has been made, they will enter the resulting society with an IQ drawn at random from the bell curve. Thus they make their choices about social policy, knowing the *distributions* of welfare that will result from different policies but without knowing where they themselves will fall.

The strength of John Rawls's concept is not weakened by the fact that the 'experiment' is in practice impossible. What it does is provide a very strong way of thinking about the problem. And in fact when reasonable people, who do have different interests, are having a serious political argument, one can often see them trying to argue from the point of view of 'society as a whole', rather than their own interests. Although they are unlikely to know of John Rawls's idea, they argue as if they do.

---

1   John Rawls, *A Theory of Justice*, 1971, in References.

Rawls's imaginary procedure is, in fact, a kind of way of *defining* the interests of society as a whole. Faced with Figure 5.2, how would the disembodied spirits decide, and what happens if they disagree? The answer is that each voting quite *self*-interestedly will vote for the society that gives them the *best chance* of welfare. That result is the result obtained by someone who is eventually awarded an average IQ. And the best society for a person with average ability is the society with maximum total welfare. Therefore, still assuming they are perfectly informed, our decision makers will all choose, in Figure 5.2, 'a better way'. The problem of disagreement will not arise, because they will always agree.

Of course, when the plan is put into operation, some, in the light of the IQ they actually receive, will begin to agitate for change. In principle, they should not. In making the original choice, justice was done and is still being done. That is the luck of the draw. The real case for agitation, of course, is that in the real world, justice was not done, because the experiment never actually happened.

Despite the theoretical character of John Rawls's argument, it is my experience that once one has understood it (and many people who think they do, do not[1]) one never looks at the world the same way again. In particular, it is impossible, after Rawls, to think of any reason for not supporting the principle of choosing economic policies to maximize total welfare.

---

1 Unfortunately, Rawls, having brilliantly invented the imaginary decision procedure, got into a muddle about the voting criterion. Instead of a theoretical distribution of prospective welfare, his imaginary spirits were in effect faced with a distribution of earnings, rather roughly grouped. One large group represented the prospective outcome for the 'least advantaged', ie a class of people who in my story would eventually draw low IQs. He then applied what is called the 'maximin' principle; one chooses the policy which, given all the alternative outcomes from different IQs, maximizes, not the average result, but the worst result. Sometimes the two will be the same, sometimes not. The most lucid critique of Rawls on this point I know is that of John Harsanyi, who later received a Nobel Prize in economics for other contributions in game theory. (See Harsanyi, 1976, in References.) Because this error led Rawls to appear to conclude that the imaginary choice should always favour societies with economic systems biased in favour of below-average IQ (the least advantaged), rather than the average, he violated the principle of maximizing total welfare and, as a result, has had less influence than he should have done.

Welfare and morality

Given that we cannot actually carry out Rawls's experiment, how in the world of practical politics, should we judge economic situations and the policies that bring them about?

Many people, including Pareto-supporting economists, will answer, 'from morals'. 'Value judgement' is, I think, another name for moral judgement. The problem is, where do moral judgements come from if not from 'Benthamite' principles? The Rawls principle is basically a sophisticated version of 'the greatest good for the greatest number'. (For 'greatest number' read the mode of the expected distribution.)

Personally, the only other answer I know to the question is from religion. Religiously minded people (I must say frankly that I am not one) are especially noted for supporting moral principles some of which they derive directly from their scripture and theology. Many moral principles supported by religious people are similar to those upheld by non-religious people. But there is a sense in which those morals of a religious person which are derived from the religion itself are not open to 'rational' debate. For example, I could not usefully protest that a taboo on certain agricultural practices was disadvantageous to total welfare, because my protest would be deemed irrelevant. In effect, and I say this without I hope disrespect, religion more often than not speaks of higher things than economic welfare.

Protestant Christianity is often seen as favouring free markets and laissez faire, the suggested explanation lying in the Calvinist doctrine of pre-destination. God has assigned you an IQ and that is that. In Britain at the present time, however, the English Church is exceptionally concerned about the underclass.[1] The Catholic Church, while usually opposing socialism, has nevertheless an important tradition of favouring economic balance between the social classes. I will therefore close the chapter with a quotation from a famous Papal Encyclical which, in the year 1931, said some interesting things about economics:

> The opportunity to work must be provided to those who are able and willing to work. This opportunity depends largely on the wage and salary rate, which can help as long as it is kept within proper limits, but which on the other hand can be an obstacle if it exceeds these limits. *For everyone knows that*

---

1   See, for example *Staying in the City*, Church of England, 1995, in References.

an excessive lowering of wages, or their increase beyond due measure, causes unemployment. This evil .... has plunged workers into misery and temptation, ruined the prosperity of nations, and put in jeopardy the public order, peace, and tranquillity of the whole world [emphasis added].[1]

In 1931 the world was in the throes of a huge Keynesian slump, but it was to be five years before Keynes published his book[2] explaining unemployment. In Chaper 1 I pointed out that 'Keynesian' unemployment, in contrast to 'classical' unemployment, was not affected by the wage level. So, in retrospect, the Pope had the wrong theory (he was probably advised by good Catholic professional economists). As far as I am concerned, however, his heart was very much in the right place. Notice that he does not refer to God. He gives his own reasons for his concern, the assumption being, I assume, that his reasons would be God's reasons also.

One reason he gives is the peace of the world, another the prosperity of nations. And what is the latter but total welfare? Why do those of us who are fortunate enough to be 'well-endowed', care about the underclass? Religion gives one answer, Rawls, supported by myself, another, and both answers are the same.

---

1   From the encyclical 'Quadragessimo Anno'. See Carlen, C., *The Papal Encyclicals*, in References.

2   Keynes, the 'General Theory', 1936, in References.

Appendices to Chapter 5

A.   The Buchanan doctrine

Social scientists have identified two kinds of problems about voting for economic policies. The first, which can be called the 'committee problem' is due to logical difficulties if voting is used to choose between more than one pair of alternatives: many people have experienced the situation where the procedure produces a result that is not at the top of anyone's list. The second is the problem at issue in this chapter, namely that even with only one choice to make, the majority vote does not necessarily select the highest welfare. To be sure of that, one would need to give extra votes to people who would be likely to have high marginal utility of money, ie to people with low incomes and/or less intelligence – an interesting and logical idea but obviously fraught with practical difficulties.

The committee problem was brought to the attention of economists by Kenneth Arrow, in the famous Nobel-winning work wherein he proved that once you accept denial of inter-personal comparisons it is impossible to draw up a logically consistent procedure whereby public policies can be evaluated from the preferences of individuals.[1]

The 'welfare' problem was originally brought up by James Buchanan,[2] who also gained a Nobel Prize, but led him to virtually the opposite conclusions from mine. Buchanan is a passionate believer in the Paretian philosophy but drew far more conservative conclusions from it than anyone before. In effect he denied not only interpersonal comparisons but also value judgements. Since a change in an economic situation could be justified only if it were Pareto optimal, proposals to change the status quo should be accepted only if the voting was unanimous: only by that means could one be sure that the change would make everyone feel better off. Consequently, in the case of the example shown in Figure 5.2, it would be wrong to move from 'American way' to 'A better way' *even if a majority did vote for it.*

Despite James Buchanan's formidable reputation, I have to say that this seems to me the most ridiculous and illogical proposition ever to be taken seriously. The situation depicted in 'American way' was not handed down by God. It was the result of the accumulation of *previous changes*. In 1970, the economic system was less unfavourable to the less intelligent. So something like 'A better way' was once itself the status quo. As a result of the various causes described in the previous chapters of this book, we went from one 'status quo' to another. The causes represented changes in the economic system. Since unanimous voting was not employed to decide whether to allow these changes to occur, Buchanan would have to say they

---

1   Arrow, 1951, in References.

2   See Buchanan, *The Calculus of Consent*, 1962, in References.

were illegitimate. So he has proved that it is illegitimate to be where we are and illegitimate to go back to where we were![1] Que sera, sera. By the same reasoning, it would be wrong to abolish Communism if, on a free vote, a single citizen voted for retention. And, by the same token, if an uncomfortably large number of Russians now vote to return to Communism, that would be wrong also!

B.   The algebra of organization

Let an organization be structured in authority levels, numbered 0, 1, 2, 3 etc.
At every level every supervisor has S supervisees at the level below.
The number of people at level L is N_L.
The salary of a person at level L is Y_L.
The salary at any level is β times the salary at the level below, where β typically is a number greater than one and less than, say, ten, eg $\beta = 1.5$.

Then,

$$N_L = N_0 / S^L \qquad or \tag{1}$$
$$\log N_L = \log N_0 - L (\log S) \tag{2}$$
$$Y_L = Y_0 \beta^L \qquad or$$
$$\log Y_L = \log Y_0 + L (\log \beta) \tag{3}$$

Hence,

$$\log N_L = \log N_0 - \alpha (\log Y_L - \log Y_0) \tag{4}$$
$$\text{where } \alpha = \log S / \log \beta$$

(3) can be written in simplified form,

$$n = 1/ y^\alpha \tag{5}$$

– where n is the ratio of the number of people at a given level to the number of people at the lowest level and y is the corresponding ratio of salary at that level to the salary at the lowest level.

If the salary increment factor, β, increases relatively to span of control, a larger salary is awarded for given responsibility. In that event, α decreases.

When α decreases, the income distribution is stretched out to the right: as would be expected, inequality has increased.

---

1   For a particularly lucid discussion of this point see David Reisman, *The Political Economy of James Buchanan*, 1990, in References.

6. A Better Way

This book has explored the nature and causes of the 'underclass syndrome' – the state of affairs where, in the midst of affluence, a significant percentage of the population are likely to experience poverty; where another significant proportion feel a risk of poverty and where there has been a general spreading out of the income distribution both between and within economic groups.

We suggested that the trouble was the result of a developing **'SM'** (severe meritocracy) caused in turn by inadequate economic growth (of output, capacity and the demand for labour), interacting with and exacerbated by the five additional factors of 'technology', 'trade', 'services' 'women' and 'public policy'.[1]

In the chapters which followed we explored this causal nexus in more detail. The main findings are summarized at the beginnings of the chapters. From these, some specific discoveries stand out:

(1)   On both sides of the Atlantic, but much more so in Europe than in the US, there has been since 1970 a growing gap between total employment and the 'effective' labour supply (Chapter 1, Figures 1.4 and 1.5 and text).

(2)   The smaller employment gap in the US is offset by the fact that real wages of lower paid Americans have fallen well below the corresponding figures in Europe (Chapter 2, Figure 2.8).

(3)   On both sides of the Atlantic, since 1970, there has been a massive reduction in the proportion of the population who received only a 'basic' education ('Low-Eds'; see Chapter 2, Figures 2.1 to 2.4).

(4)   But among those who were left out of this education revolution, especially young males, not only in Europe, but also in the US, 'non-employment' has also become widespread (Figures 2.5 and 2.6).

---

1   *See page 19.* Reminder: 'Technology' *referred to the role of the IT revolution in changing the income distribution.* 'Trade' *referred to the export of the Third World's wage structure to the old 'First' world.* 'Services' *referred to the natural economic shift of consumer demand to services.* 'Women' *referred to the huge increase in the proportion of mothers desiring paid employment.* 'Public policy' *referred to the tightening up of requirements for social security payments.*

(5)   *In the middle and upper segment of the distribution of incomes from employment, the upper tail has become more stretched out to the right and has also spread down into the middle. This is probably mainly due to the IT revolution (see Chapter 5 page 148 and after).*

(6)   *The growth slow-down after 1973 was a not a long term technical-productivity phenomenon. We found strong evidence (Chapter 3, Figures 3.5 to 3.7) that the <u>apparent</u> supply-side productivity slow-down was <u>induced</u> by demand-side slow-down.*

(7)   *The demand-side slow-down was initially caused by the oil shocks of the nineteen-seventies, and later prolonged by the political and economic aftermath of these; also by misunderstanding the mechanism of wage inflation in the modern economy; by high real long term interest rates; by perverse expectations in the financial markets (both these last partly government-induced) and by excessive stock-market take-over activity (Chapter 3, last section).*

(8)   *The 'trade' effect is theoretically inevitable and has been quantitatively significant, especially when taken in conjunction with the fact that increased trade has especially affected oligopolistic industries with strong labour unions (Chapter 4, on de-industrialization).*

(9)   *The explanation of **SM** is helped by recent research in brain science. The tendency for the market to convert the symmetrical distribution of IQ into a skewed distribution of earnings cannot be avoided. What can be avoided is an unnecessarily bad outcome for people born with below-average IQ. The answer is the recovery of economic growth.*

(10)   *Otherwise, the current situation can be described by two 'ways'; 'American' and 'European'. The former, as compared with the latter, has lower wages and less non-employment. Therefore there is a different distribution of well-being between the IQ 'haves' and 'have-nots'. In my opinion total economic welfare is higher in the European Way, but others disagree. In any event, neither situation is satisfactory.*

So the task of the present chapter is to consider what must be done to achieve a better way. This does not mean creating employment for the sake of employment. The over-arching goal is to increase, or to prevent further declines in <u>total welfare</u> (for definitions see Chapter 1 page 9 and Chapter 5 page 157 and after).

Increased employment, reduced statistically reported unemployment, reduced actual non-employment, are all changes which could increase welfare, provided they did not also involve other changes going the other way. The same could apply to 'increased competitiveness' (whatever that really means) provided it does not also mean a fall in real wages. Finally the same applies to economic growth. The objective of faster and stabler long term economic growth, so strongly supported in the preceding pages, is an 'intermediate' objective. It will not inevitably raise the future average real income per head (although, if it induces faster productivity growth, it will) but it will inevitably create better employment opportunities at good wages for the less favoured segment of society.

The chapter begins by discussing the conclusions and recommendations of Robert Reich and Hernstein and Murray, criticising all three, in varying degree, for pessimism.

Two questions are then discussed – the possible contribution of more progressive taxation and the problem of middle class insecurity. The former may be desirable on the criterion of total welfare, but will not necessarily command a majority in elections. The latter in logic requires an increase, rather than a decrease in the generosity of the welfare-state safety net.

Twelve specific proposals – aimed at changing government priorities in order to raise the sustainable growth rate of real demand, of capacity, of output, of the demand for labour and of the real wages of the lower paid – are then set out. We also discuss the means for reducing real interest rates and for dispelling the perverse contemporary tendency (discussed in Chapter 3 pages 104-7) for operators and dealers in financial markets to hold expectations of a kind that, however rational from their point of view, are obviously irrational for society.

Having briefly discussed and rejected as immoral and/or unfeasible the 'populist' remedy of a First World reversion to protectionism, the international dimension is discussed from the point of view of various bodies such as the UN, the EU and the OECD.

Finally, I revert to the proposition that if the growth programme fails, the nations of the world, under the heading of 'damage limitation', will need permanent 'welfare states' to protect not just the most vulnerable members but also the total welfare of their societies. That is the final conclusion of the book.

However, before starting the discussion above, it is desirable to pause to think again about geography.

		Weighted averages of data for:	
Table 6.1 The Anglo Saxons and the Continentals			
		UK and US	France, Italy and Germany
1.	Level of Low-Ed male non-employment in 1995	35%	27%
2.	Increase in total male non-employment 1970 to 1995	10 points	16 points
3.	1970-1995 total employ-ment gap	10.5%	14%
4.	Per capita GDP growth slow-down, pre mid 70s to early 90s	1 point	4 points

Sources:
   (1) As Figure 2.7, p 52.   (2) As Figure 1.7, p 37.
   (3) Table 1.1, p 25.   (4) As Figure 3.1, p 78.

A pause for Europe

Throughout the preceding chapters, the situation in continental western Europe (or *CWE*) has not become entirely clear. We have seen that in France and Germany both official unemployment and the real wages of the lowest paid workers have been, and are, higher than in the UK and the US. But we have also seen that this is not matched, as conventional economics would predict, by higher Low-Ed non-employment. Non-employment among male Low-Ed workers is on average *lower* in France and Germany than in the UK and the US. Does this mean that *CWE* is a paradise, marred only by general overvaluation of 'Deutchmark zone' currencies in the 1990s, where Anglo Saxon sin does not occur? Few people, on either side of the North Sea, are likely to answer 'yes'. Most especially in France, in the middle nineties there is a general sense of economic pessimism. Throughout *CWE,* there is deep concern about employment.

Now that our statistical work is complete, it is possible, by taking details from several different chapters, as in Table 6.1 above, to see the explanation of this contradiction. As the table shows, the increase in *total* (as compared to Low-Ed) male non-employment has been very markedly higher in France and Germany than in the UK and the US. The same applies to another statistic relating to total, rather than Low-

Ed, labour, namely the cumulative deficiency, 1970 to 1995, of labour demand in relation to effective labour supply (the 'employment gap'). Finally, we know that in a crude sense, although France and Germany were, up to 1990 (but not thereafter) growing faster than the US in terms of GDP per capita, their post-mid-seventies slow-down was very large. They slowed down very sharply from a previously very fast rate. Whatever the expanation may or may not be,[1] this massive slow-down happened, and inevitably had major labour-market effects. Putting these points together, the story that emerges from Table 6.1 is that *CWE* has indeed suffered severe demand deficiency in her labour market, caused by inadequate growth, but on account of the different or 'Catholic' social regime (and, in Germany especially, educational system) the adverse effects, *rather than as in UK and US, concentrating on Low-Eds, have spread more evenly over the whole working population.* The problem in the *CWE* is not strictly a problem for an underclass, it is general problem, and, as such, a very serious one. Alternatively, to the extent that the problem does have a distributional dimension, this arises from a hidden aspect, ie the presence of low wages and high non-employment among immigrant people who do not feature in the official education and employment statistics.

The need for constructive optimism
Both Hernstein and Murray (discussed in Chapter 5[2]) and Robert Reich (discussed in Chapter 1[3]), starting from opposite ends of the political spectrum, arrive near the end of their respective books with significantly similar pessimistic views of the future. Both envisage

---

1   For a discussion see page 84.

2   See 1994, in References. I have made my view of the political aspect of H & M (I hope, abundantly) clear. I have also made some major statistical criticisms. (See Chapter 5, pp 142 and after). To remind the reader, my position was and is that H & M's basic statistical propositions are probably sound, but I derive from them almost opposite political conclusions. Since Chapter 5 was typeset, I have come across a survey of the controversy that has followed their book in the London *Economist* (13 July 1996, p 94). The writer concludes, 'Enraged academics have spent the past two years producing rebuttals. So far the results are disappointing.' I think this supports my position.

3   1991, in References.

two increasingly diverging 'nations'[1] of ability-haves and have-nots. In H & M the haves are characterised by IQ, in Reich by function as symbolic analysts. Both books foretell a kind of 'secession' of the haves, as also described by Reich in his 1996 speech at the University of Maryland reproduced in Chapter 1.[2] H & M then paint a local American picture of a 'cognitive elite' fed up with crime and welfare dependency, turning to a 'custodial' society – trying to 'reclaim the streets' by virtually locking away the underclass. (Eerily, just after I write these words, my television gives me a picture of the British Home Secretary proudly announcing a plan for 12 new prisons.) Robert Reich sees the same kind of tendency, reflected in ever-increasing income inequality, enhanced by the fact that his elite of symbolic analysts have acquired additional bargaining power by virtue of global mobility.

Having reached a nadir of pessimism, each book then in about ten pages expresses a form of constructive optimism based on a recognition that the pessimistic scenario, seen in the longer span of human social history, must be self destructing. H & M, in a manner entirely consistent with the logic of my Chapter 5 above, ask,

> How should policy deal with the twin realities that people differ in intelligence for reasons *that are not their fault* and that intelligence has a powerful bearing on how people do in life?[3]

Robert Reich in a passage that every modern citizen should read,[4] points up the barrenness of two distinctive adverse modern tendencies, *'zero-sum nationalism'* (meaning a false belief that what other nations or regions gain, my nation or region must lose and vice versa), dangerously prevalent among general public and populist politicians; and *apathetic cosmopolitanism* among the elite: they sense the global moral problem but lack incentive to do much about it. In my opinion, the first tendency is currently increasing in Britain, fuelled by our notorious 'tabloid' press. The second tendency can be seen in the way national leaders, speaking in international fora, spin words lamenting

---

1   A 21st century version of Benjamin Disraeli's 19th century picture, as described in his *'Sybil: The Two Nations'* (Disraeli, 1861, in References) ?

2   Page 10.

3   Herstein and Murray, 1994, in References, p. 535.

4   Reich, 1991, Chapter 25.

the plight of the underclass while implying that the only practical 'solutions' are reducing welfare benefits.

After these preliminaries, each book, appropriately displaying the respective conservative and liberal viewpoints of the authors, proceeds to practical proposals, as follows:

A better way according to Hernstein and Murray

(1)   'Simplify the rules': the cognitive elite has gradually compli- cated tax forms, welfare applications, small-business regula- tions, professional qualifications and etc. Practical conclusion; 'stop it and strip away the nonsense.'

(2)   Also simplify criminal law so that people understand the crimes they are committing and the consequences.

(3)   Remove the legal and financial responsibility of natural fathers for illegitimate children.

(4)   Increase the economic incentives for 'trying hard'. One way or another the proportion of earned income exempt from tax should be increased. (The recommendation is not sufficiently clearly stated to indicate whether it implies an increase or a decrease in the progressiveness of the taxation of all earned income.)

General comment: I leave the reader who has covered the preceding pages of this book (mine, not H & M's) to judge the likely practical contribution of these items to the economic problem as I have outlined it. My personal reaction, after 550 pages of H & M, is 'damp squib'. Although I have some personal sympathy with item (3) I doubt if it will help save the underclass. Maybe I have missed something, but it seems to me it would either merely redistribute income between adult males and adult females or cause an increased taxpayer cost for single mothers. The proposal would also cause great excitement in the current British Conservative government, who recently set up a whole new agency to pursue exactly the opposite policy. In the case of item (4), economists, fiscal experts and politicians have wracked their brains for many years to find ways of reducing the marginal tax on low earned incomes without an unacceptable loss of revenue or increased 'burden' on the overclass.

A better way with Robert Reich

(1)   Citizens – the general public – should take primary responsibil- ity for enhancing (by education, training and re-location

programmes) the productivity of others, at home and abroad.

(2) Everyone should recognise an overarching goal of *global welfare*. This means absolute opposition to protectionism as a (false) solution to the trade problem.

(3) More public expenditure on pre-school, primary and secondary education, child-care and pre- and ante- natal care, targeted towards the underclass.

(4) Subsidies to firms, whether home or foreign managed, undertaking economic activities tending to draw out value added from people who would otherwise be in the underclass.

(5) Inter-governmental subsidies for international productive high-science research such as decoding human DNA or space exploration.

(6) Grants and subsidies to ease the transition from technologically redundant industries.

(7) Encouragement, rather than discouragement, of the process, described in Chapter 4 above, whereby the old Third World countries undertake an increasing proportion of the whole world's high-volume industrial production.

Obviously, I have more sympathy with this list. It is clearly more substantial. Given what I have said in Chapters 4 and 5, I particularly like Robert Reich's point number (2). But equally obviously I must fault the absence of the macro dimension. (3) to (5) are concrete proposals for government expenditure which in my opinion could be seriously considered within the context of the over-arching goal of adequate macro growth.

A better way with me

With all due humility (tempered by a degree of professional confidence) I believe I can offer some policy recommendations that have a greater degree of economic solidity. Because they are quite specific, however, they are bound to face the problem of 'political feasibility'.

The problem of political feasibility

When academic persons, such as myself, come up with specific, technically-feasible policies intended to improve the world, as often as not we face the response that the proposals, however intrinsically desirable, are not 'politically' feasible. What does this actually mean? The answer is that it can either refer to the voting problem I discussed in Chapter 5, or to something else. If the latter, what?

The voting problem is that a majority procedure, applied to economic policy, does not necessarily choose maximum welfare. As I described the problem, the situation could be likened to that in an imaginary referendum being held between the 'American way' and the 'European way' as depicted in Figure 5.2. But a large proportion of the decisions affecting the problems discussed in this book are necessarily decided by civil servants, parliaments, congresses, ministers and other executives such as presidents or chairpersons. Often, especially in the US, the decisions result, *de facto*, from the interplay of multiple leaders with varying constituencies. So if, when we describe a proposal as 'politically unfeasible' we mean more than merely that we believe the people, if fully informed, would not vote for it, we must mean we believe that, for some *other* reason, the elected leaders would not do it. These other reasons can only be of two kinds, ideological conviction (or prejudice) or personal interest.

I have special aversion, not to people who are frank about their prejudices but to those who hide vested positions behind supposed ideals. The costs they impose on the welfare of the world is enormous. Many economists are deliberately pragmatic, tailoring conclusions to the world's manifold 'political' constraints. They have a good argument that it is better to achieve a step in the right direction than none at all. Other economists are patently ideological. They go beyond pragmatism to positively create theories whose assumptions lead to conclusions reinforcing, consolidating, rationalizing or otherwise advancing this or that ideology. It is no coincidence, for example, that many (though not all) economists who deny inter-personal comparisons (eg Lionel Robbins) tend to be of the conservative persuasion. Another example is the current phenomenon of a kind of unholy intellectual convergence between contemporary ex-Marxists and contemporary conservative laissez-fairists. They unite to support a reaction against Keynesian economics, positive macro demand management, and targeted economic growth. The one dislikes the idea that capitalism cannot work without demand management, the other that capitalism could ever been made to work at all. The latter group (who sadly include a number of personal friends of mine) particularly annoy me. The more influential either group, the gloomier the future prospects of the people about whom one should care the most, ie the underclass.

So in the remainder of this book I am going to be ferociously politically naive. I believe economists have a duty to be that. Otherwise there is intellectual inertia. 'Unfeasible' options cease to be explored. The argument for one step forward in place of no steps forward is displaced by arguments for no steps forward in place of some steps back. Horizons shrink. The process is patently apparent in contemporary discussions of growth and growth targets.

Anatomy of the general problem

In Chapter 1, I described our basic problem as having three aspects,

(1) The situation of the underclass

(2) The insecurity of the middle class

(3) The general stretching-out of earnings at all levels.

We have now gone over the facts and causes of (1) and (3) in some detail. All three aspects interact, in the sense that the total adverse effect on welfare is more than the simple sum of the individual effects. In that respect, however, (1) stands apart. It would quite obviously be a bad thing, even if (2) and (3) had not occurred. By contrast, I would argue, neither (2) nor (3) in isolation would necessarily reduce welfare. Why?

The special problem of the J-stretch

In Chapter 5 we saw how the total distribution of personal earnings was apparently made up of three subsidiary distributions relating to the bottom, middle and top ends, respectively. The top distribution was approximately a 'Pareto Curve' (ie a highly skewed distribution which turns into a stretched-out straight line on a double-log scale), about which we reached three rather confident conclusions:

(1) The shape was the result of the following sequence of causes:

   1.1 the productivity of people working in this segment affects the productivity of others, the more so the further up one goes,

   1.2 it therefore pays society to have able people in the higher positions, and to reward them, at least to some extent, for beneficial effects of their own productivity as it acts not only on the productivity of those with whom they are in immediate contact but also on those whom they affect through others,

   1.3 if people are thus arranged in a partly-hierarchical structure of salaries and responsibilities, with superiors paid proportionately more than 'inferiors' or 'subordinates'[1] according to their degree of responsibility, the resulting earnings distribution *is* a Pareto distribution.

(2)   Since 1970 the top-end distribution has become more skewed: the downward slope of the straight line in the double-log chart has been reduced, stretching it further to the right, because:

    2.1   the information revolution, in reducing control and communications errors, has increased the net productivity-enhancing capacity of productivity enhancers,

    2.2   consequently 'superiors' are being paid more for given responsibility.

(3)   The Pareto curve, which used mainly to affect the top 20 per cent of earners, has probably spread further down.

We could call the story, 'trouble in the stratosphere'.[2] It is not completely obvious why we should be upset about it. Imagine a history where the changes listed above had occurred, but no others – no increased insecurity for the middle class, no increased poverty for the underclass. Further imagine that following the changes, every group, from top to bottom, gains enhanced rewards related to their enhanced productivity. This means gains not only for people who enhance others' productivity, but also for those whose productivity is enhanced. The gains of the latter, proportionately, are less than the gains of the former, but are still absolute. Clearly, total welfare has increased, so why should we lament the situation?

The answer is that we may dislike the fact that *relative* inequality has increased.

Taxation and the Rawls criterion

Is that a 'value judgement'? To understand why the answer must be

---

1   Neither word is satisfactory. Suppose John is in a relationship with Tom, Dick and Harry, such that he influences their productivity (by giving leadership, guidance and information) but they do not greatly influence his. John however has a boss called Jane, who also has three other Johns (or Joes, or whoevers) reporting to her. Jane not only influences the productivity of her Johns, but also, via them, of Tom, Dick and Harry. For convenience we not only say Jane is John's superior, but also that John is T, D & T's 'superior'.

2   A reference to Robert Reich, 1991, in References. See Chapter 1.

'no' we can turn back to John Rawls (see last section of Chapter 5). If I did not know what my IQ was going to be, I would prefer the new situation to the old because in it, my most probable level of welfare is higher. But that is not the end of the matter. It is possible, given the new technology, to create a third society, namely one where part or all of the gains in the upper reaches of the Pareto curve are re-distributed by a more progressive income tax – the effect of which, of course, is to make after-tax income distribution not equal, but more nearly symmetrical, or bell-shaped. Unfortunately, as a million high-IQ economists have pointed out, taxes on incremental income may cause high-IQ, high-responsibility people to choose to make less effort or work shorter hours (always supposing that they are paid by results). If this actually happens, the productivity of others will suffer, and so the average productivity of the whole system. Total welfare may not be increased. Therefore, as we have mentioned before, economists such as James Mirrlees[1] have tried to find optimal tax structures to get the best balance between the two effects.

This is a tricky question, because, to the extent that our problem today arises from a meritocracy based on inherited IQ, it is difficult to see how the 'incentive' effects really work. I cannot wake up in the morning, learn that the rate of income tax has increased, and reduce my IQ. I am still better off getting the best gross wage that I can with the IQ that I possess. What progressive taxation does, in effect, is to change the value of the distribution coefficient in the Pareto curve in much the same way as if the market itself were offering lower rewards for given responsibility.

On the other hand, there is the point that progressive taxation of actually earned income is not a nice thing; it imposes a pain on the payers that seems to go beyond the economic cost. First you earn it, then you have it, then you must give it up. I have worked a hard slog for quite some months to finish this book. I do not enjoy the prospect that the more successfully I have worked the more I shall have to pay my beloved Queen – a feeling that is not fully suppressed by remind-ing myself that she might use the money to help the underclass.

Nevertheless, the concept of optimal taxation is very valuable in judging the morals of the J-curve. Suppose taxation was actually

---

1   See Chapter 1 and also Mirrlees in References.

optimal before and after the changes. Which society would I prefer? The answer has to be the new one. Both societies have optimum welfare, but in the new society, because of the technological changes, optimum welfare is higher welfare.

A policy conclusion
Now comes the rub. *It is possible that the progressiveness of the new optimal tax structure will be greater than the old.*

It follows that if the 'J-curve problem' (increased skewness of the basic income distribution to the right, caused by the new technology) occurred in isolation, what I mean by a better way for society is that we may need to adopt a more progressive tax structure.

Interestingly, in the UK, since 1980, exactly the opposite has occurred. This was the result of decisions made by a properly elected government. Furthermore, it is widely believed that in the 1992 election, the accusation that the opposition party was planning to increase the progressiveness of taxation caused its defeat. As a result, at the time of writing, the 'new' Labour Party is extremely fearful of repeating that experience. If their political judgement is correct, and it may well be, we have a perfect example of the proposition that majority voting cannot guarantee to optimize welfare.

Either we abandon democracy therefore, or we must accept that if we cannot succeed with political persuasion, we may be able to do *nothing* about the J-curve problem, in isolation, as such.

Following this conclusion, for the rest of the book, I shall treat the J-curve problem as of special additional importance only to the extent that it enhances other problems. By making life more difficult for people with below-average IQ, it obviously does. The solutions there, however, lie with those problems as such. It is not conceivable to help the underclass by some means, whatever they might be, that reduced the productivity of the overclass. Nor, in a market economy, is it possible to repress the process whereby people are rewarded for their productivity.

None of this implies, of course, that we cannot help the underclass by redistributing more income from the right hand, high up, 'Pareto'

end of the distribution as a whole, towards the left hand, low down,
bell-like end of the distribution as a whole.

The problem of insecurity

The working classes were always insecure. Before World War II they
were very insecure. They were basically hired on a weekly basis and
even in good times, many micro events could cause a person to be out
of work from one week to the next. And before World War II, even in
the best of times, although new jobs could be found, it was never easy.

Then came the golden age. Working-class 'contracts' of employment, such as they were, never exceeded a week. The difference was
that if one lost a job, or chose to give one up, one could usually find
another. Some middle-class people called this 'over-full' employment.
There were no more servants. But it was a situation which, with the
benefit of hindsight, gave great freedom, now lost, to many young
people. They did not necessarily desire secure employment. They
desired to be free to quit a job and maybe travel abroad. That was
much more practical if one knew that with reasonable effort and
adaptability one could get back into employment when needed. That
life has not disappeared, but it is not what it was.

Since the middle or early eighties, however, there is a new factor
in the situation – middle-class insecurity. Consequently the problem
has become topical: it is a fundamental modern political fact (at the
heart, of course of the voting paradox) that today the middle class has
more votes than the underclass. Will Hutton was surprised by the sales
of his book. The Group-of-Seven summit on employment problems,
held in the northern French city of Lille on April 1 1996, sent out
statements from thoughtful British and American representatives (the
latter being one of the world's leading economic theorists, Joe Stiglitz)
concerning the problem. The Stiglitz position (see box) was that
although lifetime jobs were no longer possible we should aim for
security of *employability*. The British Conservative-government
position was that the problem did not really exist: it was basically a
state of mind.

The reader will have noticed that I have not discussed the insecurity

The Stiglitz Plan for Employability

In an informal presentation at the late March 1996, Group of Seven Summit meeting at Lille, France, Joe Stiglitz, US Chairman of the Council of Economic Advisors is reported to have suggested the following elements in a programme aimed to reduce the costs and increase the benefits of job mobility:

1 A good rate of macroeconomic growth to create new jobs replacing lost jobs,
2 High quality general education facilitating re-employability,
3 State assistance and guidance to help redundant workers, where appropriate, to re-target their careers,
4 Public housing policies facilitating geographical mobility,
5 Increased portability of pensions,
6 Increased portability of health insurance.

The reader will have no difficulty in seeing that the Stiglitz emphasis on the interaction between the demand and supply sides of the problem is exactly in line with the general theme of this book. Without growth, the jobs are not there and points (1) through (6) can do nothing. With growth, they can be potent.

problem at all since I first mentioned it in Chapter 1. There are two reasons. I think the cause of middle clas insecurity is an offshoot of the same technical and organizational forces which generally created the J-curve problem. As a result of the IT revolution, the process whereby people contribute to the productivity of others is now much more susceptible to out-sourcing. Out-sourcing increases insecurity because small specialized organizations, by the laws of statistics, not only experience larger fluctuations than large organizations, but also have proportionately smaller financial resources to carry people over trade cycles. In some sectors of the economy, this has created a state of affairs where virtually every professional is effectively a freelance.

The other side of the coin is that average productivity has probably increased, and, as we have seen, in the UK *average* real earnings have increased. 'Insecurity' is part of the price of the higher earnings. Many 'freelances' have more work than they can cope with. (I have more than one friend who, after the shock of redundancy from what they thought was a life-time job, followed by some difficult months or even years, have succeeded in re-establishing themselves as free-lances, and are now earning so much more money that even if the opportunity offered, they would not go back.) In consequence, by an argument paralleling the argument of the middle part of the previous section, we cannot say that, from this factor in isolation, total welfare has been affected, on balance, adversely.

To that conclusion there is an important qualification, namely that it is possible, if not likely, that middle-class people today have less choice than before as between secure and insecure careers. Among the working classes, the more insecure a job, the worse it was paid. Among the middle classes, there was, over a certain range, the opposite choice. In some fields, however, even if one would have preferred the freelance life, the choice was not freely available, because the large organizations, holding, for good economic reasons, in-house staff, had little incentive to out-source. Now, in the same fields, the in-house type of job may no longer exist. Such a loss of choice represents a loss of welfare.

Here again, however, I do not see how we can put the clock back. Small out-sourcing firms are very productive. Whether the tax system needs some adaptation to reflect the full situation of freelances is an open question. At first sight it does seem hard taxing people at a rate of progression based on current earnings, but many freelances are taxed as businesses, with various rights to carry forward losses, so the total situation is unclear.

The worry of insecurity is partly the worry caused by not knowing where one's next commission is coming from, even though, on the odds, it will be there. Or for insecure employees, it is the fear that almost anyone in the firm is liable to sudden redundancy. Or that the firm itself, being small, however good it is, has a high risk of insolvency. The worry is there for people who do not actually experience adversity as well as for those who do.

The worry is a worry of general loss of control of one's destiny and also, for the middle-class, of falling into relative deprivation. Not many end up qualifying for income support, but today the fears of both the deprivation and possibly the actual disgrace are always there. It is my impression that this was also very much the case, among the middle classes, in Victorian times.

My policy conclusion is exactly the opposite of current conventional wisdom. The best way to reduce the worry is to reduce the consequences which are worried about. This clearly means increasing the 'generosity' of the welfare safety net. Let me not beat about the bush and make my heresy clear. If one is a person who is seriously concerned about the loss of total welfare caused by the worry of middle-class insecurity, one should make income support available in case of redundancy or bad business, *at rates related to previous earnings*. Something not unlike that has been in place in the countries such as the Netherlands for some time past. For fiscal reasons, it is under re-consideration. And that is the point. More generous benefits mean higher taxes, which would, and should, mainly be paid by the overclass. Properly informed of the calculations, will they vote for it? If the answer is 'yes', I will vote for it also; if not I will not.

The priority of growth

The upshot is that the central problem is the underclass and the central cause of that problem insufficient long term economic growth – in the sense of demand for goods, supply of capacity and demand for general labour. Other causes (such as technology, trade, services, women and public policy) have been major supplementary factors. All, however, interact with growth. And as we have looked into them further, we have found that most were inevitable, positively desirable or both. Generally we have found they are clocks which cannot and/or should not be put back.

The issue of protectionism

In the case of trade, with all respect to Sir James Goldsmith, whose two books[1] deserve more intellectual credit than some have given them, I think he is essentially proposing an international version of Hernstein and Murray's 'custodial' society. He advocates increased tariff barriers and increased migration barriers, and he has a general programme with similarities to those of American populists such as Perot or Buchanan. Because he recognises the potential effects of trade on income distribution, like other populists, his programme is not conventionally conservative. 'Liberals' cannot dismiss it out of hand for having no prospect of increasing, or forestalling further decreases in total welfare in the North. It is morally objectionable however because unless one believes that the economic situations of the First and Third Worlds have already been reversed, by pulling world income distribution back from South to North, the Goldsmith programme is likely to decrease, or forestall an increase, in the welfare of the world. Unless one is a racist, the programme thus fails the John

---

1   *The Trap*, 1993, and *The Response*, 1995, in References.

Rawls test. Clearly, if one is not a racist, one must assume that when the imaginary spirits make their imaginary choices not knowing who they will be, among the future things they do not know is their country of birth, or the colour of their skin.

Beyond all that, I think most informed observers of the current scene would say that the Goldsmith programme is also physically unfeasible.

The response to technology

The role of technology in stretching out the Pareto (ie upper) end of the income distribution has already been discussed. Technology, in increasing *average* productivity in the mid-range distribution, relative to that in the low-range, has obviously also contributed to the problem of the underclass. There are also the findings of Borjas and Ramey discussed in Chapter 4.[1] If technology destroys low-end jobs, growth should re-create them. That used to happen. Now it doesn't. Why? The blame cannot be laid at the door of the technology, and in any case, how can we reverse the technology? The blame for the adverse macroeconomic effects of the technology must be laid at the door of the growth slow-down.

The welfare state as damage limitation

The reader can easily see that similar arguments apply to all the other supplementary causes bar public policy. Public policy in the Anglo-Saxon countries in the nineteen-eighties and early nineties exacerbated the situation. But it was clearly not the only factor. Reversing just those policies will not cure all. Much of what we have to say below will, however, imply a general *bouleversement* of current 'Anglo-Saxon' policy (more precisely the policy of the post-Thatcher Conservative government and the policy of the majority party in the Congress; the policy of the Clinton Administration is another matter).

Therefore much of the remainder of this chapter and this book will be devoted to growth.

The problem of globalization

The following destructive trio of propositions is often heard in debates on growth policy:

(a)   On account of 'globalization' of financial markets, it is difficult

---

1   1995, in References.

      if not impossible for the government of any economy other than the US or China (? + Japan) to pursue a significantly independent macroeconomic policy.

(b)   On account of 'political constraints' it is also impossible to envisage a practical coordinated international programme.

(c)   Ergo, it is impossible to do anything about anything.

So many people are openly or subconsciously impregnated with these ideas that I have a major difficulty of presentation. I want to describe first a 'national' then an 'international' policy, the latter flowing naturally from the former. But, as I proceed along my 'national' path of description, I am constantly challenged by the ghosts of the triad. 'You can't do that', they cry, 'because the other countries won't, and the markets won't allow you to go it alone.' The problem is not that there is no truth in the warnings. The problem is that discussion is blocked. We want first to find out what is good for the peoples and nations of the world, then maybe discuss why political leaders or 'markets' oppose it. Not in this book, but maybe elsewhere, there could then be a discussion of how to get the bastards out of their blocking positions and put away, maybe, into one of Anglo-Saxonia's new prisons.

    Therefore I proceed in a way which conservatives always find naive. I first discuss a 'national' policy as if the government in question was the government of virtually the whole OECD, possibly, but not necessarily, excluding Japan. In order to keep our feet on the ground this policy will in fact be cast against the back-drop of an imaginary real country looking rather like the contemporary UK, only very much larger.

    This imaginary country, being extremely large, is free of 'global' constraints. (To some extent it *is* the globe.) Then, and only then is it useful to discuss the international dimension, ie what the nations need to do collectively to free the programme of globinical shackles.

A policy for growth

The fundamental problem of macroeconomic growth policy is a conflict between the short term and the long term. In the short term the economy's capacity to produce goods and employ labour is constrained by physical capital, business organization and micro markets. In the long term it is precisely this capacity we desire to increase. One group of factors influencing the long term can be called 'supply side', the other is the demand side.

On the **demand side**, it is a *necessary* but not sufficient condition that businesses, in contemplating expansion should not only expect that demand will be growing, but that it will be growing reliably. Looking into the future, managers face the opposing risks of being caught with too little or too much capacity. The one implies loss of *potential* profit, the other the danger of losing one's job in a liquidity crisis. The strength and firmness of business confidence in the growth of macro demand crucially affects the balance between the two.

But, and it is the unkindest but of all, the only obvious way to create expectations of future growing demand is to create the reality of current high demand. That process, however, is constrained by fear of inflation. After a long period of low investment, the level of capacity in the British economy, now in the middle nineteen-nineties, is low. Demand expansion may yet quite early collide with capacity constraints, possibly encouraging sellers to push up margins and either, therefore, reducing real wages or stimulating nominal wage claims. Demand side policy is therefore a balancing act. At any one moment, the constraints are biting. Success in pushing against the constraints, without generating unacceptable inflation fear, leads to faster growth of capacity and hence to reducing the constraints. In the short term, therefore, there is a limit to the *sustainable growth rate*. In the long term, the fundamental aim of demand-side policy is to *increase* the sustainable rate.

The fundamental aim of **supply side** policy is to increase the *flexibility* of the sustainable rate. That is to say, we desire that business is as 'bullish' as possible for *given* expectation of demand growth. The greater the amount of capacity expansion business is disposed to venture, with given profits and demand expectations, the more *flexible* the sustainable growth rate, and the less daunting the task of demand side policy. Thus the fundamental role of supply side policy is to reduce the conflict between the long term and the short term.

The demand side

It immediately follows that the most important general change of policy is a heavily emphasised government indication that a large increase in the sustainable rate of growth is the first priority of all its policies. For example, the Chancellor (chief economic minister) instead of saying, as he is recently reported to have said,[1] that it was his ambition to reduce inflation to zero, should have said it was his ambition to increase by half the sustainable rate of growth. Notice that such a statement does not abandon the desire for inflation control. Sustainable growth *requires* that inflation be no more than an acceptable maximum.

As a matter of fact, since growth is actually an intermediate target, it would be better still for the government to frame its fundamental priorities in a way that is more relevant to the distribution problem. Therefore, the government could better state its target in real wages. For example the government could state an ambition *to increase by half over a period of years the real hourly wage rates of low paid workers while at the same time <u>reducing</u> Low-Ed non-employment* (taking account of forecast trends of the effective labour supply).

The government should also set a '**target-maximum' for inflation** in the sense that provided inflation, as measured by actual, rather than proxy indicators, is below the target maximum rate or, if near the target rate, not rapidly accelerating, the government will undertake always to *expand* (not merely hold constant) macroeconomic real demand. Brisk

---

1   See page 94 above. One hopes the reported statement was no more than one Mr. Clarke's famous off-the-cuffs, for it obviously makes no economic sense. Who would benefit if inflation came down to zero? Subsequently on June 30, 1996, Mr. Clarke gave a long interview to *The Times*, in which he said many remarkable things, including the proposition that the fundamental aim of economic policy should be to promote *rising living standards and secure employment* for the general mass of the people. At that point he sounded indistinguishable from his official political opponents, the Labour Party, who two weeks later issued a manifesto (*New Labour*, 1996, in References) where fear of inflation was emphasised at least as much as desire for faster sustainable growth. In the same interview, however, Mr. Clarke also indicated that he would regard a growth rate of real output of 4 per cent per annum as a sign that the economy was overheating, thus giving yet another example of the problem of 'irrational expectations' we discussed in Chapter 3 (pp 104-7).

growth of macroeconomic real output will not be taken as a danger signal as such. Rapid declines in the official unemployment rate, however, if forecast to generate such rapid wage increases that, after allowing for productivity increases expected with rising output, there is a concrete forecast of inflation above the target rate, can be accepted as genuine danger signals.

A reasonable figure for the target maximum inflation rate would be four per cent.

The supply side

The latter part of Chapter 3[1] discussed the reasons why the adverse effects of the troubles that began in the mid nineteen seventies had stayed around so along, continuing and exacerbating the problem of the underclass. For the moment leaving aside the international dimension, the discussion found that in addition to the general persistence of fear of inflation over desire for growth, three specific additional factors had been at work: excessive real interest rates,[2] perverse financial-market expectations[3] and excessive take-over activity.[4]

In the case of **interest rates**, the fundamental task of policy is to create a permanent expectation of substantially lower future nominal short rates relative to expected inflation. If that is achieved real long rates will fall.

Creating the expectation of lower future short rates depends not only on bringing down actual current short rates (expanding the money supply as necessary) but also on creating the belief that the reductions are permanent. The negative effect on this endeavour of the historical accumulation of public debt has probably been exaggerated, but it is a 'real' factor in the perceptions of the markets and hence the factors affecting long term credibility.

---

1   Page 92 and after.
2   Page 96 and after.
3   Page 104 and after.
4   Page 108 and after.

It follows that, provided it is not obsessive, the general aim of restraining government borrowing is valid: in the long run excessive government borrowing does have a negative net effect on the sustainable growth rate and total welfare.

It is also necessary to create an expectation of reduced *variability* in future short rates, in order to reduce the risk premium of long over short rates which has been increased by governments relying on the short term nominal interest rate as an instrument of macroeconomic management.

Both for the purpose of reducing long-term interest rates and for the purpose of reducing perverse financial-market expectations, it must be a determined aim of policy to reduce reliance on short term interest rates as the instrument of macroeconomic management. Macro management needs a battery of weapons, including fiscal policy.

Reasonable interest-rate targets would be that expected future short rates should be little greater than expected inflation, in the hope that real long rates can be reduced to their 1950-70 and 1880-1900 levels, ie to around two and a half per cent.

In the case of **take-overs**, the essential objectives of policy would be to reduce the intensity of take-over activity and encourage *long-term* efficiency in business management while minimizing adverse effects on short term efficiency or management complacency.

We need a combination of legal and fiscal measures designed to create moderate bias in favour of retained profits and, in the event of take-over or merger offers, in favour of incumbent managements. One is aiming to moderately twist rewards towards existing management and employees, and correspondingly away from shareholders, so that the net effect on the flexibility[1] of the macroeconomic sustainable growth rate – after allowing for offsetting effects from the lowered return to new equity investment – is positive.

---

1   See p 191.

The international dimension: general considerations
There are two specific ways in which the international economic system may inhibit an individual country from pursuing a positive growth policy.

First, if it attempts to achieve a faster actual growth rate than the average of other countries, it may (but of course – witness Japan – by no means necessarily will) experience an increasing external deficit.

The solution to this problem is **creeping devaluation** of the real exchange rate, ie the actual exchange rate relative to the domestic price level.

However, in a **currency union** (eg the EMU), with devaluation ruled out, it is essential that target rates for sustainable growth be harmonized. In effect this means that a currency union must either contain a *de facto* central macroeconomic government or the members must adopt some other effective procedure. If they fail to do that, the currency union is as likely to *reduce* as to increase the total welfare of the population of the union.

Second, there is the problem of 'global irrationality' as discussed in Chapter 3:[1] owing to the huge increase in speculative currency movements, relative to government foreign-exchange reserves, governments fear that 'go it alone' policies may provoke currency crises, with de-stabilizing economic and political effects that are likely to vitiate the policies themselves.

The solutions are governmental and inter-governmental fiscal and legal measures to reduce the ease of and increase the cost of short-term international money movements.

In this connection governments should give extremely serious consideration to the 'Tobin Plan'. This is a proposal first made, with

---

1   Page 107 and after.

the foresight of genius, nearly a quarter of a century ago[1] by Yale Keynesian economist and Nobel Laureate, Jim Tobin. The basic idea is a turnover tax, set at a very low rate – between a quarter and a half of one per cent – on every transaction where one currency is bought or sold for another. For a person or institution needing foreign exchange for long or medium term purposes, for example for business travel or basic medium term commercial transactions, the cost would be very small relative to all the other costs involved in the activities concerned. But for a currency trader who may go into or out of a foreign 'position' as many as a hundred times a year, the calculated cost becomes weighty, and quite sufficient to reduce materially the profitability of frequent as against less frequent transactions. Tobin forcefully argued that the total effect would be to make markets less volatile and thus strengthen the defences of governments in general. Consequently, it seems clear that the Tobin Tax would inevitably promote general economic growth and total welfare.[2]

The international dimension: specific bodies

The Group of Seven

Government ministers of the United States, Canada, Japan, Germany, France, Italy and the UK hold periodic 'summit' meetings to discuss the affairs of the world. In recent years these meetings have been widely criticized as ineffective, especially with regard to economic

---

1   To be precise, in 1972. For full details and discussion of pros and cons, including technical objections (which do not seem very weighty), see the recent authoritative conference report on the subject, edited by the Cambridge-trained distinguished Pakistani international economist and administrator, Dr. Mahbub al Haq, and two others. See Haq, Kaul and Grunberg, *The Tobin Tax*, 1996, in References.

2   The tax would be agreed collectively by the major governments and then collected at domestic points of sale. The total revenue (of the order of a thousand billion dollars a year) would however be pooled, part kept for international projects (eg UN peacekeeping) and the rest returned to countries in proportions based on internationally negotiated criteria. The prospective revenue from a relatively painless tax (with minimal distorting effects on desirable incentives) is a major additional merit.

growth.[1] On April 1 1996 they held a meeting in Lille, Northern France, to discuss employment. The US sent a strong delegation consisting of the Finance Secretary, Labor Secretary Robert Reich and the Chairman of the Council of Economic Advisors, Joe Stiglitz, an extremely famous economist from Cambridge Massachusetts who probably has an IQ at least half a standard deviation higher than that of anyone else who was present.

The French sent the President of their country, M. Jacques Chirac, and the OECD (see below) sent its Secretary General. Significantly, the British were represented by a junior Treasury Minister, William Waldegrave, and Gillian Shephard, Minister for Education (whose brief on 'insecurity' has already been mentioned) – the Conservative government having recently given a good indication of its priorities by abolishing the long-standing Department of Employment (previously the Ministry of Labour) and merging it with Education.

According to reports,[2] Stiglitz, apart from his suggestions about the insecurity problem, already noted above, also reported research indicating some encouraging developments in the US economy that appear to have occurred under the Clinton Administration: the 'quality' of new jobs (value-added, technological orientation) created has been high, real wages have made some gains and the rise of inequality has slowed down and possibly halted.

Both President Chirac and Jean-Claude Paye, Secretary General of the OECD,[3] referred in effect to the comparison of 'The American way' and the 'European way' as characterized in Chapter 5, Figure 5.2 (low wages[4] v non-employment) above. M. Chirac looked for a 'third way', but M. Paye, while conceding that neither way was without defects, said personally he would prefer the American or 'Anglo-

---

1   For example, Fred Bergsten, extremely experienced and respected international economist and administrator, founder-Director of the Washington, DC, Institute for International Economics (and closely associated with the Democratic Party) was reported in London *Observer* on 9 June 1996, as saying, 'The G-7 countries have failed to act on a wide range of issues in which world leadership was desired'.

2   See *The Times* and *The Financial Times*, London, April 2, 1996.

3   M. Paye retired from the post in June 1996.

4   The term used, as is the current convention, was not 'low' but 'flexible'. Obviously what is meant is flexible downwards.

Saxon' model.

The reader will recognise that the problem with M. Chirac's position, as reported, is that he made no mention of economic growth: if my arguments are accepted, without faster growth, no third way exists. The problem with M. Paye's statement is that we do not know whether it was intended to be scientific or a 'value judgement'.[1] Did he have data for something I personally do not find credible, ie that he is sure that average total welfare is higher in Anglo-Saxonia than in western continental Europe? Or is he merely indicating a rather likely probability that persons such as himself tend to be better off in the former model than in the latter? The reader knows that the problem here is the one identified by John Rawls and discussed above in the later sections of Chapter 5. I feel, however, that, more than anyone, the head of an international organization should view the world from the point of view of the disembodied spirit, rather than of someone who already knows who they are and where they come from.

More generally, my reaction to the reports of the April-96 G-7 summit is not totally pessimistic. Although the nations' leaders clearly have a hundred miles to go in understanding the link between problems discussed at Lille and economic growth, they do appear to have the beginnings of a mental framework. President Chirac, as reported, seemed furthest along the line in that he could reasonably be interpreted as openly perceiving that the problem is one of comparing alternative income distributions – something that others, such as the British Conservatives or M. Paye, if they understand it, do not desire to admit.

The European Union

For me, this is a very sad story. I happen to be a lifelong supporter of the idea of a strong European economic and political union, so strong that it would be a *de facto* 'federal' nation state. This puts me in a minority position in many circles, not only in my own country but also on the Continent. My basic reasons, like the reasons motivating my opponents, are largely subjective: my patriotism to my own country, which is very strong, is emulated by my patriotism to Europe. Today that motive is enhanced by the proposition that if Britain and Europe

---

1   See page 161.

want to save *their* underclass, it is *in principle* much easier, given the global environment, to do so from the basis of a strong regional grouping. Sadly, *in practice* it is another matter.

The whole history of the EU is bedevilled by the problem of 'political feasibility' as I have discussed it above. In logic it is a project for total economic union or it is nothing. After the full Maastricht programme is implemented, the only remaining independent macroeconomic powers left to the member governments will be taxation. However, as the experience of the United States clearly shows, with free trade, free movement of capital and labour and a common currency, the effective scope for local variations in taxation is small. Local income tax in the District of Columbia is maybe effectively five points higher than down the road in Maryland, yet many people remain content to reside within the District boundary; but if the difference were large, things would obviously be different. The absence of an overt tax-harmonization process in the EU is already producing absurd spectacles of southern English residents rushing back and forth across the Channel loaded up with, among other things, cans of *English* beer.

But for 'political' reasons it has always been necessary to present the EU project as falling far short of federation. In the resulting programme of illusion, it turned out to be feasible to sell the idea of a common currency so long as little was said about taxation and little or nothing about macroeconomic demand management or economic growth. Then, however, as the currency union began to seem like a political practical reality, the German government, using the bargaining power of her own strong currency, insisted on including macroeconomic elements reflecting her own popular ideology – fear of inflation, more fear of inflation, and an obsession with the intrinsic wickedness of fiscal deficits, irrespective (see above) of causes and origins. Hence the famous Maastricht 'convergence' criteria which actually say nothing about economic convergence at all.

It is now widely recognized that the countries who are currently preparing themselves, under the terms of the Treaty, for the advent of the common currency are suffering from the obvious deflationary bias of the plan. I have said repeatedly that I believe that total welfare is still currently higher in western Europe than in the UK or the US, but with the slow pace of total growth, and the sharp rise of open unemployment, that situation may not long survive. The failure, if it occurs, will be due to the perversity of the Maastricht criteria. The whole 'Deutschmark area' probably needs to devalue against the world, but Maastricht provides no mechanism for such an adjustment.

The research and papers of the EU Commission are widely criticized as confused.[1] Although they speak of the employment-creating role of economic growth, they seem unable to distinguish between the demand-side and supply-side of the relationship. They employ a complex statistical economic model which at heart suffers from the type of confusion, explained in Chapter 3,[2] concerning the nature of the relationship between real wages and the demand for labour. The member governments fare no better; in Edinburgh, Scotland, in late 1992 they vaguely agreed to an expenditure pro-gramme intended to boost, in more or less 'Keynesian' fashion, EU investment and output. But the sum agreed was equivalent to well under one per cent of EU GDP and was, in fact, never spent: the EU has strong powers to regulate bathing beaches, but little power over economic growth.[3] And perhaps the most frightening omen of all can be found in an early April 1996 report from the putative European Central Bank (EMI[4]) which simply takes for granted that the run-up to the union will be an unpleasant deflationary experience. What else is new? More serious is the prospect that the plan, if unrevised, will yield unpleasant experiences for ever. The countries concerned are of course the same countries whose data are represented in the figures for France and Germany presented in Table 6.1. We have seen how those figures suggest that in continental western Europe, the adverse effects of demand deficiency in the labour market, rather than being concen-trated on an underclass, appear to spread more widely (as compared to

---

1　This is particularly marked in the important Commission White Paper on growth and employment, 1993, in References.

2　See page 70.

3　Four years later, Mr. Monti, the EU single-market Commissioner, said in an interview with *The European* newspaper (20 June, 1996) that the single market 'has not delivered as we had hoped at the macroeconomic level'. He gave several explanations (one of which was that the single market was incomplete or incompletely enforced!) none of which even hinted at the obvious one, namely that the community had no growth-oriented macroeconomic management.

4　European Monetary Institute. Reports in London press, April 3, 1996.

the UK and the US) among the whole population. That being so, it is absolutely certain that the deflationary bias of the Maastricht criteria will reduce the total welfare of the whole region.

Although I am more 'pro-European' than 99 per cent not only of my countrymen but also of all Europeans, if I had to participate now in a referendum on the EMU plan in its present (1996) form, I would not know how to vote. So let me conclude this section by asking how in my opinion the Treaty would need to be revised so that a person who supports my type of economic policy could vote for it. The answer is as follows:

1 Provisions relating to fiscal deficits to be revised to be more pragmatic: the only essential objection to public debt is via the extent, if any, of the adverse effect on the ability of governments to hold down interest rates without creating excessive inflation.

2 Every country joins the system fully accepting that membership implies commitment to the 'real' objectives of the type of growth policy described above.

3 The provisions for an embryo central bank be replaced by a comprehensive system of macroeconomic government based on the assumption that the task will be to accept both the long term concepts and the *day-to-day, month-to-month, year-to-year operation* of the growth policy in respect of monetary policy, interest rates and taxation and fiscal policy.

4 Given that in any monetary union, interest rates denominated in the common currency will necessarily converge, it will be the commonly accepted objective to bring down expected short term real rates substantially and permanently so as to aim for a target of resulting long term real rates not much above two per cent.

5 As well as 'harmonization' of tax policy the revised treaty would also envisage fairly brisk progress towards harmonization of public expenditure patterns and the structure of the welfare state.

Any reader with a minimal knowledge of the political history of the Maastricht treaty is likely to regard this list as extremely unrealistic. Could one consider something less that would get my vote for a Europe redesigned to protect and raise the total economic welfare of the region? The only answer that I can give, in 1996, is that if the present British economics minister, Kenneth Clarke, somehow freed from all effects of his current membership of the British Conservative

Party, plus the present leader of the British Labour Party, Tony Blair, plus the President of France, M. Chirac, plus other good people such as Romano Prodi, Prime Minister of Italy, plus like-minded leaders from EU countries such as Sweden got together, I have little doubt that they could come up with an economically and politically acceptable and feasible project. This they could then present to the German government in a form it could accept, especially now that employment has become a major issue in that country.

As things are, the actual EMU project, with or without British membership, may well be sabotaged by its own contradictions. The deflationary situation in Europe has apparently produced, horror of all the ultimate horrors, a budget deficit in Germany. Hoist by her own petard,[1] Germany could in theory be prevented from joining the scheme of her own particular devising.

The OECD (Organization for Economic Cooperation and Development)

This is another very sad story. We have a prestigious inter-governmental body, with a historic reputation for detached, high quality statistical and economic policy-analysis, which has taken the appearance of a centre-right think-tank. First came the appointment as chief economist, some years back now, of my friend David Henderson who has given brilliant lectures explaining why he doesn't believe in macroeconomics at all. Then came the appointment of M. Paye, whom I have never met and of whom I have only the query (but it is big one) concerning the logic of his preference (discussed above) for the 'American way'. Then came the notorious supply-sider Jobs Study,[2] already criticized directly or implicitly a number of times in these pages and finally, with apparently excellent timing on the eve of the Lille summit, the organization published a hymn of praise for the current British economy, which may be compared with the more complex picture we have found in Chapters 2 and 3, above.

After this diatribe, I should say that I have received substantial help in preparing this book – in time, data and constructive advice – from

---

1　Meaning loosely, 'blown up by one's own bomb'. 'Petard' was a mediaeval nickname for an explosive charge, derived from a French word meaning 'young fart'.

2　OECD 1994, in References.

the staff of the OECD, who have pointed out to me, when I have made my comments, that it is an organization designed to reflect the views of governments. I quite agree that it reflects the views of the Anglo-Saxon governments of the nineteen-eighties and early nineties. Present and future governments are another matter. It is obvious the OECD does not reflect the views of the current US Labor Secretary, and it is my impression that the same is true, at least to a degree, with respect to the whole current US Administration. And after the next British election, who knows?[1]

There is not much more to be said. My simple recommendation with regard to the OECD is: read this book, agree with it, and act accordingly. That will not save the underclass, but will surely help.

The United Nations

The United Nations standing conference on trade and development (UNCTAD), whose headquarters is in Geneva, has produced reports, commissioned from consultants, directly bearing on the problem of non-employment and economic growth, that – in clarity, research depth and logical coherence – stand out from those of other organiza-

---

1   Written in May, 1996. On *18 July, 1996,* the organization published its annual *Employment Outlook* (not in References) accompanied by a press release which showed that they had now come a little way in the right direction but still have a long way to go. They said,

> 'High and persistent unemployment is only one manifestation of the poor labour market performance in many OECD countries. OECD societies also confront some worrying inequalities which are straining the social fabric. In some countries, such as the UK and the US, earnings have have become considerably more unequal.... The risk now facing a number of countries is that labour market exclusion can easily turn into poverty and dependency. Social protection systems can alleviate poverty, but they cannot promote participation in society unless they are closely tied to measures to tackle labour market problems. ...The OECD *Jobs Study,* which was endorsed by Ministers in 1994, sought to provide answers to this and related questions. Work over the past two years has confirmed that the *Jobs Study* recommendations were the right ones.'

Tiptoeing past the complacency of the last sentence one can say it is good the authors have belatedly discovered what has been happening to poverty and the Anglo-Saxon wage distribution, but extremely distressing that they still cannot understand that the general problem is as much a macro problem, involving both the demand and supply sides of the economy, rather than a specific problem of a structurally misfunctioning labour market.

The main body of the report, containing what looks like a very valuable statistical study of earnings inequality, is much better. The discussion of the causes of increased inequality however, is superficial, and apparently makes no reference at all to economic growth or the macro demand for labour.

tions. The reader who desires to test this assertion need only sample the listings under Eatwell and Rowthorn in the References. No doubt it is not a coincidence that both these persons, friends and ex-colleagues of mine, are also ex-Marxists. What a pity that well-trained professional economists, of no particular political orientation, working in Brussels or Paris are not permitted, owing to the exigencies of inter-governmental political reality, to do work of similar quality.

Damage limitation and the welfare state

The concept of failure

It has to be admitted that the policy programme advocated in this book may fail. By that I would mean that over the next ten or twenty years real earnings at the bottom end of the income and IQ-distribution failed to make a substantial gain in absolute terms: male non-employment does not decline and bottom-end real hourly wages make only small increases. The reason could be either that, although my diagnosis placing heavy emphasis on growth is valid, the governments are unable to act on it. Alternatively, my diagnosis may be wrong. In either case the implications are quite grave because, as we have seen, in a weak labour market more specific remedial or palliative measures (education, training employment subsidies) are unlikely to increase either wages or total employment.

Of course, there will still be many jobs, some at not impossible wages and conditions, for Low-IQ/Low-Ed people who seek them out. To celebrate the fact that I have almost finished this book, I go out of the house, along the banks of the river Thames, to my favourite pub, which also serves good coffee. The sun is shining, it is Easter Friday, and many people and families from all walks of life are sitting around drinking, eating and watching the rowing crews practising for next day's Oxford v Cambridge Boat Race. I go inside and order a coffee. While I wait at the bar, a male person, 25-30, with a Slavic accent, comes up and in limited English asks the head barman for full-time work as a dish washer. By the time my cappucino has been poured, he has been hired! I happen to know what the wage will be, about £3 (probably worth about $3 in Montana) an hour. Quite surprised, I remark on the incident to two obviously fully-employed female secretaries who are enjoying glasses of wine. 'Well, it's better than sitting around doing nothing on the dole,[1] isn't it', we all agree. 'Anyway, he's probably an illegal, and can't get the dole.'

I contemplate that if 'inflexibilities' in the labour market had made it impossible to hire that person so quickly, at so low a wage, he would have been worse off and my coffee would either have been slower served, less politely served, more expensive or all three. That is what this book has been all about. But suppose that man, in truth, if the dole had been available to him, for one reason or another preferred to accept it rather than work at such a wage, can one necessarily morally blame him?

The implication is that the moral basis of the welfare state is completely different in a weak labour market than in a strong one. The weak state of the market is *not the fault* of the people who suffer in it. At that moment, the welfare safety net becomes a obligation on society and should have no moral strings attached. Furthermore, in those circumstances we must have an ambivalent attitude to 'welfare scroungers'. Do we really want them trying too hard to seek work? If they are successful, who knows whose job they will take away?

It has lately become fashionable among economists to get excited about the problems, costs and supposed inefficiencies of the welfare state. On this, Tony Atkinson has rather nicely written,

> The Welfare State has in recent years been rediscovered by economists. When I first began work on the economics of social security in the 1960s, the subject scarcely appeared in the economics literature.... The situation has now changed dramatically.... Reform of the Welfare State is seen as one of the key policy issues of the 1990s.[2]

Another good quotation is, yet again, from Chancellor Clarke. He was

---

1 English slang for unemployment money.
2 Atkinson, 1995, in References.

recently reported as saying,[1]

> The whole country is now seized with the feeling that the welfare state has to be reformed in some way, to be made affordable. I do find that interesting but I don't think we should be panicked into doing things which would damage the welfare state. A modern European state requires a strong welfare state to increase people's willingness to accept change.

Many people, I think including Atkinson, believe that much of this discussion is a diversion. On account of the problems discussed in this book, the fiscal pressure of the safety net has increased, and the taxpayers do not like it. There are, however, no doubt some real concerns over the long-term transfer burden of maintaining people after retirement (the 'pensions' problem) and in different forms in different countries there are chronic problems with health care. But what about the 'problem' of the cost of social security, the actual safety net – all those payments in cash or kind (in the UK, income support, housing benefit, unemployment benefit and sickness and invalidity benefit) which people may receive because (for one reason or another) otherwise they will starve, freeze or be forced to accept work at wages below any acceptable local minimum? The answer is that at the present time, in the typical OECD country the fiscal cost of the whole net tends to be a figure equivalent to about eight per cent of GDP. A fully-employed person pays between 30 and 40 per cent of their income in direct and indirect taxes, about a quarter of which goes to the safety net. If things get worse, the quarter could become a third.

What do I mean by things getting worse? I mean that if the labour market does not improve, or deteriorates, we will be morally bound to *increase* the 'generosity' of the safety net and also that there may be more claimants. This is the price of damage limitation and on that note I rest my case.

---

1   London *Observer*, 12 May 1996. In the subsequent June 30 *Times* interview already quoted (p 192) he said jocularly, 'The British welfare state doesn't need reforming. I've already reformed it.' More seriously he was referring to his previous Ministerial posts, including Health, where he instituted changes intended to make public services more cost-effective: in strong words he favourably compared efficiency of the British health system with that in the US (of which he was highly critical). Maybe Kenneth Clarke also has other motives. It is pure speculation, but could it be, that with his love of jazz, he knows there is great music that without the welfare state might never have been played?

Summary of the policy recommendations

The following is a list of the specific policy recommendations we have made in this chapter after the subheading on page 190, 'A policy for growth':

1   Governments should indicate that their first priority is the achievement of a substantial increase in the sustainable rate of growth. The same priority also desires an increase in the *flexibility* of the sustainable growth rate, ie an increase in the response to be expected from the supply side of the economy for a given increase in macroeconomic real demand.

2   In the UK and the US, practical ambitions for growth should best be put in the form of a substantial desired increase, over a period of years, in the real hourly wage of the lowest paid workers, accompanied by a decrease, rather than an increase, in non-employment among Low Ed workers. On the west European continent this is modified to read as a general reduction in male non-employment without a general reduction in real salaries and wages.

3   There should be a target maximum for actual inflation below which, in general, policy will always be aiming to expand the real economy (rather merely holding it constant). Actual expansion of the real economy should not be taken as a warning sign. Rapid declines in unemployment, however, would be accepted as warning signs if on established statistical relationships, they suggested an early probability of actual cost inflation accelerating beyond the target maximum inflation rate. A suitable figure for the target maximum inflation rate would be four per cent.

4   Governments should aim to create a permanent reduction in expected future short term interest rates with the ambition of bringing down permanently expected future real long rates to little over two per cent.

5   With the twin aims of helping reduce the risk premium gap between long and short rates (and thus facilitate the reduction of long rates) and of eliminating socially-irrational expectations behaviour in financial markets generally, governments should reduce their reliance on short term interest rates as a weapon of

short term macroeconomic management. They should make more use of fiscal and other policy instruments.

6   In the case of mergers and take-overs, there should be a combination of legal and financial measures designed to create moderate systematic bias in favour of retained profits, incumbent management and long term management efficiency.

7   If a country with a floating exchange rate finds that a positive growth policy is inhibited by slow growth in other countries, the government should encourage a creeping devaluation of the real exchange rate.

8   Fiscal and other measures (such as the Tobin tax) intended to reduce the comparative profitability of short term, as against long term, currency transactions should be very seriously considered.

9   The Group of Seven should put the long growth of output and the demand for labour permanently at the top of its economic agenda and should clarify its understanding of the relation between growth and total welfare.

10   If the European Monetary Union is to avoid having the effect of reducing the total welfare of its member population, it must be drastically revised to adopt a more pragmatic approach to fiscal deficits, a binding commitment to the type of positive growth policy described above, a powerful, operational, central macro-economic government, a binding commitment to effective policies to bring down long term real interest rates to a level not much higher than two per cent, and a brisk programme for harmonization of taxes and public-expenditure patterns.

11   The OECD Secretariat should completely revise its current political and economic outlook (which seems near to an ideology) in order to be closer to the likely outlook of its member governments at the turn of the century, and thus better able to contribute to the total welfare of its member populations.

12   If policy succeeds in increasing the actual growth of the real economy, the demand for labour and the real wages of the less advantaged, while also reducing non-employment, most current apparent 'problems' of the Welfare State will tend to fade away.

13   If (12) fails, a strong and 'generous' Welfare State, financed if necessary by higher taxes on the able and successful, will

become a moral imperative. As such it ought to command, but will not necessarily command voting majorities.

Encouraging developments

As we go to press the climate of political and intellectual opinion is improving. It is not improbable that by the year 2000, elected governments representing the majority of the population of the OECD will be governments which could be sympathetic to much of what has been said in this book.

I therefore conclude by reporting some developments that occurred while the manuscript was being copy edited.

1 *'Creating Capacity'* – an essay collection published by Oxford University Press edited by Jonathan Michie and John Grieve Smith[1] – a rich collection of applied studies supported by a wealth of analysis deconstructing contemporary anti-Keynesian arguments.

2   *Wisdom from Felix Rohatyn* – well-known US banker and economic commentator wrote an article in the *Wall Street Journal* which is reported to have attracted the attention of the leader of the British Labour Party. Among other things, he said,

> The social and economic problems we face include job insecurity, enormous income differentials, significant pressure on average incomes, urban quality of life and many others. All require different approaches but the *single most important requirement is the wealth and revenues generated by a higher rate of economic growth.*[2] [emphasis added]

3 *Rich argument from Gordon Brown*

Britain's 'shadow' Chancellor of the Exchequer has made speeches which are historically remarkable coming from a person who expects to be minister of finance. In 20 pages of textual argument there are only three on the subject of public finance. The great weight of what he had to say concerned the human side of total welfare.

Final comments

The reasons for welcoming such developments are obvious. It is not churlish to note that our treatment of economic growth has been

---

1   1996, in References.

2   From an edited version published in the London *New Statesman*, May 3, 1996, p 12.

different from that of Mr. Rohatyn. He appears to be speaking of productivity, whereas (in Chapters 1 and 3 and at the beginning of the present chapter) I have defined growth as the capacity to create both goods *and* employment: unless productivity growth is accompanied by corresponding growth of macro demand and capacity, it is inevitably *damaging* to employment. But we are all speaking in the same cause and we all, I think, share the same compassion.

In the Mitchie and Grieve Smith book there is a powerful chapter[1] called '*The Death of Keynesian Europe*'.

On the resurrection of Keynesian Europe depends the future of the European underclass.

The last remark is in short-hand. The UK and the US have an underclass problem whose causes and cures have been the subject of this book. In addition, continental western Europe, also, has suffered a severe deficiency in the demand for labour, whose effects, however, have been spread more widely through the general population. In 1996, with the exception of the element in the British government represented by Chancellor Kenneth Clarke, the Clinton Administration has a far better understanding of the Keynesian nature of the problem than any government in Europe. Thus the future of the underclass, on both sides of the Atlantic, depends on the resurrection of Keynesian Europe and the continuation of Keynesian America.

---

1   By Grahame Thompson.

References

Adnett, N., and A. Dawson, 1996, Wage subsidies and European unemployment, *Economic Issues*, 1, March, 1-22.

Aitchison, J., and Brown, A., 1969, *The Lognormal Distribution,* Cambridge: Cambridge University Press.

Albert, M., 1991, *Capitalisme Contre Capitalisme,* Paris: Du Seuil.

Arrow, K., 1951, *Social Choice and Individual Values*, New Haven, Conn: Cowles Commission, Yale University.

Atkinson, A., 1983, *Social Justice and Public Policy*, Brighton, England: Wheatsheaf.

Atkinson, A., 1995, *Incomes and the Welfare State*, Cambridge: Cambridge University Press.

Baldassarri, M. (ed), 1994, Equity, Efficiency and Growth: the future of the welfare state, 1, 2, *Rivista di Politica Economica*, 84, 11,12, Nov, Dec, Rome: SIPI.

Barclay, P. (ed), 1995, *Inquiry into Income and Wealth*, Vol 1, York: Joseph Rowntree Foundation.

Barro, R., 1991, Economic growth in a cross-section of countries, *Quarterly Journal of Economics*, 106, 2, May, 407-43.

Barry, B., 1965, *Political Argument*, London: Routledge.

Bartel, A., and F. Lichtenberg, 1987, The comparative advantage of educated workers in implementing the new technology, *Review of Economics and Statistics,* 69, Feb, 343-59.

Batra, R., 1993, *The Myth of Free Trade,* New York: Charles Scribner.

Baumol, W., 1986, Productivity growth, convergence and welfare: what the long-run data show, *American Economic Review*, 76, 4, Dec, 1155-59.

Baumol, W., S. Blackman and E. Wolff, 1989, *Productivity and American Leadership:* the long view, Cambridge, Mass: MIT Press.

Becker, G., 1964, *Human Capital*, New York: Columbia University Press.

Borjas, G., and V. Ramey, 1995, Foreign competition, market power and wage inequality, *Quarterly Journal of Economics,* 110, Nov, 1075-1110.

Bound, J., and G. Johnson, 1992, Changes in the structure of wages in the 1980's: an evaluation of alternative explanations, *American Economic Review,* 82, June, 371-92.

Bridel, P., and G. Busino, 1987, *L'Ecole de Lausanne de Léon Walras à Pasquale Boninsegni,* Lausanne, Switzerland: University of Lausanne.

Buchanan, J., 1962, *The Calculus of Consent,* Ann Arbor, MI: Michigan University Press.

Burtless, G., 1993, The Contribution of employment and hours changes to family income inequality, *American Economic Review,* 83, 2, May (Proceedings), 131-135.

Burtless, G, R. Freeman and R. Solow, 1994, in *Widening Earnings Inequality*, Jane Norwood (ed), Washington, DC: Urban Institute.

Campbell, J., and R. Shiller, 1989, *Yield Spreads and Interest Rate Movements:* a birds-eye view, Discussion Paper No. 66, LSE Financial Markets Group, London: London School of Economics.

Carlen, C., 1981, *The Papal Encyclicals*, 1903-1939, Raleigh, VA: McGrath Publishing Company.

Churchland, P., 1995, *The Engine of Reason*, Cambridge, Mass: MIT Press.

Church of England, 1995, *Staying in the City*, London: Church House Publishing.

Commission of the European Community, 1993, *Growth, Competitivenes and Employment:* the challenges and ways forward into the 21st century, Brussels: EC, COM(93) 700.

Cornwall, J., 1977, *Modern Capitalism:* its growth and transformation, London: Martin Roberston.

Crick, F., 1994, *The Astonishing Hypothesis:* the scientific search for the soul, New York and London: Simon and Schuster.

Cutler, D., and L. Katz, 1991, Macroeconomic performance and the disadvantaged, *Brookings Papers on Economic Activity*, 2, 1-74, Washington , DC: Brookings.

Danziger, S., 1995, *America Unequal,* Cambridge, Mass: Harvard Press.

Debreu, G., 1959, *Theory of Value:* an axiomatic treatment of equilbrium, New York: John Wiley.

Denison, E., 1989, *Estimates of Productivity Change by Industry,* Washington DC: Brookings.

Disraeli, B., 1861, *Sybil:* the two nations. Republished, 1980, Oxford: Oxford University Press.

Domar, E., 1947, Expansion and employment, *American Economic Review,* 37, March, 34-55.

Downs, A., 1957, *An Economic Theory of Democracy,* New York: Harper and Row.

Dupuy, M., and M. Schweitzer, 1994, Are services sector jobs inferior, *Economic Commentary,* Federal Reserve Bank of Cleveland, Feb 1, Cleveland, Ohio: FRBC Research Dept.

Edey, M., and K. Hviding, 1995, *Financial Reform in OECD Countries,* Economics Department Working Paper No 154, Paris: OECD.

Eatwell, J., 1995, *Disguised Unemployment:* the G7 experience, Discussion Paper No. 106, Geneva: UNCTAD.

Eatwell, J., 1996, *International Capital Liberalization*: an evaluation, UNDP Report SSA 96-049, New York: United Nations.

Edleman, G., 1992, *Bright Air, Brilliant Fire:* on the matter of the mind, New York and London: Basic Books and Allen Lane.

Education and Employment Dept Analytical Services, 1995, *Education Statistics for the UK,* London: HMSO.

Elmeskov, J. and K. Pichelmann, 1994, Interpreting Unemployment: the role of labour force participation, *OECD Economic Studies,* No 21, Winter, 139-160, Paris: OECD.

Freeman, R., 1993, How much has de-unionization contributed to the rise in earnings inequality, in S. Danziger and P. Gottschalk, (eds), *Uneven Tides:* rising inequality in America, New York: Russell Sage.

Freeman, R., 1995, Will globalization dominate US labor market outcomes? *Conference on Imports, Exports and the American Worker,* February, Washington, DC: Brookings.

Freeman, W., *Societies of Brains,* Lawrence Erlbaum: Hillsdale, NJ.

Frisch, R., 1959, A complete scheme for computing all direct and cross demand elasticities in a model with many sectors, *Econometrica,* 27, 2, April, 177-96.

Gallup, 1995, *Gallup Political and Economic Index,* London: Gallup House.

Gilbert, M., and I. Kravis, 1954, *International Comparisons of National Products and the Purchasing Power of Currencies,* Paris: OEEC.

Goldsmith, J., 1993, *The Trap,* London: Macmillan.

Goldsmith, J., 1995, *The Response,* London: Macmillan.

Goldstein, M., and J. Frenkel, 1988, *International Coordination of Economic Policies:* scope, methods and effects, WP/88/53, Washington, DC: International Monetary Fund.

Goldstein, M., 1992, *Improving Economic Policy Coordination*: some new and not-so-new proposals, July conference paper, Perugia: Banca d'Italia.

Goleman, D., 1996, *Emotional Intelligence,* London: Bloomsbury.

Gomulka, S., 1990, *The Theory of Technological Change and Economic Growth,* London and New York: Routledge.

Goodwin, R., 1967, Growth cycles, in C. Feinstein (ed), *Capitalism and Economic Growth,* Cambridge: Cambridge University Press.

Goodwin, R., M. Krüger and A. Vercelli, 1984, Non-linear models of fluctuating growth: an international symposium, Siena, in *Lecture Notes on Mathematical and Economic Systems,* 228, Berlin: Springer-Verlag.

Gosling, A., S. Machin and C. Meghir, 1994, What has happened to wages, *Commentary* No. 43, London: IFS.

Gosling, A., and S. Machin, 1995, Trade unions and the dispersion of earnings in British manufacturing establishments, *Oxford Bulletin of Economics and Statistics,* 57, 167-84.

Gottschalk, P., 1995, Changes in the inequality of family income in seven industrialized countries, *American Economic Review,* 85, May (AEA Proceedings), 137-141.

Grilliches, Z., 1994, Productivity, R&D and the data problem, *American Economic Review,* 84, 1, March, 1-13.

Grubb, D., 1982, *Ability and Power over Production in the Distribution of Earnings,* London: Centre for Labour Economics, London School of Economics. Republished, 1985, *Review of Economics and Statistics,* 67, 2, May, 188-194.

Haq, M., I. Kaul, and I. Grunberg, eds, 1996, *The Tobin Tax*: coping with financial volatility, Oxford: Oxford University Press.

Harrod, R., 1939, An essay in dynamic theory, *Economic Journal,* 49, March, 14-33.

Harsanyi, J., 1976, *Essays on Ethics, Social Behaviour and Scientific Explanation,* Dordrecht, Netherlands: Reidel.

Hart, O., and J. Moore, 1993, Debt and seniority: an analysis of the role of hard claims in constraining management, *American Economic Review,* 83, 568-585.

Hart, O., 1993, Optimal capital structure and managerial discretion, in M. Blair (ed), *The Deal Decade,* Washington, DC: Brookings.

Hernstein, R. and C. Murray, 1994, *The Bell Curve:* intelligence and class structure in American life, New York: Free Press.

Heston, A. and R. Summers, 1991, *The Penn World Tables* (diskette), Cambridge, Mass: National Bureau of Economic Research.

Hills, J., 1993, *The Future of Welfare,* London and York: London School of Economics and Rowntree Foundation.

Hills, J., 1995, *Inquiry into Income and Wealth,* Vol 2, York: Rowntree.

Homer, S., and R. Sylla, 1991, *A History of Interest Rates,* New Brunswick, NJ: Rutgers University Press.

Hunt, E., 1995, The role of intelligence in modern society, *American Scientist*, July.

Hutton, W., 1995, *The State We're In*, London: Cape.

International Monetary Fund, 1995, *International Financial Statistics,* Washington, DC: IMF.

Johnson, G. and F. Stafford, 1993, International competition and real wages, *American Economic Review,* 83, May (Proceedings), 128-32.

Kaldor, N., 1966, *Causes of the Slow Rate of Economic Growth of the United Kingdom,* Cambridge: Cambridge University Press.

Kaldor, N., and J. Mirrlees, 1962, A new model of economic growth, *Review of Economic Studies,* 29, 2, June.

Keynes, M., 1936, *The General Theory of Employment, Income and Money,* London:Macmillan.

Kravis. I., A. Heston and B. Summers, 1978, *Comparisons of Real Product and Purchasing Power,* Baltimore: Johns Hopkins Press.

Kravis, I., 1984, International comparisons of real product and prices, *Journal of Economic Literature,* 22, 2, Mar, 1-35.

Kreuger, A., 1991, *How Computers have Changed the Wage Structure*, Mimeograph, Princeton, NJ: Economics Department, Princeton University.

Krijnse-Locker, H., 1984, On estimation of purchasing power parities on the basic heading level, *Review of Income and Wealth,* June.

Krugman, P., 1994, *Peddling Prosperity*, New York: Norton.

Krugman, P., and R. Lawrence, 1994, Trade, jobs and wages, *Scientific American,* April, 44-9.

Labour Party, 1995, Labour's macroeconomic framework, in *A New Economic Future for Britain,* Conference Document, London: Labour Party.

Labour Party, 1996, *New Labour: new life for Britain*, London: Labour Party.

Lawrence, R., and M. Slaughter, 1995, *Trade and US Wages:* great sucking sound or small hiccup, June, Washington, DC: Brookings.

Lawrence, R., 1995, *Single World, Divided Nations,* Paris: OECD Development Centre.

Leamer, E., 1993, Wage effects of a US-Mexican free trade agreement, in P. Garber (ed), *The Mexico-US Free Trade Agreement,* Cambridge, Mass: MIT Press, 57-125.

Lindbeck, A., and D. Snower, 1996, Reorganization of firms and labour market inequalities, *American Economic Review*, 86, May (Proceedings)..

Machin, S., 1996, Wage inequality in the UK, *Policy Studies,* Spring.

Maddison, A., 1987, Growth and slowdown in advanced capitalist economies, *Journal of Economic Literature,* 25, June.

Maddison, A., 1991, *Dynamic Forces in Economic Development,* Oxford: Oxford University Press.

Maddison, A., 1995 (a), *Monitoring the World Economy, 1820-1992,* Paris: OECD.

Maddison, A., 1995 (b), *Explaining the Performance of Nations,* Aldershot, England and Brookfield, Vermont, USA: Edward Elgar.

Malinvaud, E., 1977, 1985, *The Theory of Unemployment Reconsidered,* Oxford: Blackwell.

Malinvaud, E., 1984, *Mass Unemployment,* Oxford: Blackwell.

Malinvaud, E., 1994, *Diagnosing Unemployment,* Cambridge: Cambridge University Press.

Mark, J., 1987, Technological change and employment: some results from the BLS research, *Monthly Labor Review,* April, 110, 26-9.

Marney, J., 1995, Endogenous growth: a survey of surveys, *British Review of Economic*

Issues, 17, 43, July, 1-30.

Marris, R., 1964, *The Economic Theory of Managerial Capitalism,* London and New York: Macmillan and Free Press.

Marris, R. and D. Mueller, 1980, The corporation and competition, *Journal of Economic Literature,* 18, Mar, 32-63.

Marris, R., 1982, How much of the slow down was catch up, in R. Mathews (ed), *Slower Growth in the Western World,* London: Heinemann.

Marris, R., 1984, Measuring the wealth of nations, *Journal of Economic Literature,* 22, 2, Mar, 36-42.

Marris, R., 1987, Corporate economy, in *The New Palgrave Dictionary of Economics,* London: Macmillan.

Marris, R., 1991, *Reconstructing Keynesian Economics with Imperfect Competition:* a desk-top simulation, Aldershot, England: Edward Elgar.

Marris, R., 1992, R. F. Kahn's fellowship dissertation: a missing link in the history of economic thought, *Economic Journal,* 102, 1235-43.

Marris, R., 1996, Yes! Mrs. Robinson: the General Theory and imperfect competition, in G. Harcourt and P. Riach, (eds), *The Second Edition of the General Theory,* London: Routledge.

Marris, S., 1987, *Deficits and the Dollar:* the world economy at risk, Washington, DC: IIE.

Mathews, R. (ed), 1982, *Slower Growth in the Western World,* London: Heinemann.

Michie, J., and J. Grieve Smith, 1996, *Creating Industrial Capacity,* Oxford: Oxford University Press.

Minford, P., et al, 1995, *The Elixir of Trade,* Discussion Paper No. 1165, London: CEPR.

Minford, P., et al, 1995, Germany's social disease, *Quarterly Economic Bulletin,* 16, 3, Oct, 26-28, Liverpool: Research Group in Macroeconomics.

Mirrlees, J., 1971, An exploration in the theory of optimal income taxation, *Review of Economic Studies,* 38, 175-208.

Mishel, L. and J. Bernstein, 1994, *The State of Working America,* New York: EPI.

Mitchell, B., 1991, 1993, *International Historical Statistics,* London: Macmillan.

Mueller, D., 1988, The effects of mergers, in T. Calvani and J. Siegfried (eds), *Economic Analysis and Anti-trust Law,* Boston: Little Brown.

Mueller, D., 1989, (ed) Mergers (symposium), *International Journal of Industrial Organization,* 7, special issue, March, 1-10.

Mueller, D., 1992, Mergers: Theory and evidence, in G. Mussatti, (ed), *Mergers, Markets and Public Policy,* Dordrecht, Netherlands: Kluwer Publishers.

Murphy, K., and F. Welch, 1993, Occupational change and the demand for skill, 1940-1990, *American Economic Review,* 83, May (Proceedings), 123-25.

Nickell, S., 1996, The low-skill, low-pay problem: lessons from Germany for Britain and the US, *Policy Studies,* 17, 1.

Nickell, S., and B. Bell, 1995, The collapse in demand for the unskilled, *Oxford Review of Economic Policy,* 11, 1, 40-62.

Nield, R., 1963, *Pricing and Employment in the Trade Cycle:* a study of British manufacturing industry, 1950-61, Cambridge: Cambridge University Press.

Noble, E., 1993, The dopamine receptor gene: a review of association studies in alchoholism, *Behavior Genetics,* 23, 2, 119-129.

Nölling, W., 1993, *Monetary Policy in Europe since Maastricht,* London: Macmillan.

Norman, P., 1981, *Shout:* the true story of the Beatles, London: Hamilton.

OECD, 1992, *Historical Statistics* (diskette), Paris:OECD.

OECD, 1994, Facts, Analysis, Strategies, *The OECD Jobs Study,* Paris: OECD.

OECD, 1994, Evidence and Explanations Part 1, Labour Market Trends and Underlying Forces for Change, *The OECD Jobs Study,* Paris: OECD.

OECD, 1994, Evidence and Explanations Part 2, The Adjustment Potential of the Labour Market, *The OECD Jobs Study,* Paris: OECD.

OECD, 1995, *Labour Force Statistics 1995,* Paris: OECD.

OECD, 1995, *Education at a Glance,* Paris: CER, OECD.

OECD, 1995, *Economic Outlook,* 58, Dec, Paris: OECD

Olson, M., 1965, *The Logic of Collective Action,* Cambidge, Mass: Harvard Press.

Olson, M., 1982, *The Rise and Decline of Nations,* New Haven, Conn: Yale University Press.

Ormerod, P., 1994, *The Death of Economics,* London: Faber.

Orr, A., M. Edey, and M. Kennedy, 1995, *The Determinants of Real Long-term Interest Rates:* 17 country pooled-time-series evidence, Economics Department Working Paper No. 155, OECD: Paris.

O'Mahony, M., 1995, International differences in manufacturing unit labour costs, *National Institute of Economic Review,* 54, Nov.

O'Mahony, M., 1995, *Manufacturing Productivity:* data base, privately supplied, London: NIESR.

Pareto, V., 1897, *Cours D'Économie Politique,* Geneva: Droz.

Pareto, V., 1906, *Manuale D'Economia Politica,* Milan: Libraria.

Pareto, V., 1916, *Trattato di Sociologia Generale,* Florence: Barbera. English, 1935, *The Mind and Society,* New York: Harcourt Brace.

Patel, I., 1995, *Equity in a Global Society,* Centenary Lecture, London: London School of Economics.

Roy, A., 1950, The distribution of earnings and individual output, *Economic Journal,* 60, Sept, 489-505.

Phelps, E., 1994, Low-wage unemployment subsidies versus the Welfare State, *American Economic Review,* 84, 2, 54-58.

Phillips, C., 1981, *Strange Fruit,* Ambergate, US: Ambergate Press.

Pullan, B., 1971, *Rich and Poor in Renaissance Venice:* the social institutions of a Catholic state, to 1620, Oxford: Blackwell.

Ramey, C., 1996, *At Risk Does Not Mean Doomed:* the plasticity of early intellectual development, Baltimore: Kennedy Krieger.

Rawls, J., 1971, *A Theory of Justice,* Cambridge, Mass: Harvard University Press.

Reich, R., 1991, *The Work of Nations:* a blueprint for the future, New York: Simon and Schuster.

Reisman, D., 1990, *The Political Economy of James Buchanan,* London: Macmillan.

Robbins, L., 1932, *An Essay on the Nature and Significance of Economic Science,* London: Macmillan.

Robinson, J., 1956, *The Accumulation of Capital,* London: Macmillan.

Romer., P., 1986, Increasing returns and long-run growth, *Journal of Political Economy,* 94, 1002-1037.

Romer., P., 1994, The origins of endogenous growth *Journal of Economic Perspectives,* 8, 3-22.

Rosen, S., 1982, Authority, control and the distribution of earnings, *Bell Journal of Economics,* 13, Autumn, 311-323.

Rowthorn, R., 1975, What remains of Kaldor's Law, *Economic Journal,* 85, 2, March, 10-19.

Rowthorn, R., 1994, *Unemployment, Trade and Capital Formation in the OECD,* Geneva: UNCTAD.

Rowthorn, R., 1995, Capital formation and unemployment, *Oxford Review of Economic Policy,* 11, 1, 26-39.

Rumelhart, D., et al, 1986, *Parallel Distributed Processing,* Cambridge, Mass: MIT Press.

Sachs, J., and H. Shatz, 1994, Trade and Jobs in US manufacturing, *Brookings Papers on Economic Activity,* 1, 1-84.

Salter, W., 1960, *Productivity and Technical Progress,* Cambridge: Cambridge University Press, re-issued, 1969.

Schmitt, J., 1990, *The Changing Structure of Male Earnings in Britain,* 1974-88, Discussion Paper No. 122, London: Centre for Economic Performance, London School of Economics.

Sembenelli A., and L. Rondi, 1991, Testing the relationship between the growth of firms and the growth of the economy, *International Journal of Industrial Organization,* 9, 251-259.

Sen, A., 1977, Rational fools, *Philosophy and Public Affairs,* 6, 317-44.

Sen, A., and J. Drèze, 1990, *Hunger and Public Action,* Oxford: Clarendon Press.

Sen, A, 1992, *Inequality Re-examined,* Cambridge, Mass: Harvard Press.

Shackleton, J., 1996, *The Skills Mirage,* London: EPI.

Simon., H., 1957, The compensation of executives, *Sociometry,* March.

Snower, D., 1994, Converting unemployment benefits into employment subsidies, *American Economic Review,* 84, 2, 65-70.

Snower, D., 1994, *The Low-Skill, Bad-Job Trap,* Discussion Paper No. 999, London: CEPR.

Solow, R., 1962, A contribution to the theory of economic growth, *Quarterly Journal of Economics,* 70, 1, 65-94.

Sowell, T., 1984, *Civil Rights:* rhetoric or reality, New York: Morrow.

Sraffa, P., and M. Dobb (eds), 1951, *The Works and Correspondence of David Ricardo,* Cambridge: Cambridge University Press.

Sternberg, R. (ed), 1995, *Encyclopedia of Human Intelligence,* New York: Macmillan Corporation.

Summers, R., and A. Heston, 1991, The Penn World Tables Mark 5: an expanded set of international comparisons, 1950-1988, *Quarterly Journal of Economics,* 106, 2, May, 327-368.

Taylor, J., 1993, *When the Clock Struck Zero:* science's ultimate limits, London: Picador.

Taylor, J., 1995, *Towards the Ultimate Intelligent Machine,* Presidential Address, World Congress on Neural Networks 1995, London: King's College.

Tease, W., A. Dean, J. Elmeskov and P. Hoeller, 1991, *Real Interest Rate Trends:* the influence of saving, investment and other factors, OECD Economic Studies, 17, Autumn, Paris: OECD.

US Government, 1994, *Statistical Abstract of the United States,* Washington, DC:US.

US Government, *Employment Trends,* 1995, Bureau of Labor Statistics, Sept, Washington, DC: US.

Van Ark, B., 1990, Manufacturing productivity in five countries, *Oxford Bulletin of Economics and Statistics,* 52, 4, No, 343-375.

Van Ark, B., 1995. Manufacturing prices, productivity, and labor costs in five economies, *Monthly Labour Review,* US Department of Labour, July.

Verdoorn, P., 1949, Fattori che regolano svilluppo della produtività del lavoro, *L'Industria,* 1, 45-53.

Wills, C., 1993, *The Runaway Brain:* the evolution of human uniqueness, New York and London: Basic Books and HarperCollins.

Wood, A., 1978, *A Theory of Pay,* Cambridge: Cambridge University Press.

Wood, A., 1991, Global trends in real exchange rates 196-84, *World Development,* 19, 4, 317-332.

Wood, A, 1994, *North-South Trade and Income Inequality,* Oxford: Oxford University Press.

Wood, A, 1995, How trade hurt unskilled workers, *Journal of Economic Perspectives,* 9, Summer.

Williamson, O., 1970, *Corporate Control and Business Behavior*, Prentice-Hall.

Young, A., 1928, Increasing returns and economic progress, *Economic Journal,* 38, 4, Dec, 527-42.

Young, M., 1958, *The Rise of the Meritocracy, 1970-2033*: an essay on education and equality, London: Thames and Hudson.

Index